WASHINGTON, D.C., with Kids

5TH EDITION

SANDRA BURT
LINDA PERLIS

FODOR'S

D1402318

With love to our favorite traveling companions: nine terrific men—our husbands, Barry and Jeff; and our sons, Aaron, Andrew, Cliff, Daniel, Jonathan, Roy, and Stephen; our six wonderful daughters-in-law, Alissa, Allison, Debbie, Emily, Jessie, and Kristin; and six precious grandchildren, Elliot, Gabrielle, Jasper, Nathan, Samuel, and Zoe.

Published by Fodor's Travel, a division of Random House, Inc.

Fodor's is a registered trademark of Random House, Inc.

www.fodors.com

All products mentioned in this book are trademarks of their respective companies.

Every effort has been made to make this book complete and accurate as of the date of publication. In a time of rapid change, however, it is difficult to ensure that all information is entirely up-to-date. Although the publisher and authors cannot be liable for any inaccuracies or omissions in this book, they are always grateful for corrections and suggestions for improvement. Please feel free to visit www.parentsperspective. org and send your comments and corrections to parentsper@gmail.com.

Cover photo (Museum of Natural History): Corbis.

Illustrations and maps by Nathaniel Levine.

Special thanks to Coffman Publications for permission to use photo images.

Interior photos © Keith Stanley (pages 12, 47, 51, 62, 73, 114, 142, 150, 167, 205, 267, 352, 367), © Russ Finely (pages 17, 45, 56, 87, 192, 225, 281, 322, 323), © White House Historical Association (page 92), © RWC-A (pages 105, 117, 131, 297), © Parks and History Association/Carol M. Highsmith (page 122), © Finley-Holiday Films (pages 200, 288, 314), © Impact/John Wagner (page 34), © Photo Disc (page 9), John Wagner (pages 125, 277, 292), Barry R. Perlis (pages 219, 232, 339, 338), Maury Sullivan (page 165), Alexandria Convention and Visitors Association/Anna Frame (page 308), Alexandria Convention and Visitors Association/Eric Kvalsvik (page 315).

Library of Congress Cataloging-in-Publication Data on File.

Previously published by Prima Publishing.

Fifth Edition

ISBN 978-1-4000-0428-7
ISSN 1940-3275

Printed in the United States of America

10 9 8 7 6 5 4 3 2 1

Contents

List of Maps x
List of Quick Guides xi
Icons xii
Preface to the Fifth Edition xiii
Washington, D.C., Region Map . . . . xiv–xv
Acknowledgments xvii
Introduction xix

Chapter 1 Preparing to Go   1
Getting There Map *2*
When to Go 3
Planning Your Itinerary 4
Media Resources 7
Movies, Books, & Games 8
Expense Planning 9
Where to Stay 12
What to Bring 14
Getting Here 15
Getting Around 18
Keeping Safe 22
The Capital Scavenger Hunt 24

Chapter 2 Capitol Hill   26
Capitol Hill Map *28*
★ The United States Capitol 29
Quick Guide to Capitol Hill Attractions 32–33

U.S. Botanic Garden 39
★ Library of Congress 40
Folger Shakespeare Library 42
★ Supreme Court Building 44
National Japanese American Memorial 46
Victims of Communism Memorial 48
The National Guard Memorial Museum 49
National Postal Museum 50
★ Union Station 51
Where to Stay in the Capitol Hill Area 52
Answers to Smart Stuff Questions 53

Chapter 3   The National Mall   54

★ Smithsonian Visitor Information Center ("the Castle") . . . 55
The National Mall Map *57*
The Freer Gallery of Art 58
The Arthur M. Sackler Gallery 59
Quick Guide to the National Mall Attractions 60–61
The National Museum of African Art 62
Arts and Industries Building 63
Hirshhorn Museum and Sculpture Garden 64
★ National Air and Space Museum 66
National Museum of the American Indian 69
The Voice of America 70
★ National Gallery of Art 71
National Gallery of Art Sculpture Garden
    and Ice Skating Rink 75
★ National Museum of Natural History 76
★ National Museum of American History 78
Where to Stay in the National Mall Area 80
Answers to Smart Stuff Questions 81

Chapter 4   White House & Foggy Bottom   83

★ National Aquarium 84
White House Visitors Center 85
White House & Foggy Bottom Map *86*

The White House. 87
Quick Guide to White House &
    Foggy Bottom Attractions 88–89
Lafayette Square. 93
St. John's Church 94
Decatur House 95
Renwick Gallery. 95
Eisenhower Executive Office Building 96
The Octagon 96
Corcoran Gallery of Art 97
★ DAR (Daughters of the American Revolution)
    Museum. 99
Organization of American States Building 101
State Department, Diplomatic Reception Rooms 102
George Washington University. 103
★ Kennedy Center for the Performing Arts 104
Where to Stay in the White House &
    Foggy Bottom Area 106
Answers to Smart Stuff Questions. 106

Chapter 5 Tidal Basin   109
Vietnam Veterans Memorial. 110
Tidal Basin Map. *111*
Quick Guide to Tidal Basin Attractions 112–113
Constitution Gardens and Reflecting Pool 116
★ Lincoln Memorial 117
District of Columbia War Memorial. 119
★ National World War II Memorial. 120
Korean War Veterans Memorial 121
★ Franklin Delano Roosevelt Memorial. 121
★ Jefferson Memorial. 124
★ Bureau of Engraving and Printing 126
U.S. Holocaust Memorial Museum 127
Washington Monument 131
Where to Stay in the Tidal Basin Area. 133
Answers to Smart Stuff Questions. 134

Chapter 6 Georgetown & Embassy Row   135

★ Chesapeake & Ohio Canal National
   Historical Park 137
Georgetown & Embassy Row Map *137*
Quick Guide to Georgetown &
   Embassy Row Attractions. 138–139
★ Old Stone House 141
Georgetown University. 142
Tudor Place 143
Dumbarton Oaks Garden and Museum 144
★ Wisconsin Avenue and M Street, NW 146
Embassy Row 148
Islamic Center 151
U.S. Naval Observatory 153
Where to Stay in Georgetown. 154
Where to Stay Near Embassy Row 154
Answers to Smart Stuff Questions. 155

Chapter 7 Dupont Circle & Adams Morgan   156

Anderson House. 158
Dupont Circle & Adams Morgan Map *158*
Quick Guide to Dupont Circle &
   Adams Morgan Attractions. 160–161
The Phillips Collection. 162
Textile Museum 164
★ Woodrow Wilson House 165
Fondo Del Sol Visual Arts Center. 167
National Museum of American Jewish Military History 168
St. Matthew's Cathedral 170
U.S. Chess Center 171
★ Explorers Hall, National Geographic Society 172
Scottish Rite Freemasonry Temple 173
Mansion on O Street 174
★ The Washington Post 174
Adams Morgan. 175

Where to Stay in the Dupont Circle &
    Adams Morgan Area. 177
Answers to Smart Stuff Questions. 178

Chapter 8   Chinatown & Gallery Place   179

Chinatown & Gallery Place Map. 180
National Museum of Women in the Arts 181
Quick Guide to Chinatown &
    Gallery Place Attractions 182–185
Willard Inter-Continental Hotel. 187
Freedom Plaza 188
Ronald Reagan Building and International
    Trade Center 189
★ Pavilion at the Old Post Office. 190
★ National Archives. 191
★ Newseum. 194
U.S. Navy Memorial. 195
National Museum of Crime and Punishment 196
★ Ford's Theatre. 198
Smithsonian American Art Museum
    and National Portrait Gallery. 201
★ International Spy Museum. 203
Chinatown Friendship Archway 204
Marian Koshland Science Museum. 205
National Law Enforcement Officers Memorial 206
National Building Museum 207
Lillian and Albert Small Jewish Museum 208
Mary McLeod Bethune Council House 209
African-American Civil War Memorial. 210
Howard University. 211
Lincoln Theater 212
Where to Stay in the Chinatown &
    Gallery Place Area 212
Answers to Smart Stuff Questions. 213

Chapter 9 Uptown & Suburban Maryland 214

★ National Zoo 215

Uptown In Map 216

Uptown Out Map 217

★ Washington National Cathedral 219

Quick Guide to Uptown & Suburban
Maryland Attractions 220–223

American University 226

Hillwood Museum and Gardens 227

Rock Creek Nature Center 228

Peirce Mill 231

Peirce Barn 232

National Museum of Health and Medicine 232

The Kreeger Museum 233

Glen Echo Park 234

Discovery Creek Children's Museum 236

Clara Barton National Historic Site 237

Woodend Sanctuary 238

The Washington Temple and Visitors Center of the
Church of Jesus Christ of Latter-Day Saints 239

The Dennis & Phillip Ratner Museum 240

National Capital Trolley Museum 242

University of Maryland 243

National Cryptologic Museum 243

Where to Stay in the Uptown Area 244

Where to Stay in Suburban Maryland 245

Answers to Smart Stuff Questions 245

Chapter 10 Northeast & Southeast 247

Northeast & Southeast Map 248

Catholic University 249

Quick Guide to Northeast & Southeast Attractions . . . 250–251

★ Basilica of the National Shrine of the
Immaculate Conception 252

Franciscan Monastery 254

President Lincoln's Cottage 255

Gallaudet University. 255
U.S. National Arboretum 256
Lincoln Park. 258
Eastern Market. 260
Washington Navy Yard 260
Anacostia Community Museum. 262
★ Frederick Douglass National Historic Site 264
National Harbor. 265
Kenilworth Park and Aquatic Gardens 266
Where to Stay in Northeast & Southeast D.C. 268
Answers to Smart Stuff Questions. 269

Chapter 11 Northern Virginia 270

Arlington Map *271*
★ Arlington National Cemetery. 272
Quick Guide to Northern Virginia Attractions. 274–275
United States Air Force Memorial. 291
Iwo Jima Memorial. 291
Netherlands Carillon 292
Theodore Roosevelt Island 294
DEA Museum 296
The Pentagon. 296
National Weather Service 298
Steven F. Udvar-Hazy Center 299
Where to Stay in Arlington. 299
Answers to Smart Stuff Questions. 300

Chapter 12 Olde Virginia 301

Alexandria Map *302*
★ Old Town Alexandria 303
Quick Guide to Olde Virginia Attractions 304–305
★ Claude Moore Colonial Farm at Turkey Run 320
★ Mount Vernon 321
George Washington's River Farm 325
Collingwood Library and Museum on Americanism. 326
Woodlawn Plantation. 327

Pope-Leighey House 328
National Museum of the Marine Corps 329
Where to Stay in Olde Virginia. 330
Answers to Smart Stuff Questions. 331

Appendix I For the Fun of It   333

Seasonal Events. 333
Sports. 346
Spectator Sports 354
Entertainment & the Arts. 356

Appendix II Tours: Washington, D.C.,
Inside & Out   369

Bike 369
Boat 370
Buses & Other Vehicles 371
Recorded Tours. 374
Self-Guided Tours. 374
Walking 376
Media Tours 377

Appendix III Now What?   379

The Capital Scavenger Hunt. 379
Sharing Your Washington Experiences 379
Individual & Group Project Ideas. 381
A Few More Ideas to Think About 384
Scavenger Hunt Answers 384

Index   387

List of Maps

Washington, D.C., Region . . . . xiv–xv
Getting There. 2
Capitol Hill 28
The National Mall 57

White House & Foggy Bottom 86
Tidal Basin 111
Georgetown & Embassy Row 137
Dupont Circle & Adams Morgan 158
Chinatown & Gallery Place 180
Uptown In 216
Uptown Out 217
Northeast & Southeast 248
Arlington 271
Alexandria. 302

List of Quick Guides

Capitol Hill Attractions 32–33
The National Mall Attractions 60–61
White House & Foggy Bottom Attractions. 88–89
Tidal Basin Attractions 112–113
Georgetown & Embassy Row Attractions 138–139
Dupont Circle & Adams Morgan Attractions 160–161
Chinatown & Gallery Place Attractions 182–185
Uptown & Suburban Maryland Attractions 220–223
Northeast & Southeast Attractions 250–251
Northern Virginia Attractions. 274–275
Olde Virginia Attractions 304–305

Icons

Every chapter contains symbols to help locate specific tips:

Smart Stuff

Helpful Hint

Money-Saving Tip

Time-Saving Tip

Parents/Teachers Take Note

★ Major Site

Watch for Smart Stuff questions throughout the book. Answers appear at the end of each chapter.

Preface to the Fifth Edition

As we complete this fifth edition of *Washington, D.C., with Kids,* we are grateful that so many readers have found the earlier editions helpful. We continue to be delighted with readers' suggestions and support. Those of you familiar with the book will note some new sites to explore and activities to try. We hope your next trip to our nation's capital is a fun-filled one!

We are always happy to have reader input. Please visit www.parentsperspective.org and send us your comments and suggestions.

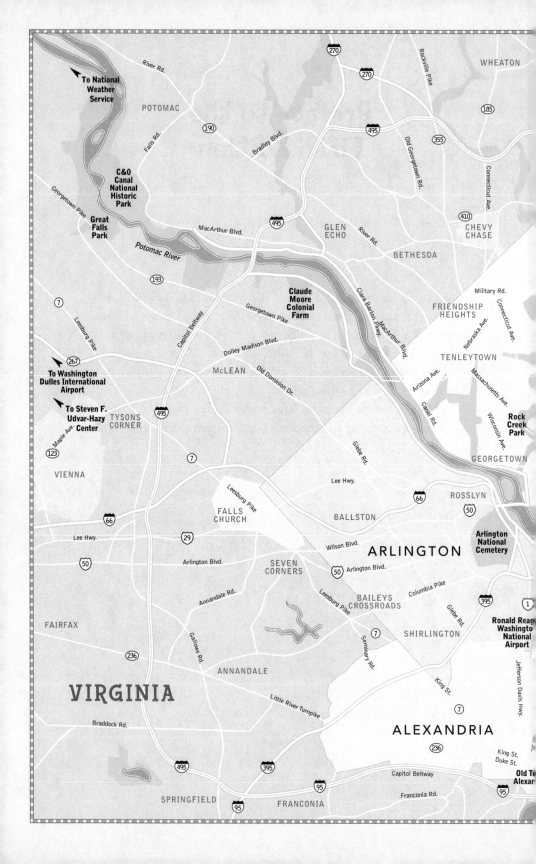

Acknowledgments

Little did we suspect that our journey rediscovering our hometown of Washington, D.C., would become a genuine expedition. The suggestions and support of numerous people have made this book a reality. And along the way, we have been the fortunate recipients of much encouragement.

As chief scout, our agent and dear friend Sara Camilli has kept us on course, all the while making us feel cared for and empowered. Our editor for the past few editions, Mark Sullivan, has been encouraging and supportive. Jess Moss, who has worked with us on this fifth edition has been a supportive guide throughout this process. As always, the staff members involved have used their impressive talents to enhance our project. Nathaniel Levine's maps and illustrations continue to set the book's welcoming tone.

The Washington, D.C., Visitor Information Center, the Alexandria Convention and Visitors Association, and the Hirshhorn Museum Education Department, as well as museum educators, librarians, and other specialists, including Lauren Beyea (Ford's Theatre), Julia Neubauer (Textile Museum), Sheila Brennan (Navy Museum), Evelyn Espinueva (National Law Enforcement Officers Memorial), Rachel Goldberg and Suzanne Wright (Phillips Collection), Sallie E. Altizer (National Museum of Women in the Arts), Dee Hoffman (Children's Concierge), Michelle Shuster and Suzanne Carbone (Montgomery County Public Libraries), Sari Hornstein (historian), Eva Sarelle (Board of Jewish Education), Elizabeth Pagano (Metropolitan Washington Airports Authority), Phyllis Bolden (Office of the Capitol Curator), Alden O'Brien (DAR Information), Ann

Piccoli (National Capital Trolley Museum), Matthew Mathias (Audubon Naturalist Society), Laura Overstreet (Alexandria Convention and Visitors Association), and Keith Stanley (professional photographer), have kindly shared their materials and expertise.

Teachers and students across the country gave us the benefit of their experiences visiting Washington, D.C. Alex Cutler, Diana Epstein, Patricia Lambert, Michael Moore, and Joreta Speck were particularly generous with their time and suggestions. Our special thanks go to Rochelle Follender, librarian, for her thorough research, Tami Ishaeik and Julie Gasway, for their superlative people-finding; Linda and Jon Goldman, for their dependable information-gathering; and Peggy Waitt, for her thoughtfulness.

For their enthusiastic contributions, Barry Perlis, Ruth Cass, the late Millard Cass, and Evelyn Sacks have our deepest thanks. Jessica Bennett, Jonathan Burt, Stephen Burt, and Nell Minow weighed in with guidance on appropriate movies and books to recommend; two thumbs up for their kind assistance. Jeff Burt generously gave us the benefit of his legal skill and personal concern. For this our fifth edition, we were blessed with a whole host of volunteers: Ginny Frank, Carole Kaminsky, Shelah Landsman, Joyce Lipman, Sharla Neuberger, Andi Sacks, Ada Sheinbaum, and Madeline Shere. Many thanks for their stellar phone and computer skills, and much-valued time and energy. The continued patience and support of both of our families through the first, second, third, fourth, and now the fifth edition of this book have been invaluable. We are also thankful for the thoughtful feedback from so many of you who "road-tested" the book.

Together we have weathered yet another adventure, a trip neither of us could or would have taken alone. And for all the bumps along the road, we've discovered that each of us is the other's best shock absorber. We hope you enjoy your own journey of discovery in our nation's capital.

Introduction

Why Visit Washington, D.C.?

Visitors to Washington, D.C., arrive year-round from all over the world. They come with their families, classes, Scout troops, youth groups, 4-H clubs, and friends. Washington, D.C., is the capital of the United States of America, the capital of the free world, and the capital of our modern world's first democracy.

Washington visitors can both watch and participate in activities that only happen in the United States. They can see representatives debate bills and craft laws, they can sit in on congressional committee hearings on subjects they read about in the daily newspapers, and they can hear arguments before the Supreme Court. In contrast to many other governments, this one welcomes both American and foreign visitors.

Smart Stuff

Why is Washington called the District of Columbia? (A.)

Washington, D.C. (or the District, as locals call it, short for District of Columbia) owes a debt to Frenchman Pierre L'Enfant, a brilliant engineer who envisioned a city of grand boulevards radiating out from a central Capitol building. Like L'Enfant's beloved Paris, Washington has green spaces, parks, and beautiful trees throughout the city. From Japan came a major contribution to the

Parents/Teachers Take Note

Journals are wonderful learning tools and mementos of travels. It's fun for kids and teachers or parents to keep separate journals of what they see and think about. They can write down adventures that are funny or of special interest. After the trip, comparing different people's versions of the same places and experiences will be fun!

city's beauty—the cherry trees that draw thousands of tourists when they blossom every spring.

Washington is a city built on a human scale. The maximum building height allowed within city limits was set at 110 feet, to keep the Capitol visible from everywhere in the city. Downtown Washington is pedestrian-friendly. The broad expanse of the Mall, stretching from the west front of the Capitol all the way to the Lincoln Memorial on the Potomac River, is designed for walking. It's lined with major sites and beautiful areas for recreation and relaxation, where numerous festivals and fairs take place throughout the year.

Smart Stuff

For Tykes . . . Washington is a city of statues of famous (and not-so-famous) people. If you could choose a statue to put in your school, who would it commemorate? Draw (or build) your design for a statue.

For any American, coming to Washington is like coming home—it is your city, no matter where you actually live. It's a city whose builders represented much of the diversity of our country. Quaker geographer Andrew Ellicott, whose family founded Ellicott City, Maryland; African-American astronomer Benjamin Banneker; Scottish physician William Thornton; Irish architect James Hoban; and English architect and engineer Benjamin Latrobe all contributed to the planning, design, and building of this capital city created by a newborn nation. Washington, D.C., is also a bargain: there are more free attractions here than in any other U.S. city! In fact, unless otherwise specified, all sites described in *Washington, D.C., with Kids* are free.

Smart Stuff

For Tweens and Teens . . . Which Native American nations populated the area where Washington, D.C., is now? What was their frightening prophecy? (B.)

What Can This Trip Do for You?

Travel exposes everyone to experiences beyond the familiar. Kids particularly respond to new places and events, integrating them into their developing view of themselves and the world. When they encounter sites they have read or heard about, they can better understand their connection to a new ingredient in their environment.

Sharing experiences and adventures with their peers promotes camaraderie among young people. Coming from the same base (family, hometown, school, or group), youngsters can more easily help each other interpret their experiences. They enjoy what they're discovering even more when they share. Each member enriches the group with his or her individual contributions.

Adults can help children focus their attention, and can help them interpret what they see and hear in a context they can more easily understand. Adults provide responsible guidance, support, and safety. An extra bonus for adults who travel with children is the benefit of their youthful perspective and energy.

As anyone who deals with kids knows, we need to be flexible, and that is especially true with travel. Things don't always go according to plan. We recently heard a story about a class that came to Washington for two days and awoke to a major snowstorm on the first morning. (This probably happened in February!) Even the museums were closed—a rarity in Washington. Via television, students and their chaperones learned that D.C. hospitals were requesting volunteers to make up for staff who couldn't reach their workplaces. So being right there in the city, students eagerly filled in. Their experiences at the hospitals made them feel much more important than they would have felt after a day of cruising the monuments. It proved to be an unexpected but treasured highlight of their trip. We wish you better weather, of course, but similar satisfaction. (By the way, we could always use leaf-rakers, yard-workers, or garage cleaner-outers, if you're hard up for activities while you visit D.C.!)

Brief Historic Background

The earliest Caucasian visitors arrived here by boat in early summer of 1608, when Captain John Smith led the first expedition up the Potomac River. For more than 100 years afterward this area was a quiet backwater—until the new nation needed a capital. How appropriate that Washington, a city of political give-and-take, was established through a compromise. Shepherded through the Congress of 1790 by Alexander Hamilton and Thomas Jefferson, the Residence Act, establishing the capital city at its present location, was passed. Both the North and the South had wanted the capital in their own jurisdictions. They were also divided on whether the federal government should assume payment of individual states' Revolutionary War debts. The North agreed to establish the capital in a southern location when the South agreed that Congress should assume the states' war debts. President George Washington chose the site, and the U.S. geographer general, Andrew Ellicott, drew the boundaries.

The city is grateful to a daughter of Virginia Quaker parents, who rescued the portrait of our first commander in chief from a burning White House. On August 23, 1814, when the British invaded and burned Washington, Dolley Madison, wife of President James Madison, remained in the White House until the last possible moment. She took Gilbert Stuart's famous portrait of Washington, along with the most important state documents and works of art, to safety.

During the Civil War, Washington, D.C., became a city ringed with forts. To reduce the city's vulnerability to Confederate troops, the Union built 68 forts, one of which was visited by President Abraham Lincoln, who came to view the conflict. Standing more than 6 feet tall and wearing his stovepipe hat, he made a notable target on the ramparts of Fort Stephens. To keep him from harm's way, an army officer next to him

Smart Stuff

For Tweens and Teens . . . In which eight cities did the U.S. government meet before the capital was established in the District of Columbia? (C.)

shouted impulsively, "Get down, you fool!" Fortunately, Lincoln did. The army officer turned out to be a pretty sharp fellow. His name was Lieutenant Colonel Oliver Wendell Holmes, later a justice of the U.S. Supreme Court. Lincoln had government buildings converted into barracks, and fields in the city became pastures for grazing animals. The forts and batteries are maintained by the National Park Service. Children can climb up on the mounds that once served to protect the capital city.

Following the Civil War, a construction boom modernized much of Washington with paved streets, sidewalks, streetlights, and a sewer system. Over the ensuing years such notables as landscape architect Frederick Law Olmsted, sculptor Augustus Saint-Gaudens, and first lady Lady Bird Johnson became involved in the beautification of the city.

Between 1910 and 1935 Washington saw the birth of many new museums, galleries, and concert halls, including the Smithsonian's Natural History Museum, the Folger Shakespeare Library and Theatre, the Freer Gallery, the National Theater, and the Lincoln Memorial.

Beginning with World War I and the Wilson era, Washington's voice in world affairs became more powerful. Government began an expansion that increased dramatically by World War II. Buildings proliferated in several areas of the city to accommodate living and working space for the ever-increasing federal workforce. The Pentagon building, across the river in Arlington, Virginia, accommodates 40,000 employees.

Smart Stuff

For Tweens and Teens . . .
What famous woman was
responsible for obtaining
the blossoming cherry trees
for Washington, D.C.? **(D.)**

Washington again became the focus for thousands of people during the 1960s. Marches to end hunger, promote civil rights, and conclude the war in Vietnam were all staged in the nation's capital. Emotion-filled events such as Marian Anderson's performances in 1939 and 1952 and Dr. Martin Luther King Jr.'s famous "I Have a Dream" speech in 1963 took place on the steps of the Lincoln Memorial. And through the beginning of the 21st century even more museums, art galleries, and monuments have been added. Who knows what significance these landmarks will hold for the future?

From the Bonus Marchers of World War I to the occupants of the "Poor People's Tent City" on the Mall to the Million Mom March for gun safety, citizens of the United States look to their nation's capital as the place where their voices can be heard. Continuing national rituals, such as the presidential inauguration on the steps of the Capitol and the ensuing parade, funerals of presidents and national leaders, and ceremonies for visiting heads of state, take place in Washington, D.C. Sites like Arlington National Cemetery and the Vietnam Veterans Memorial continue to evoke emotional responses.

What's in This Book and How to Use It

Washington, D.C., with Kids is divided into 11 geographic chapters, with additional sections on entertainment, tours, and follow-up. Each chapter includes maps of city areas, lists of recommended sites, and the appropriate information for visiting them, along with ideas and activities to enhance children's learning about the city. Always call before you go, because of constant changes in security measures. Child-friendly accommodations and restaurants are featured as well. Throughout the book, icons identify money-saving tips, time-saving tips, "smart stuff" (brain teasers), and so forth. Age-appropriateness for each site is indicated by the terms *tykes* (children 6 and under), *tweens* (ages 7–12), or *teens* (ages 13–19).

Especially for Out-of-Towners and the Physically Challenged

The DC Visitor Information Center (202/289–8317; 866/DC–IS–FUN; www.itcdc.com; www.dcchamber.org) is at 1300 Pennsylvania Avenue, NW, in the Ronald Reagan Building and International Trade Center. Up-to-date information is available here, with brochures, maps, souvenirs, assistance with hotel and restaurant reservations, a food court, public phones, and public restrooms. This center is a valuable resource, no matter where you're coming from.

Destination DC (901 7th Street, NW; 202/789–7000; 800/422–8644; www.washington.org) has a free booklet titled the *Washington, D.C. Visitors Guide*, updated twice a year and filled with sightseeing tips, maps, and contacts. The National Park Service also has a useful Web site (www.nps.gov), as does the Smithsonian Institution (www.si.edu).

The Meridian International Center (1630 Crescent Place, NW; 202/667–6800; www.meridian.org) offers services specifically for international visitors, and can tailor programs for groups. A new Web site also designed to help tourists visiting the United States from other countries is www.usawelcome.com.

Washington, D.C., is one of the most accessible and welcoming cities in the world for the physically challenged. Most government buildings, museums, galleries, hotels, restaurants, and shopping areas have wheelchair ramps and accessible restrooms and water fountains. There are also Braille menus, telephones for the hearing-impaired, and large-print brochures. Ask for a disability guide (*The Washington, D.C. Access Guide*) detailing accessibility in the capital city (www.disabilityguide.org).

What if You Get Sick While You're Here?

Getting sick or having an accident while away from home can be alarming. Be sure everyone brings all prescription medications, extra eyeglasses or contact lenses, health insurance information, and frequently used over-the-counter medications (such as for allergies, motion sickness, or upset stomach). A hotel concierge is a good source for finding a doctor. The Washington Hospital Center (202/877–3627) offers a referral service during the week, 8 AM to 4 PM, and can help you locate a doctor as close as possible to where you're staying. However, visitors often have to go to the nearest hospital for help. Some emergency rooms have walk-in clinics for non-life-threatening problems, and service there is much less expensive than in the emergency room itself. Some local hospitals include: Washington Hospital Center Emergency Room (110 Irving Street, NW; 202/877–5515; www.whcenter.org); Children's National Medical Center Emergency Room (111 Michigan Avenue, NW; 202/884–5203; www.childrensnational.org); George Washington University Hospital Emergency Room (901 23rd Street, NW; 202/715–4911; www.gwhospital.com); Georgetown University Hospital Emergency Room (3800 Reservoir Road, NW; 202/444–2119; www.gumc.georgetown.edu); Sibley Memorial Hospital Emergency Room (5255 Loughboro Road, NW; 202/537–4080; www.sibley.org); and Howard University Hospital Emergency Room (2041 Georgia Avenue, NW; 202/865–1141; www.huhealthcare.com). There are several 24-hour CVS pharmacies in the area, including branches at 1199 Vermont Avenue (Thomas Circle; 202/628–0720) and at 6–7 Dupont Circle (202/785–1466).

Some Suggestions for Reading

Books and games about Washington, D.C., places and people include the following: *Underground Train,* by Mary Quattlebaum (tykes); *I'm Going to Washington to Visit the President,* by Tanya Roitman (tykes); *N is for Our Nation's Capital: A Washington, D.C. Alphabet,* by Roland and Marie Smith (tykes); *Washington Is Burn-*

Helpful Hint

The White House, Smithsonian Institution, Kennedy Center, Library of Congress, and some other attractions offer brochures in a number of languages. All foreign embassies and legations offer information and assistance to visitors from their countries. It's a good idea to contact them in advance. Telephone numbers are listed in the District of Columbia telephone directory's Yellow Pages under Embassies and Legations. You can access the D.C. Yellow Pages at any library (in your hometown) and on the Internet at www.yellowpages.com.

All airports serving the Washington, D.C., area and Union Station (trains) offer information desks for arriving visitors.

ing, by Marty Figley, et al. (tweens); *Look Out, Washington, D.C.!*, by Patricia Reilly Giff (tweens); *Building the Capital City*, by Marlene Brill (tweens); *Lives of the Presidents: Fame, Shame, and What the Neighbors Thought*, by Kathleen Krull, a book about the lives of presidents as husbands, fathers, pet owners, and neighbors (tweens); *Eyewitness to Power: The Essence of Leadership, Nixon to Clinton*, by David R. Gergen (teens); and *Anything Goes!: What I've Learned from Pundits, Politicians, and Presidents*, by Larry King (teens).

Just the Facts: Fun Facts of American History (tweens and teens) is a video about the evolution of the United States, its customs, origins of its symbols, and even new inventions. An interesting DVD is from a public television presentation: *Washington, D.C.: Our Nation's Capital* (teens). Tweens and teens will have fun putting together the 1,000-piece United States Presidents Jigsaw Puzzle, a 24" by 30" composite of colored pictures of the U.S. presidents. *Run-Off: The Game of Presidential Campaigning* is a board game (tweens and teens) enabling players to collect electoral votes with their knowledge of U.S. politics, history, and geography. A game of humor and politics, power and prestige, *Democracy* would also be fun for teens to play.

> An international chain of hotels, food, and hospitality services was begun inauspiciously with a root-beer stand at 14th Street and Park Road, NW, in 1927. The young entrepreneurs did quite well in the end; their names were Alice and J. W. Marriott.

And, believe it or not, there's even a children's *map* of Washington, D.C., by Guy Fox.

Have a safe and happy visit!

Oh, and by the way, please keep in touch. To help us update suggestions and information, we need to hear from readers. Visit www.parentsperspective.org, or send an e-mail to parentsper@gmail.com.

Answers to Smart Stuff Questions

A. In 1871 Congress passed a law making Washington a federal territory. Since 1802 it had been a city simply called Washington, with a mayor appointed by the president, as well as a city council. After the Civil War, corruption was rampant in city governments across the country, and Washington was no exception. In an attempt to keep the capital from being moved to a different part of the country, Congress instituted territorial status (no more local government). Because the United States was known as Columbia (for Christopher Columbus), the new capital was named the District of Columbia.

B. Algonquin and Iroquois. They believed that strangers from across the ocean would come and destroy their people.

C. Philadelphia, PA; Baltimore, MD; Lancaster, PA; York, PA; Princeton, NJ; Annapolis, MD; Trenton, NJ; and New York, NY.

D. Helen Herron (Mrs. William Howard) Taft received the ornamental cherry trees as a gift to the United States from Japan.

CHAPTER

1

Preparing
to Go

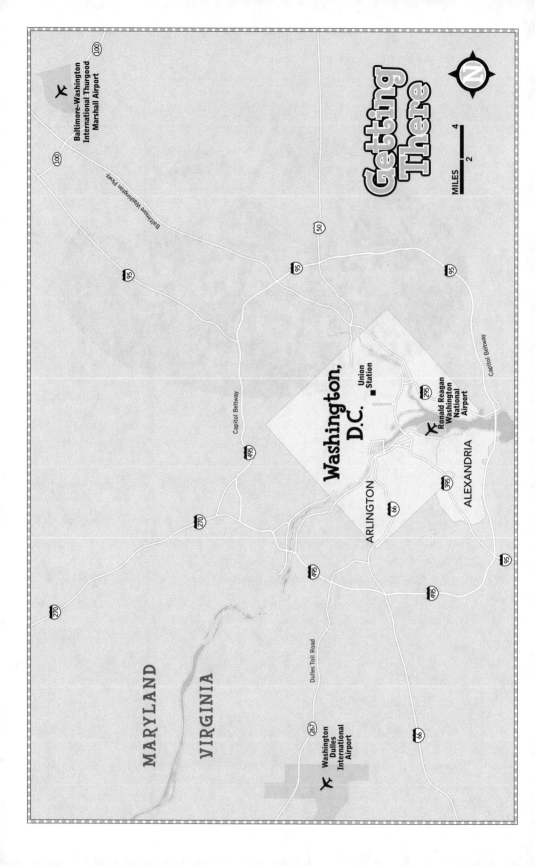

Washington, D.C., is a wonderful city for visitors at all times of the year. In spring its famous cherry blossoms festoon the Tidal Basin and adjoining Potomac Park with ribbons of pastel pink. In summer visitors can enjoy the annual Smithsonian Folklife Festival spread out across the Mall. Thousands come to sit under the stars on the grounds of the Washington Monument every Independence Day and marvel at the canopy of fireworks crackling in magnificent displays overhead. In addition to the beauty of leaves changing color in a city filled with trees, fall brings the opening of the Supreme Court and the return of Congress from its August recess. Winter is always a season of surprises, from glittery frost and snow to bright, clear days when the white marble buildings reflect the sunlight against a deep blue sky. Winters are normally mild and not crowded with tourists, except during the holiday season; a short subway, bus, or taxi ride can get you quickly to almost any destination in the city.

When to Go

Tourists crowd into all of Washington's most popular attractions and forms of transportation at cherry blossom time and in the hot, humid summer months when school is out. The best times to avoid a mob scene are before Memorial Day, when the weather is lovely and the crowds are lighter, and after Labor Day, when most schools have reopened and the weather is more comfortable. Weekends can be a challenge at any time of year, however. November brings lighter numbers of travelers and welcome fall temperatures. Although unpredictable weather-wise, winter (except for the last few weeks of December) is the least crowded season of all, and brings the added bonus of a full and accessible cultural scene. Daytime spring temperatures average from the low 60s to the mid-70s; summer sizzles with temperatures regularly in the 80s and sometimes into the 90s (don't forget about Washington's famous humidity); fall begins in the 70s and ends in the 50s; and winter temperatures hover normally in the 30s and 40s—but there *can* be stretches of bone-chilling weather and snow.

The winter holiday season in Washington is popular because of the many colorful events open to the public, but this does mean long waits for some activities. Saturday brings peak numbers of visitors all year long. Monday through Wednesday is the least crowded time at most sites. But be sure to call and check days and hours of operation.

Planning Your Itinerary

The logical question is whether to pull children out of school to visit Washington, D.C. What more educational city could a child visit? If the visit is a family trip or a school trip, parents and teachers together need to facilitate a workable plan, so that a youngster doesn't return home to enormous loads of make-up work and uses his travel experience productively. A creative teacher might prepare a list of questions as a framework for the child's written response (see "The Capital Scavenger Hunt" at the end of this chapter).

Every monument, gallery, and museum has free (or inexpensive) informative guides and brochures to enhance your visit. Encourage children to collect information and reflect on and discuss what they see and hear. They might even like to buy a postcard at

Parents/Teachers Take Note

Everywhere you go in Washington there will be pictures and papers to collect, so it's a good idea for each young person to prepare a scrapbook to save these in after the trip. Some people might choose to select a specific theme for a scrapbook, such as architecture, monuments and/or statues, or maps and charts. Gallon-size resealable plastic bags make good storage containers for these treasured items. Pack a few in backpacks and label each with a sticker.

Needless to say, everything that pertains to children and trips needs a name and address label (except, perhaps, the child!). Three-dimensional objects that cannot be pasted in a scrapbook can be saved in a memory box, a container specifically purchased or made by your child to showcase these items after you get home. And don't forget about those *journals*.

Autograph collectors, bring your autograph books. In addition to collecting signatures, you might want to preserve a meaningful name from the Vietnam Veterans Wall, for example. You can hold a page up against the name and rub the side of a pencil or crayon over it; the name will appear on your page.

each site for future journal or scrapbook use. (Journals come in handy here.)

If possible, arrange in advance with your legislator's office to obtain passes to watch Congress in session. Students can often meet senators and representatives at their offices when picking up the passes. If not, free timed-entry passes (one per person) are given on a first-come, first-served basis for tours of the Capitol, at the kiosk opposite the Botanic Gardens. Also, check the local newspapers for notices about Congressional hearings and committee meetings that are open to the public. These hands-on experiences can be more memorable than any class in (or lecture on) U.S. government. Come see how your tax dollars are spent.

Contact the Smithsonian Information Center (202/633–1000; www.si.edu) to request a free copy of *Planning Your Smithsonian Visit.* When you need information you can't find in other materials, try one of these helpful telephone numbers: Dial-a-Park (202/619–7275 recording); National Park Service (202/619–7222; www.nps.gov); and the D.C. Department of Parks and Recreation (202/673–7646; www.dpr.dc.gov).

Need help coming up with activities that the kids will enjoy? The Children's Concierge (301/309–6601 or 877/888–5462; www.childrensconcierge.com) designs itineraries for groups and families, offering ways, such as scavenger hunts, to involve kids interactively in Washington's cultural and historical sites.

Don't forget to check out the great ideas from the editors at Fodor's (www.fodors.com).

Once you've arrived, there are still more resources. All three major airports that serve the city have trained staff members on hand to help with the kinds of problems travelers encounter. The National Park Service has two kiosks—on the Ellipse and near the Vietnam Veterans Memorial—open all year to assist visitors. Other kiosks around the city are open seasonally.

Helpful Hint

When it comes to finding out about Washington, online resources abound. The official Web site for the D.C. Convention and Visitors Association is www.washington.org, where event calendars and travel tips are generally kept up-to-date. This site also enables you to make hotel reservations online. The organization publishes *The American Experience,* a helpful pamphlet, as well as seasonal calendars of events and clear visitor maps. Don't forget the D.C. Visitor Information Center, which has online information at www.dcvisit.com.

Media Resources

The *Washington Post* (www.washingtonpost.com), a favorite with local news junkies, is especially valuable for its Friday edition, which includes the "Weekend" section. Here's where to find tips for what's hot during the time you're in town. The newspaper has a "Today in Congress" column that details the times and locations of House and Senate sessions and committee hearings, as well as which are open to the public. There's a similar column called "Washington Daybook" in the *Washington Times* (www.washingtontimes.com). *City Paper* (www.washingtoncitypaper.com), a free Generation X–friendly alternative weekly, is a good source for information on arts, theaters, clubs, and popular music, as well as reviews of current movies. *The Washington Informer* (www.washingtoninformer.com) provides coverage of D.C.'s black community. *Washington Jewish Week* (www.washingtonjewishweek.com) lists synagogues and kosher restaurants, in addition to community news and events. *Washingtonian* (www.washingtonian.com) is a monthly magazine with all sorts of events listings, restaurant write-ups, and special features. Numerous publications focusing on specific communities are available at newsstands, including *News World* (1001 Connecticut Avenue, NW; 202/872–0190). It's open weekdays 6 AM to 8:30 PM and weekends 7 to 7. Hotel desks provide the ubiquitous, free *Go* and *Where* brochures that list what's going on around town.

On the airwaves, Washingtonians have a variety of choices. Around the clock, newsaholics (of which there are many here) can watch or listen to C-SPAN, broadcasting coverage of congressional events. (On the radio, it's 90.1 FM.) Local news here is often national news; you may see yourselves on a local channel if you've spent the day visiting a government event or congressional hearing. Several radio stations focus on news, talk, and sports programming, including 630 AM, 1500 AM, and 820 AM. "Parents' Perspective," a national and international parenting program, airs on 1500 AM and 820 AM at 7 PM on Sunday evenings. Everyone's musical tastes can be satisfied by at least one D.C.–area radio station; check the Web or *Washington Post* for listings.

On the Web, you can access *D.C. Urban Moms* (www.dcurbanmom.com), a daily compendium of advice and suggestions to and from area parents. *Our Kids* (www.our-kids.com) has resources for families in the D.C. area. *Our Kids Weekly,* an e-mail newsletter with tips on family- and child-centered area events, is available by subscribing online (info@our-kids.com).

Movies, Books, & Games

Heat up the popcorn; watch a film. Some fine movies with a Washington, D.C., connection that are good for older tweens and teens include *Independence Day* and *Air Force One,* action movies with very active presidents, and *All the President's Men,* a gripping whodunit that just happens to be a real-life story. Kids need to be reminded that the work two reporters began resulted in the only resignation of a president in U.S. history. Teens might also enjoy *Thirteen Days*, about the Cuban missile crisis; *Charlie Wilson's War,* a frightening exposé of foreign policy; and *Wag the Dog*, an eye-opening look at how information can be manipulated in politics.

Book lovers will especially enjoy delving into the rich selection of works on Washington, D.C. For tykes, take a look at *What's in Washington, D.C.?*, by Laine Falk, and *A Kid's Guide to Washington, D.C.*, updated by Miriam Chernick (tweens might like this, too). For tweens there's *The Mystery in Washington, D.C.,* by Gertrude Chandler Warner, a mystery set in many Washington sites; and *Washington: An Adventure for Kids*, by Martin Weston. *The Capital Mysteries Series*, by Ron Roy, also for tweens, includes *Who Cloned the President, Skeleton in the Smithsonian,* and *A Thief at the National Zoo.* Tweens and young teens may like *The Case of Capital Intrigue,* by Carolyn Keene, another exciting mystery, this time about a theft in the nation's capital. Teens might like *Murder in the Executive Mansion* and *Murder in the West Wing: An Eleanor Roosevelt Mystery,* two popular titles in a series of mysteries set in the capital city that was written by Eleanor and Franklin Roosevelt's son Elliot; *Washington, D.C.: Ghosts, Legends, and Lore*, by E. Ashley Rooney and Betsy Johnston; and *The Street Lawyer,* by John Grisham, where the famous mystery writer does it again, this time taking his hero from the plush offices of his high-priced firm to the gritty world of the homeless. The Dan Brown thriller *The Lost Symbol* is set in Washington; it's an engrossing read for teens.

If teens are interested in Washington's natural world, two suggestions are *Spring in Washington,* by Louis J. Halle; and *Specimen Days,* by Walt Whitman, describing the city and its surrounding areas during the Civil War era. For older teens, there's *Undercover Washington: Touring the Sites Where Infamous Spies Lived, Worked, and Loved,* by Pamela Kessler, a guide to places in and around D.C., complete with true stories about dastardly deeds. Other picks for older teens are *Murder in Foggy Bottom,* part of a well-received crime series by Margaret Truman (she should know the territory—she's former President Harry Truman's daughter); *The Incumbent: A Washington Thriller,* by Brian McGrory, about a Boston journalist who gets involved in an assassination plot; and *Washington, D.C.: A Novel,* by Gore Vidal, a searing look at politics, politicians, and others from the New Deal to the McCarthy era.

For wonderful options for kids and their families, check out *Surfing the Net with Kids* (www.surfnetkids.com). Here you can find up-to-date lists of games about Washington. And if you just feel like sitting on the floor together for hours, you can indulge in *Washington, D.C., Monopoly.* Here you really can own the Treasury!

Expense Planning

What will a trip to Washington, D.C., cost? There are certain built-in expenses such as transportation, lodging, meals, souvenirs (if you indulge), and

A good map is essential. Do you know if your destination is NW or NE?

entertainment. The good news, however, is that in this city most tourist attractions are *free*. Well, not exactly—you've already paid for them with your tax money. Unless otherwise noted, all museums and galleries we describe charge no admission fees.

Rates for everything, except local transportation, change according to season. Your best ammunition is to ask questions. As with the "rack rates" for hotels, there are always alternatives, but you have to learn what the options are. Check out special rates for students, senior citizens, tours, groups, AAA members, AARP members, union members, and any other group you've ever been associated with! Ask, "But do you have anything for *less?*" Some universities make dormitory space available for their students who come to work or study in Washington; contact your local university to see if they have vacancies in their D.C. facilities.

Money-Saving Tip
International Student/Teacher Identity Cards
Special discount ID cards are available for students and for teachers, but they have to be obtained in advance of the trip. For information, contact STA Travel (212/627–3111 or 800/552–9046; www.statravel.com). Outside the United States, contact www.istc.org.

Money-Saving Tip
Telephone calls from hotel rooms can be quite pricey; most hotels tack on extra fees beyond the change you would spend at a pay phone. Come prepared with quarters— or better yet, a cell phone.

Most travelers already know that it's not wise to carry wads of cash. Depending on your preferences and the spending habits of your traveling companions, it's a good idea to plan generously and end up with cash for last-minute, take-home items. Since traveler's checks are fast becoming an anachronism, some advance planning is in

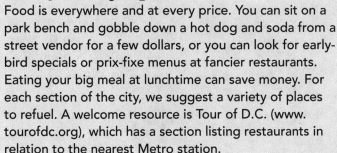

Money-Saving Tip

Food is everywhere and at every price. You can sit on a park bench and gobble down a hot dog and soda from a street vendor for a few dollars, or you can look for early-bird specials or prix-fixe menus at fancier restaurants. Eating your big meal at lunchtime can save money. For each section of the city, we suggest a variety of places to refuel. A welcome resource is Tour of D.C. (www. tourofdc.org), which has a section listing restaurants in relation to the nearest Metro station.

order. ATMs offer the convenience of picking up only the money you need when you need it—as long as you plan ahead and know which of your cards is acceptable to most machines. Check in advance with your hotel, because it's always safer to use an ATM inside your hotel, or inside any building, than to stop out in the open and let everybody around know you are filling your pockets with a fresh supply of cash. Credit cards, of course, are wonderful and generally safe, but it's wise to copy the card's emergency toll-free number and keep it somewhere separate from the card. If your credit card is lost or stolen, you will have the necessary number to call and cancel it immediately. A good tip for travelers is to lighten your wallet. Carry as few cards as possible.

Bellhops receive tips of about $1 per bag, checkroom attendants expect $1 per garment, and parking lot attendants and door-

Money-Saving Tip

Tickets for theatrical and sports events can be pricey—as much as $100 for the most popular shows—but there are ways to get bargains. Check out TICKETplace (202/638-2406; www.cultural-alliance.org) for last-minute bargains. Washington offers lots of free entertainment every day . . . and it's not all in Congress. Appendix I provides all the details.

The venerable Willard Inter-Continental Hotel

men who hail a taxi for you expect $1. Waiters generally get around 20% tips, and cab drivers should get about 15% of the fare.

Where to Stay

Ah, the glories of room service and telephones in your bathroom. But when you're planning where to stay in downtown Washington you need to consider the essentials. If you're going to be exploring the city on foot, as you should do (parking on the street is nearly impossible, and some lots cannot accommodate large cars at all!), stay within easy walking distance of a Metro station. Don't worry— *Washington, D.C., with Kids* comes with its own Metro map (see front inside cover of this book). We'll tell you what accommodations are near which stops. The size of your group will also dic-

Helpful Hint

Be absolutely sure to have reservations before you come to Washington. It's a good idea to confirm a few days before your trip. George might have slept here, but you will need reservations.

tate your choices. Some larger places are delighted with busloads of teenagers, while smaller ones cater to adults or families. Count on a really good travel agent, if you can find one. Travel agents often know more places and can get better deals. You can also try the on-line agencies (www.expedia.com, www.travelocity.com, www.orbitz. com, www.priceline.com, www.kayak.com, and www.sidestep.com) or contact the companies below:

Central Reservation Service (800/555–7555; www.crshotels. com)

Hotel Reservations Network (800/964–6835; www. hotelreservationsnetwork.com)

Washington, D.C., Accommodations (800/503–3330; www.wdcahotels.com)

Capital Reservations (800/847–4832; www.visitdc.com)

One caveat for anyone taking groups of students: absolutely avoid hotel rooms with balconies!

Smart Stuff

Game time! A wonderful way to introduce kids to the layout of Washington is to have them work in groups with a large city map and a colored map of the Metro-rail system. Contact the DC Convention and Tourism Corporation (202/789–7000; www.washington.org).

Give each group six to eight places to locate on their street maps, and then have them identify which subway stops they would use to get there. The difficulty of locations and number of assignments can be geared to the ages of the participants, whether 5th graders or 10th graders. This can be a race among the groups. Washington T-shirts would make wonderful prizes.

What to Bring

In contrast to travelers who need a truck just to get their luggage to the airport, savvy travelers to Washington come with as little baggage as possible. (Everyone does bring political preferences, but these don't take up space.) Almost every place you go will welcome casual attire; however, this means clothing that will not embarrass adults. One dressier outfit is a safe bet—a jacket, slacks, dress shirt, tie, dress or skirt, and change of shoes should suffice for any special dinner, event, or religious service. Bring the most comfortable pair of shoes you've ever worn, as you could wear them out on this trip. We find it useful to pack an extra pair of spongy insoles that fit into any pair. Happy feet make happy travelers.

Summer packing is the easiest because you won't need coats or boots—but don't forget these items if you're coming in late fall through early spring. Wintry weather can arrive early and stay late. Because any season could surprise you, carry a sweater or lightweight jacket to use as a layer to stave off early-morning or late-evening chill. Layers, in fact, are always a good idea. In summer many buildings have thermostats set to arctic temperatures. For summer you might want to pack a little personal fan (a tiny machine, not a small groupie). The hot, sticky weather will require coping with sweat—yours and everyone else's. No matter when you visit D.C., raincoats and/or umbrellas are wise choices.

Especially for kids, backpacks or fanny packs offer space to stow a whole day's worth of supplies: jackets, cameras, notepads and pens, small games or toys, snacks, and drinks. We have found that when traveling with children *snack* is the most valuable word in our vocabulary, because it's the key to a child's stamina and an adult's patience. Teens also require frequent infusions of energy, and might need a reminder to be prepared.

A small notebook or a set of small note cards can serve as a journal for each traveler. Teachers and parents need to allow time each day for kids to jot down their own personal notes. Where they go, what they see, who they meet, jokes they want to remember, and thoughts, ideas, or brilliant revelations that occur to them during their travels are all worth saving. And what fun it is afterward for everyone, adults and kids alike, to share and compare their versions of the trip. Of course, every traveler should also bring some kind of camera.

If you want your group's members to stay together, plan for everyone to wear something identifiable. Sun visors, baseball caps, or bandannas—all matching—are easy to recognize. They're also helpful to tour guides so they can recognize who's in your group. Some people use T-shirts for this purpose, but, teenagers' habits notwithstanding, the shirts do need to be washed and therefore can't be counted on for daily wear. They do make nice souvenirs, though. Parents of small children might want to pin a tag onto the back of each child's shirt or jacket with a hotel or cell phone number, just in case.

Getting Here

No matter where you're coming from, the most important thing to remember when you arrive in Washington is that the time it will take to get to your specific destination depends on the time of day. At the beginning and end of each working day most Washingtonians are worried more about transportation gridlock than legislation gridlock. Rush hours are impossible, so plan accordingly. From 6:30 to 9:30 AM and from 3:30 to 7 PM, traffic snarls are everywhere—we are not making this up!—and you will have to plan at least an extra hour to drive *anywhere*. Bridges that cross the Potomac and Anacostia rivers are especially likely to become bottlenecks during rush hour. (We've heard rumors that people have met and become engaged while caught in bridge traffic.) If you're caught in this jumble, you might get better acquainted than you ever expected with the occupants of cars, trucks, or buses on either side of you, and possibly behind and in front of you as well.

Car Travel

Years ago, wise planners thought they had the solution: a highway encircling the city. They were wrong. The Capital Beltway, which consists of Interstates I–495 and I–95, can come to a complete standstill if there's an accident anywhere along the way. Connecting to the Beltway are five major highways that go off in different directions: Route

66 goes west into Virginia; Interstate 50 heads east toward Annapolis, the Chesapeake Bay, and the beaches; Interstate 95 is a north–south route that overlaps the Beltway for a while; Interstate 270 goes northwest through Frederick, Maryland; and Route 295, known locally as the Baltimore-Washington Parkway, heads northeast toward Baltimore (Route 195 is a parallel highway for this route). Exits are clearly marked, but wherever you're heading, be sure to get specific directions, including exit numbers. Fast food and lots of free informational brochures and maps on Maryland, Virginia, and Washington are available at rest stops along the major highways. Take advantage!

Parents/Teachers Take Note

Yet another way to squeeze in some culture: try the Metropolitan Washington Art Tour (703/417–0895). Free hour-long walking tours of 30 works of art at Ronald Reagan Washington National Airport are available weekdays 10 to 2. Register three weeks ahead.

Bus Travel

Buses connect Washington with cities all over the United States. The downtown bus terminal is near Union Station at 1005 1st Street, NE (an area you would not want to walk in alone at night). For schedules, contact **Greyhound** (800/231–2222; www.greyhound.com) or **Peter Pan–Trailways** (800/343–9999; www.peterpanbus.com). In recent years additional low-cost bus services have sprung up, with special deals to and from Washington, D.C., mostly from the northeast cities. Try Google or www.busjunction.com for more information on such companies as Vamoose Bus, Bolt Bus, Mega Bus, and Washington Deluxe.

Train Travel

Trains bring you right into the heart of Washington. Across the street from the Capitol is Union Station (400 N. Capitol Street, NW; 202/

371–9441; www.unionstationdc.com), one of the country's most beautiful terminals. You can easily head for any part of the city, either via Metro or one of the taxis waiting in front of the station. The many shops and restaurants inside this Beaux Arts building give families with cranky or hungry children places to relax and refuel. **Amtrak** (800/872–7245; www.amtrak.com), the country's national passenger rail system, has dozens of daily departures. The Metro has a stop right inside Union Station. Maryland Rail Commuter Service, better known as **MARC** (800/325–7245; www.mtamaryland.com), is a commuter line from Union Station to Baltimore and other places in Maryland. In Virginia, the commuter line is called the Virginia Railway Express, or **VRE** (703/684–1001; www.vre.org).

Plane Travel

Washington's three airports—**Baltimore-Washington International Thurgood Marshall**, **Ronald Reagan Washington National**, and **Washington Dulles International**—are busy at all hours. Taxis, shuttle buses, and limousine services are available at all three. Information desks help travelers who need assistance.

Reagan National (703/417–8000; www.mwaa.com) has mostly domestic flights, but also services a few international routes. BWI (410/859–7100; www.bwiairport.com) and Dulles (703/572–2700; www.mwaa.com) have extensive domestic and international routes.

A taxi from Reagan National to most downtown locations runs at least $15; from Washington Dulles International Airport it's

Washington Dulles International Airport

$45, and from BWI it's $65. There are several services that shuttle passengers to and from the airports, all of which run about $10 to $28 to downtown; if there are two people traveling together, the second person's fare is much lower. Just keep in mind that fares do change.

If you ever doubt that Washington is an international city, a ride in a D.C.–area cab will be a quick reminder. Your driver will probably be from anywhere but Washington, and most likely even from outside the United States. Conversations with these people can be especially interesting. One cab driver told us of his distress when he arrived in the United States and the authorities took away his monkey!

Washington operates nominally on Eastern Standard Time (Eastern Daylight Time in summer), but in reality everyone is on "fast-forward." Plan your travel so you won't be a member of the frantic masses. (For example, a 4 PM arrival at Dulles does not match well with a 6 PM appointment *anywhere*.) Welcome to Washington, D.C. Drivers, start your engines!

Getting Around

Washington actually does have a basic plan, and once you understand it, getting around is a lot less mysterious. Even taxi drivers might rely on *your* knowing how to get to your destination. Washington is on the east side of the Potomac River. Virginia is on the west and south side. Washington is divided into four basic sections—NW, NE, SE, and SW—with the U.S. Capitol in the center. The quadrants are in no way equal in size. NW is much larger than any other area of the city. North Capitol Street separates NW and NE, East Capitol Street separates NE and SE, and South Capitol Street separates the two southern quadrants. When visiting anywhere in the 70 square miles that make up the city, you'll need to know which quadrant you're heading for; the same address—for example, 500 C Street—can be found in all four. You have to be more specific: 500 C Street, NW, for example. Numbered streets run north–south, and lettered streets run east–west. Avenues (mostly named for states) run diagonally and often pass through traffic circles and squares. Navigating these is an interesting outdoor sport for natives and visitors alike. Although there will not be a quiz on all this information, once you consult a map, trust us, it will make sense.

By Bus

Metrobus (202/637–7000; www.metroopensdoors.com) vehicles crisscross the city all day and into the evening, with more frequent stops during morning and evening rush hours. Buses require either exact change (in bills, coins, or both) or tokens available for purchase inside the sales office in the Metro Center subway station. You can also purchase one-day bus passes for $3 or seven-day bus passes for $11.

By Car

If you crave adventure and bring your car into the city, come prepared with lots of quarters for the meters. Read all the signs *very carefully.* When it says "2-hour parking," it means just that. You *must* move your car after the allotted time has expired (meter feeding will get you a ticket). Those pricey parking lots scattered around the city are still cheaper than a $50 parking ticket.

By Subway

Metrorail (202/637–7000; www.metroopensdoors.com) is a safe, clean, and efficient subway system. For many travelers we've interviewed, D.C.'s Metro was their first experience riding subways. Most find it an exciting adventure, in addition to being quick and conven-

Helpful Hint

Keep in mind that no eating is allowed on the subway; just ask the local middle school student who was handcuffed by police for this unsavory crime.

ient. Metrorail lines have color names—Red, Yellow, Orange, Blue, and Green—and each station is marked with the letter *M* at street level. In addition to clear route maps posted at every station, there are also kiosks with attendants who can answer your questions.

Fare-card vending machines inside each Metrorail station accept coins and crisp $1, $5, $10, or $20 bills. If the machine spits your bill back out at you, try folding and unfolding it lengthwise before asking for help. Newer machines will also accept credit cards. You will use the fare card both when you enter *and when you leave* the subway platforms, so hang on to your fare card even after you board! Fares run from $1.35 to $3.90, depending on how far you travel and whether you're in rush hour. You can buy one-day passes for $6.50 and seven-day passes for $32.50.

By Taxi

Within the city all taxis are metered, and will charge you according to the distance you travel. Maps and rate charts are posted in each taxi. There are some extra fees, such as charges for each additional passenger, for luggage handling, and for rides during the morning and evening rush hours. A surcharge is tacked on when you phone for a cab. Charges more than double during snow emergencies. Fares change, so always ask a driver how much a fare will be before you climb inside; not including surcharges, a maximum fare in D.C. is currently $19. You can usually hail a taxi in front of any hotel, subway or bus station, or major site. Report problems to the D.C. Taxicab Commission at 202/645–6018.

Touring

Teachers and students we've interviewed have made touring suggestions you might find helpful. In most cases, when teachers bring large groups of students to Washington they work with tour companies well in advance of their trip. Here are some recommended companies:

Educational Travel Adventures (www.educationaltraveladv. com)

USA Consolidated Travel (www.usastudenttravel.com)

USA Educational Adventures (800/949–0650; www. usaeducationaladventures.com)

If you contact a tour company, you'll want to know what these folks can do for you. Do they pick up at your school and take your group to the airport? Do they transport you to all the sites you will visit? Do they provide guide service or just a driver? Do they arrange for accommodations, meals, and so forth? Ask to receive all details in writing and discuss all your questions with one contact person; of course, ask for references, and call and grill them. Most companies offer three-, four-, and five-day plans for visiting Washington, D.C. Some school groups from far-off places may want to spend, say, three days in Washington, two in Philadelphia, and two or three in New York City. Some groups driving to Washington also visit Gettysburg, Pennsylvania, Annapolis, Maryland, and Luray Caverns, Virginia. Teachers can plan independently, perhaps bringing groups on an early flight one morning and returning late evening the next day, spending two very full days in D.C. Teachers stress that if you use a tour company, you will want to thoroughly research the choice of guide and driver for your group.

Another wonderful source to consider is the Close Up Foundation (800/256–7387; www.closeup.org), a "citizenship education organization" founded in 1970. Close Up offers a selection of civic education activities for middle-school and high-school students. Billed as an "innovative, experiential learning program," each is a short, participatory course in U.S. history, quite different from a sightseeing tour. Students who have come to Washington for a week or so of Close Up have described their experiences with much enthusiasm. Many books and videos on topics relevant to this kind of study are also published by Close Up.

From our teachers and students, here are "the big eight" suggestions when it comes to touring Washington:

1. Be prepared. Figure out your optimum itinerary in advance, taking into account *your* group's needs and requirements.

2. Be flexible. If one site is unexpectedly off-limits, have a "B" list to substitute from.

3. Take advantage of "specials." These might be based on the time of year, specific visiting shows or performances—anything you know about in advance can become a treasured extra for your trip.

4. If possible, try to connect with at least one other student tour. Kids love meeting students from other parts of the country (or the world).

5. Use what the city has to offer. Have lunch in a public park (if the weather cooperates) or use the Metro. Walk when you can—you'll see more.

6. Fit the sites to the curriculum. Students are not enthusiastic about visiting memorials to folks they've never studied.

7. Choose your chaperones (whether teachers or parents) wisely, as they can make or break a trip.

8. Separation can reduce anxiety. For some age groups, putting boys and girls (and appropriate chaperones) on separate floors (of the hotel) gives everyone a better night's sleep.

Keeping Safe

As in any city, tourists need to be cautious in Washington. Adults traveling with children should talk with them about safety before the trip. Washington is a city made for tourists, and safety of visitors is a major priority in a place that is so dependent on income from travelers. The areas that attract the most travelers—including the Mall, Georgetown, Dupont Circle, and Adams Morgan—have a strong police presence. Additional agencies are also involved in your protection, including the U.S. Park Police, the U.S. Capitol Police, the Secret Service, Metro police, and even the Smithsonian Institution's own police force. Visitors can spot officers on foot, on horseback, on bicycles, on motorcycles, and in cars. Although monuments are open daily 24 hours, rangers are on duty at each from only 8 AM until midnight.

Smart is safe. Every kid needs to be able to recognize security people on the streets and in buildings. Whenever you enter a new site, designate a *specific* meeting spot that everyone can easily find. Someone just might get lost or separated, and everybody needs to know where to go in that situation.

The crime statistics you hear about most frequently are rarely random shootings but are instead usually connected with the drug trade, which is centered in areas far from the tourist sites. The parts of Washington that tend to have the highest crime rates are parts of Northeast and Southeast not regularly frequented by tourists. If you're visiting a site in one of those areas, go as a group and go in the daytime.

The best protection—anywhere—is always self-protection. Walk purposefully and with a group. Look like you know where you're going, even when you don't. If you have to pull out a map, go into a store or museum. Women should keep purses close to their bodies, even under a coat. Men should keep wallets in front pants pockets, not an easily-accessible-to-anyone back pocket. It's a good idea to have small bills readily available to pull out instead of a big wad or wallet packed full of twenties.

If you should ever face a crime situation, your mouth is your best weapon. Shout very loudly for help and move away quickly. Shouting "Fire!" gets more attention than "Stop, thief!" The last thing a criminal wants is for anyone to notice. If you're asked to turn over your wallet, throw it and run in the other direction. The robber will be much more interested in going after the money than going after you.

If you need to catch a taxi at a train or bus station or an airport, always use the taxi line, where properly licensed and regulated drivers and vehicles are lined up for your safety. Offers for taxi or limo rides from people on the street or in the terminals could result in major overcharges or personal harm. If you're driving and become lost at night, *do not* stop the car to ask for directions. Keep driving until you find a hotel, gas station, police station, or fire station, where you can ask for assistance.

After dark, do not travel alone anywhere in the city. Teenagers, who, of course, feel indestructible, need to remember that there is safety in numbers. Even if they're in a group, under no circumstances should young people interact with suspicious-looking strangers. This advice is appropriate for *all* travelers. People on street corners or in front of restaurants asking for money *do* have resources for food and shelter funded by the city. Your response is your personal choice.

The Capital Scavenger Hunt

One enjoyable way to keep kids' attention throughout a visit is to offer a game, and *you* get to come up with an appropriate prize. (How about a D.C. souvenir—maybe a sweatshirt or T-shirt?) We suggest a scavenger hunt, perhaps to be played in teams. Here's a sample list of items to search for during a visit to Washington, D.C.:

1. Huge bronze doors depicting the life of Christopher Columbus
2. Figure of a blindfolded lady holding scales
3. A statue topped with two graceful cranes side by side
4. Statue of A. Philip Randolph
5. A large clock with IIII instead of the traditional IV for 4
6. Washington's only round museum
7. The *Voyager*
8. A Hawaiian outrigger canoe and Alaskan kayak
9. Bronze statue of the Messenger of the Gods
10. Statue of Alexander Hamilton
11. Statue of a famous scientist seated on a bench in a grove of elm and holly trees
12. Around the top of the Lincoln Memorial are the names of the 48 states in the Union at the time the memorial was dedicated. Where are the names of Alaska and Hawaii?
13. A wall of 4,000 gold stars
14. Corn and tobacco peeking out from the coat on a sculpture of a president
15. A $100,000 bill
16. Statue of Gandhi
17. The Congress Bells (Hint: they are *not* on Capitol Hill.)
18. Quote: "What is past is prologue."

19. A shoe with a radio in the heel
20. The Presidential Box, where no President has sat since April 14, 1865.
21. Statue of a lion protecting its cubs
22. A piece of moon rock that is not in the Air and Space Museum
23. America's earliest submarine
24. An exhibit featuring a model of an important escape vessel used by a young naval officer who later became president
25. "The Growlery"
26. The mast of the USS *Maine*
27. Three tall steel spires arching skyward
28. Statue of the President who instituted our national park system
29. A traffic-stopping monument featuring a Confederate soldier

(**ANSWERS** at end of Appendix III, page 384.)

CHAPTER

2

Capitol Hill

The most important land elevation in the free world, Capitol Hill is more than a collection of buildings. It's a neighborhood of historic homes, interesting shops, and intimate restaurants and bars where blue-collar and white-collar workers mingle with members of Congress, legislative aides, and lobbyists. The heart of Capitol Hill is the main tourist attraction: the **U.S. Capitol,** with its neighbors, the **Supreme Court,** the **Library of Congress,** the **House and Senate Office Buildings,** and **Union Station.** This area is worth a full day: the combination of history and current events packed into this real estate demands your time and attention. Many of the streets are not well lighted, so be cautious here at night.

To ensure their availability, it's a good idea to request tickets for the House and Senate galleries well in advance of your visit to Washington, D.C. Tickets can be reserved through any of your legislators between three weeks and three months in advance. The names of your senators and representatives should be listed in the front of your local telephone directory, along with a local contact number. To reach your legislators while visiting Washington, D.C., call the main congressional switchboard at 202/224–3121 and ask to be connected to their offices. Only five tickets can be issued under one visitor's name. The most recent run on tickets came for

Smart Stuff

For Tweens . . . Kids might enjoy writing their own letters from the viewpoint of a youngster encountering a famous person in a historic period.

the impeachment hearings of President Bill Clinton. (Talk about watching your government at work!) Senate offices (on Constitution Avenue between Delaware Avenue and 2nd Street, NE) are open weekdays 8 to 6 and Saturday 9 to 1. House offices (Independence Avenue between 1st Street, SW, and 1st Street, SE, and corner of C Street and New Jersey Avenue) are open weekdays 8 to 6 and Saturday 8 to 1. Always call ahead, as security concerns often prompt new entry requirements.

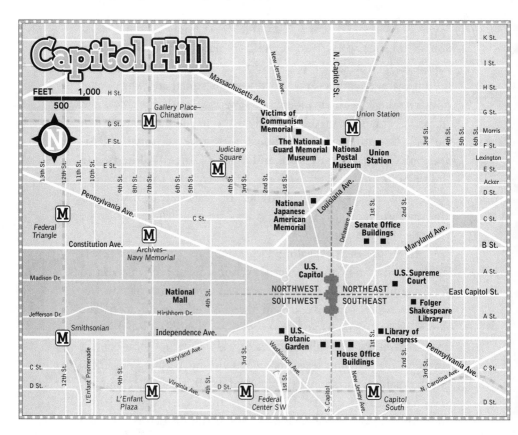

★The United States Capitol

For Tweens and Teens . . . The Capitol has seen its share of hard times. Its cast-iron dome expands and contracts as much as four inches under extreme temperatures. And to help heal the body politic, its first designer was a physician (and amateur architect), William Thornton. During the Civil War the Rotunda was used as a soldiers' barracks and then as a hospital. Noted Americans, from Henry Clay (1852), Abraham Lincoln (1865), John F. Kennedy (1963), Dwight D. Eisenhower (1969), and Ronald Reagan (2004) have lain in state in the Rotunda.

Evidently, John Quincy Adams was the beneficiary of a fascinating architectural quirk: the spot in Statuary Hall where he had his desk echoed sounds, including those whispered from the other side, so he was able to respond to opponents' arguments before they even stood to speak. Kids like to stand on the spot (a guide can point this out) and whisper, to see if a friend across the room can hear them.

Smart Stuff

For Tweens and Teens . . . In the continental United States there's one geographic location that has no voting representatives in Congress. Its residents, however, are U.S. citizens and pay federal taxes. Can you name this place? **(A.)**

Under the East Plaza of the U.S. Capitol, between Constitution and Independence avenues, is a new addition to this venerable building: the Capitol Visitor Center. On two levels, the Visitor Center houses an exhibition hall, orientation theaters, a restaurant, and gift shops. Daily activities include a variety of lectures, demonstrations, and hands-on experiences. Check the Information Desk for the schedule on the day you visit.

Begin your visit with the 13-minute film *Out of Many, One,* in one of the orientation theaters. Then join a guide on a 1-hour tour of this new facility. The Capitol Visitor Center tells the story of the design and construction of the Capitol and the history of Congress as part of the narrative of our democracy. Changing exhibits of rare documents, as well as artifacts from the Smithsonian collection, give insight into specific historic periods.

The Visitor Center gift shops on its upper level offer books, jewelry, souvenirs, and specially designed items unique to the Capitol. It's open Monday through Saturday 8:30 to 4:30. Since even the most riveting history can't fill a hungry tummy, you might want to head to The C.V.C. Restaurant, also on the upper level, which serves a variety of soups, salads, entrées, sandwiches, pizzas, and desserts—all freshly made. The restaurant is open Monday through Saturday 7:30 to 4.

The wonderful fresco in the center of the Rotunda's dome, *The Apotheosis of Washington,* was painted by Italian immigrant artist Constantino Brumidi in 1865. He lay on his back on scaffolding for 11 months to create this work. The 13 angels (representing the original 13 states) welcoming George Washington into heaven are said to have been painted using local prostitutes as models. (In a democracy, every citizen can become involved.) An enthusiastic patriot, Brumidi added after his signature the words: "Citizen of the United States."

There are 23 recent acquisitions to the Capitol's National Statuary Hall Collection, representing individuals chosen by Congress to represent the diversity of accomplished Americans. See if your youngsters can identify any of the statues. Kids can touch the 11-foot-tall model of the Capitol dome. Several interactive exhibits

Parents/Teachers Take Note

Kids will enjoy tracking down the VIP from their own state in Statuary Hall or elsewhere in the Capitol. Check online at www.aoc.gov to find the exact location. Distinguished figures represented range from Utah's Philo Farnsworth, the father of TV, to King Kamehameha of Hawaii.

in the Visitor Center will appeal to guests of varying ages and interests. If you're with tweens or teens, walk through the Library of Congress Tunnel, from the Center's upper level, and visit another national treasure.

Outside, the sculpture atop the Capitol dome (no, it's not Pocahontas or Sacajawea) is *Freedom*. Originally, she was supposed to be free of clothing, but that was too daring for the mid-1800s. So appropriately draped and crowned with feathers, she weighs an astonishing seven tons and had to be raised and lowered by helicopter in recent years for cleaning and restoration. (After 130 years, wouldn't you want a bath?)

Smart Stuff

For Teens . . . What is a fresco? Students can research the method and see if they can find other famous artists who employed this technique. **(B.)**

Among the largest equestrian sculptural groupings in the world, the **statue of President Ulysses S. Grant on his horse,** Cincinnatus, is an imposing sight in front of the U.S. Capitol (1st Street, NW, between Maryland and Pennsylvania avenues, on the Capitol's west side). Presented as a Civil War hero rather than a less-than-effective politician, Grant is shown as a brave commander leading his troops into battle. This dramatic monument is often a hit with youngsters, like the little guy whose father spent a lengthy period pointing out the significance of the statues and the importance of Ulysses S. Grant in American history. The little boy was awed by the sculptures but finally asked, as they were leaving, "Dad, who was that *riding* on General Grant?"

Frederick Law Olmstead didn't only design landscapes, he also created a delightful little **Summer House** in the shadow of the west front of the Capitol. A hexagonal brick building built around a small fountain, the Summer House is partially secluded by foliage. It's reached by a small descending stairway. Stone benches and beck-

Quick Guide to

Attraction	Location
★The United States Capitol	On Capitol Hill, at the east end of the Mall
U.S. Botanic Garden	West side of the Capitol, 1st Street and Maryland Avenue, SW
★Library of Congress	1st Street and Independence Avenue, SE, across from the Capitol
Folger Shakespeare Library	201 E. Capitol Street, SE, east of the Library of Congress
★Supreme Court Building	1st Street and Maryland Avenue, NE, facing the Capitol
National Japanese American Memorial	In a small triangular park, bounded by New Jersey and Louisiana Avenues and D Street, NW
Victims of Communism Memorial	Small triangle at intersection of Massachusetts and New Jersey avenues and G Street, NW
The National Guard Memorial Museum	1 Massachusetts Avenue, NW
National Postal Museum	2 Massachusetts Avenue, NE
★Union Station	40 Massachusetts Avenue, NE

Capitol Hill Attractions

Age Range	Hours	Details on
Tweens and Teens	Mon.–Sat. 8:30 AM–4:30 PM	Page 29
All Ages	10 AM–5 PM daily	Page 39
Teens	Jefferson Building: Mon.–Sat. 10 AM–5:30 PM	Page 40
Tweens and Teens	Mon.–Sat. 10 AM–4 PM	Page 42
Tweens and Teens	Mon.–Fri. 9 AM–4:30 PM	Page 44
All Ages	24 hours daily	Page 46
Tweens and Teens	24 hours daily	Page 48
Tweens and Teens	Mon.–Fri. 10 AM–4 PM	Page 49
All Ages	10 AM–5:30 PM daily	Page 50
All Ages	Shops open Mon.–Sat. 10 AM–9 PM; Sun. 10 AM–6 PM	Page 51

The U.S. Capitol

oning archways invite the fortunate visitor to relax and unwind.

Committee hearings, often the pulse of Congress, can offer an exciting glimpse of the give-and-take of power. Each weekday, the *Washington Post* (www.washingtonpost.com) has a "Today in Congress" column that details the times and locations of House and Senate sessions and committee hearings, as well as which are open to the public. If you'd like to know what has already happened in these hallowed halls, you might browse through the *Congressional Record* (www.gpoaccess.gov/crecord).

Smart Stuff

How can you tell from looking at the outside of the Capitol whether the House or Senate is in session? What about at night? (C.)

In addition to the regular movers and shakers toiling on Capitol Hill, young people might notice another important but less visible group: pages. These teenagers work in the House of Representatives, the Senate, and the Supreme Court. Spending a high-school semester in Washington, these students live in a dormitory and attend the Capitol Page School at the Library of Congress. Their school day begins at 6:45 AM so that their classes do not conflict with their work. They wear navy jackets and gray pants (or skirts), white shirts with ties, and black shoes. Pages receive small salaries, out of which federal and state taxes, Social Security, and their residence hall fees are deducted. Basically, pages run errands and answer phones, but regulations still stipulate that they are to "keep the Senate snuff boxes filled." Daniel Webster and Henry Clay appointed the first page in 1829. There were no child labor laws at that time; he was only nine years old.

A subway system below Capitol Hill shuttles members of Congress, staff assistants, and *you* to and from the **Rayburn House Office Building** and the House side of the Capitol; between the **Hart Senate Office Building** and the Senate side of the Capitol (stopping at the **Dirksen Senate Office Building**); and between the **Russell Senate Office Building** and the Senate side of the Capitol. Although they're not on the train routes, the **Cannon** and **Longworth House Office Buildings** are reachable by an underground passageway. Sometimes special security measures limit public access to the subway. Ask any Capitol guide how to find it—just don't call it the Metro!

In addition to being in the newspapers every day, Capitol doings make for some very good books and movies. *House Mouse, Senate Mouse,* by Peter W. Barnes, is a book with whimsical il-

Smart Stuff
What is the shortest subway in the United States? (D.)

lustrations and clear prose that helps youngsters learn about our government (tykes). *Letters from Vinnie,* by Maureen Stack Sappey, uses a wonderful fictional framework to tell the true story of the teenage girl named Vinnie Ream who sculpted the statue of Abraham Lincoln that graces the Capitol's Rotunda (tweens). An interesting read for tweens and teens is *In Praise of Public Life,* by Senator Joseph I. Lieberman. Teens might enjoy *All the King's Men* (based on the story of Congressman Huey Long), by Robert Penn Warren, and *Lord of the Flies,* by William Golding.

One of the most famous movies about Congress is *Advise and Consent* (teens), with Henry Fonda, who also starred in *The Best*

Man. Another good choice for teens is *Mr. Smith Goes to Washington*, the film that made Jimmy Stewart, who plays a naïve congressman, a star. Other films to watch are *State of the Union* (tweens and teens), with Spencer Tracy and Katharine Hepburn, and *The Great McGinty* (teens). Teens can learn about budgeting from a game by Close Up Publishing called *Slicing the Pie: A Federal Budget Game*. Players learn about issues and strategies while acting as members of Congress, lobbyists, and citizens. We don't guarantee this will improve their personal spending habits, however.

You might want to visit one of the two restaurants frequented by senators and representatives. At the far end of the House side of the Capitol is the royal-blue **Bennett Dining Room** (202/225–6300). Ask a guard for directions to Room H118—you might want to leave a trail of bread crumbs to help find your way back. In contrast to the opulent surroundings, the prices are extremely reasonable. Delicious salads, entrées, and sandwiches are all bargains. There's no official dress code, although you'll find that most men are in jackets and ties. It's open Monday, Tuesday, and Friday from 8 AM to 2:30 PM and Wednesday and Thursday 8 AM to 11 AM. It's closed to the public from 11 AM to 1:30 PM when Congress is in session.

On the Senate side is the **Senators' Dining Room,** for which you'll need a note from your senator—sort of like a school hall pass, only better. As this is the most elegant of the Capitol's restaurants, serving contemporary American cuisine, you'll have to be dressed in the proper attire, which means jacket and tie for men. It's *your* money that is supporting all these eateries, so enjoy, and enter as if you own the place. After all, you *do.*

Located on opposite sides of the Capitol Plaza, the **Senate and House of Representatives Office Buildings** are important for two reasons (besides the fact that actual work sometimes gets done there). First, this is where you pick up tickets to the House or Senate galleries or for VIP tours of the Capitol. Second, good eats are to be found within some of these marble walls.

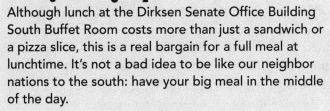

Money-Saving Tip

Although lunch at the Dirksen Senate Office Building South Buffet Room costs more than just a sandwich or a pizza slice, this is a real bargain for a full meal at lunchtime. It's not a bad idea to be like our neighbor nations to the south: have your big meal in the middle of the day.

Hungry? Capitol subways can take you to convenient and inexpensive lunch spots. The favorite seems to be the **Dirksen Senate Office Building South Buffet Room** (1st and C Streets, NE; 202/224–4249). All ages love this generous all-you-can-eat buffet. In an art deco room with white linen–covered tables and floral centerpieces, diners can indulge themselves with hot entrées, a fruit and salad bar, and a create-your-own sundae bar. Groups of six or more need reservations. Hours are weekdays 11:30 to 2:30.

If your sleepy teenagers are overwhelmed just putting on clothes before they leave the hotel and arrive at their Capitol Hill destination starving, you're in luck: the Longworth and Rayburn buildings offer food as early as 7:30. The **Longworth Building Food Court** (Independence and S. Capitol Streets, NE) offers an inexpensive breakfast and a wide selection of lunch entrées. There are pies and cakes for dessert. Just across South Capitol Street, the **Rayburn Building Cafeteria** also serves breakfast. For lunch, in addition to a grill station, servers will make salads to order. Try the cheesecake for dessert.

Next to the Hart Senate Office Building, on the northeast side of the Capitol, is the **Sewall–Belmont House** (144 Constitution Avenue, NE; donations accepted; 202/546–3989; www.sewallbelmont. org), the headquarters of the National Woman's Party, founded by Alice Paul in 1913. Paul authored the first version of the Equal Rights Amendment to the Constitution. Anyone interested in the women's suffrage movement can find party memorabilia, portraits, and even antique furniture. Look for the small sculpture of Sybil Ludington, a heroine of the Revolutionary War who, in true feminist style, made a ride similar to Paul Revere's, only four times the distance! A 28-minute videotape, *We Were Arrested, Of Course,* chronicles the history of how women got the vote. The private lives and public achievements of five of the country's women's suffrage leaders, including Alice Paul, are chronicled in *Sisters: The Lives of America's Suffragists,* by Jean H. Baker (teens). *The New York Public Library Amazing Women in American History,* by Sue Heinemann, is another book of interest (tweens and teens).

Metro: Capitol South

On Capitol Hill, at the east end of the Mall

Enter at Capitol Visitor Center, under the east plaza

Open Monday to Saturday 8:30 to 4:30; closed Sunday and New Year's Day, Thanksgiving, December 25, and Inauguration Day, but open national holidays

For information on guided tours, call 202/225–6827. To make *advance reservations* for groups of 15 or more, call 202/224–8406, weekdays 9 to noon and 1 to 3

One 40-person tour begins every half hour Monday to Saturday 8:30 to 3:30; plan to arrive half an hour early.

Free passes are required; reserve by phone 202/593–1762 or online (www.visitthecapitol.gov). Some same-day passes are available at kiosks at the east and west front entrances of the Capitol or at the Information Desk on the Visitor Center's lower level.

There are many *restrictions* on what can be brought into the Capitol, and there is *no place to check belongings*, except coats. No backpacks, duffel bags, suitcases, aerosol or nonaerosol sprays, cans, bottles, or liquids are allowed. You will not be admitted to the Capitol if you have *any* of these items with you. Call 202/225–6827 for a complete list.

202/225–3121 or 202/226–8000 for Office of Visitor Services
www.aoc.gov/cc/visit/index.cfm or www.visitthecapitol.gov

U.S. Botanic Garden

For All Ages . . . More exciting than reading about exotic plants is seeing, smelling, and touching them in the U.S. Botanic Garden. Chocolate and vanilla trees, a coffee tree, and a pineapple plant are all there for the sniffing. Visits to the Australian bunya bunya tree, the Brazilian tapioca plant, and the Chinese lychee tree don't even require a passport. Don't forget to look for the "living fossil," the 200-million-year-old plant species called the cycad. Specialty areas are devoted to orchids, medicinal plants, and endangered species. A fascinating jungle canopy walk (hold little ones' hands here) affords you a bird's-eye view of a tropical forest without having to fly from treetop to treetop. Rare flowering plants elicit wide-eyed pleasure and a furtive attempt to snatch a souvenir. *Don't!*

The National Garden at the U.S. Botanic Garden celebrates our country's history and geography. (Look for paving stones in the "Martha Washington" pattern of Colonial American quilts.) Plantings native to the Atlantic Piedmont Eastern and Coastal Plain bloom in the Regional Garden area, and a separate rose garden provides a vibrant and colorful display. And kids love the butterfly garden, featuring species from the region and those that flutter farther away.

Across Independence Avenue is lovely **Bartholdi Park,** where you can find a rock garden and changing seasonal displays. Frédéric-Auguste Bartholdi, sculptor of the Statue of Liberty, designed the fountain for the Philadelphia Centennial Exposition of 1876.

Metro: Federal Center Southwest
West side of the Capitol, 1st Street and Maryland Avenue, SW
Garden open daily 10 to 5; park open daily dawn to dusk

202/225–8333 or 202/225–7099
www.usbg.gov

★Library of Congress

For Teens . . . Thomas Jefferson made his mark here. The Library of Congress began with the books from his personal library. My, how we've grown. Some 113 million items, including 26 million books in 460 languages, sit on 532 miles of shelves in three different buildings in this one collection. Nevertheless, neither you nor anyone else, even a senator or representative, can check out a book to take home! But adults may browse here and do research.

The main building, the **Thomas Jefferson Building,** is the jewel in the crown. Standing at the base of the majestic staircases, looking at the gilt ornamentation on the walls and ceiling, it's easy to imagine what European palaces look like. Rising 75 feet from its marble floor to its stained-glass dome, the **Great Hall** graces our most elegant government building. **The Main Reading Room** is a throwback to an earlier era of dark paneling and ornate decoration. High on the walls are the seals of the 48 contiguous states, set in stained-glass windows. You can gaze down at legislative aides, college students, and government officials doing research side by side.

Start with the "American Treasures" exhibit, a permanent col-

Money-Saving Tip

In addition to reading rooms, the more modern **James Madison Building** (across Independence Avenue from the Thomas Jefferson Building) houses exhibit halls, an information center, and (are you hungry?) an elegant cafeteria on the sixth floor that has a panoramic view of the city through floor-to-ceiling windows. During the week you can get breakfast 7 to 10:30 and lunch 12:30 to 2. Snacks are available (bless them!) until 3:30. Homemade and inexpensive, too—what a bargain.

lection of more than 200 historic items, including Thomas Jefferson's rough draft of the Declaration of Independence, letters written by George Washington, and Abraham Lincoln's Gettysburg Address. Even younger visitors will be fascinated by the contents of Lincoln's pockets the night he was assassinated. Magic lovers will enjoy the scrapbooks of master magician Harry Houdini.

In the Jefferson Building, rotating exhibits are arranged by themes: Memory (history), Reason (philosophy, law, science, and geography), and Imagination (fine arts, architecture, music, literature, and sports). You can view them online at www.loc.gov/exhibits. The visitor center inside the west front entrance provides brochures and information. A 90-seat theater presents a short movie about the library. The gift shop, also on the ground floor, stocks reproductions, books, and souvenirs. A self-guiding audiotape tour of "Treasures of America" is available for $2.50.

Guided tours of the Jefferson Building begin weekdays at 10:30, 11:30, 2:30, and 3:30, and Saturday at 10:30, 11:30, 1:30, and 2:30. They take 45 minutes and depart from the ground-floor visitor center. The tours are free and require no advance reservations, although groups of 16 or larger should call ahead.

Puritanical John Adams would have raised an eyebrow at the decor of the art deco library building bearing his name. The **John Adams Building,** the second building of the Library of Congress, sits just behind the Jefferson Building, and contains a number of reading rooms devoted to specialized material. The **James Madison Building** houses exhibit halls, an information center, and a cafeteria.

Metro: Capitol South
1st Street and Independence Avenue, SE, across from the
    Capitol
Jefferson Building, Monday through Saturday 10 to 5:30
Adams Building, weekdays 8:30 AM to 9:30 PM, Saturday 8:30
    to 5:30
Madison Building, weekdays 8:30 AM to 9:30 PM, Saturday
    8:30 to 6:30
202/707–8000 or 202/707–5000
www.loc.gov

Folger Shakespeare Library

For Tweens and Teens . . . More than a library, this classic white-marble building houses a research facility, a Tudor-style great hall, and an Elizabethan theater (modeled after the Blackfriars Theater, where many of Shakespeare's plays were produced). The world's largest collection of Shakespearean works and artifacts is housed here, but unless you're doing graduate-level research you'll have to take our word for it. The library is off-limits to the rest of us *except* on one April weekend each year (the Sunday closest to April 26), when the research areas are opened to the masses in celebration of Shakespeare's birthday. Music, theatrical productions, special children's events, and food enliven the festivities.

Smart Stuff

For Teens . . . At the Library of Congress you can look up any book published in the United States by its title, author, or call number. To conduct Library of Congress research, you will need a special pass. Go to Room 140 in the Independence Avenue entrance of the Madison Building and present a photo ID with your name and address to get a User ID Card. Entering the main entrance of the Jefferson Building, go to the computer catalog center on the first floor. A reference librarian will assist you.

Try this one: 2006903816. Who are the authors? Who's the publisher? (F.)

Docent-led tours of the great hall can explain the changing exhibits of Renaissance and Shakespeare-related items, such as rare books and manuscripts, memorabilia, and paintings. From productions of Shakespearean plays to concerts to lectures and readings of poetry and fiction, the Folger (as it is known around town) is an important part of the Washington cultural scene. For evening events an admission fee is usually charged, and sometimes an invitation is required.

> Metro: Capitol South
> 201 E. Capitol Street, SE, east of the Library of Congress
> Open Monday through Saturday 10 to 4; closed federal holidays
> Free guided tours Monday through Friday at 11 and 3 and Saturday at 11 and 1
> 202/544–7077
> www.folger.edu

Parents/Teachers Take Note

The Folger sponsors festivals for high-school students each spring, complete with sword-fighting demonstrations, slide presentations, and other activities. For details, call 202/544–4600.

We know you can find any of Shakespeare's plays on your own. Here are a few other reading suggestions: *All the World's a Stage: A Pop-up Biography of William Shakespeare*, by Michael Bender (tweens); *Tales from Shakespeare*, by Charles Lamb (tweens and teens); *Stories from Shakespeare: The Complete Plays of William Shakespeare*, by Marchette Chute (teens); and *Acting Shakespeare*, by John Gielgud and John Miller (teens and adults). An interesting game, useful as a dramatic introduction to Shakespeare, is *The Play's the Thing* (teens). Other really fun games can be found online, including *"Domenic and Josh's Shakespeare Games"* (http://library.thinkquest.org/6337/games.html).

★Supreme Court Building

For Tweens and Teens . . . It's not by accident that the Supreme Court was designed to look like a Greek temple. This temple of American democracy has its motto over the door: EQUAL JUSTICE UNDER LAW.

All court sessions are open to the public, but seating is on a first-come, first-served basis. Arrive by 9 to get in line. Actually, there are two lines: one to hear an entire argument (about an hour) and one for people who just want to stay and watch for a few minutes. You'll need quarters for the lockers where you must store backpacks, cameras, and the like for security purposes.

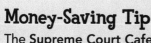

Money-Saving Tip

The **Supreme Court Cafeteria** is a supreme bargain among the government buildings' food offerings. Fresh-baked goods are featured at breakfast, and soups, salads, sandwiches, and hot entrées are all offered at lunchtime. Wednesday is ethnic cuisine day, with a different region highlighted each week. The snack bar sells inexpensive homemade desserts. Breakfast is served weekdays 7:30 to 10:30; lunch is 11:30 to 2. Snack bar hours are weekdays 10:30 to 3:30 when the Supreme Court is in session.

Visit the ground-floor exhibit hall (near the Maryland Avenue entrance) to learn about the building and the justices who have served here. On this floor, in the small theater, you can view a 20-minute film that explains the judicial process through interviews with a number of justices.

Books that help demystify the workings of the court include *Marshall, the Courthouse Mouse,* by Peter W. Barnes, a good read for tykes. For tykes and tweens, there's *Learning About Equal Rights from the Life of Ruth Bader Ginsburg,* by Brenn Jones. Tweens will like *Sandra Day O'Connor: Supreme Court Justice,* by Lisa McElroy, while

The Supreme Court

tweens and teens will enjoy Meish Goldish's *Our Supreme Court,* which explores the court and some of its famous justices and their rulings. For teens, there's *Sandra Day O'Connor: How the First Woman on the Supreme Court Became Its Most Influential Justice,* by Joan Biscupic; *Thurgood Marshall, American Revolutionary,* by Juan Williams; and *Pursuit of Justices: Presidential Politics in the Selection of Supreme Court Nominees,* by David Alistair Yalof. There's also *Night of January 16th,* by Ayn Rand, which is actually a play script. It's an informative and fun way to explore the courtroom—it even has a choice of endings (teens).

Parents/Teachers Take Note

Middle-school and high-school students enjoy presenting their own versions of courtroom dramas like the movies listed.

Movies can also enrich this visit for tweens and teens. Such classics as *Twelve Angry Men, Inherit the Wind,* and *To Kill a Mockingbird* bring home in dynamic fashion the importance of the judicial branch of our legislative system. Teens would also enjoy *Gideon's Trumpet.*

A small museum, a gift shop, a snack bar, and a cafeteria are on the ground floor.

Parents/Teachers Take Note

The movie *Gideon's Trumpet* deals with an imprisoned itinerant worker named Clarence Earl Gideon (portrayed by Henry Fonda), whose poverty prevented him from hiring legal counsel. His cause was championed by an attorney named Abe Fortas, who brought it to the Supreme Court. The case was a landmark decision affirming the right of *everyone* to legal representation. Abe Fortas later served as a Supreme Court justice.

A nearby restaurant with a hybrid name, Thai Roma (313 Pennsylvania Avenue, SE; 202/544–2338) was an Italian restaurant that found its Thai menu was getting raves. Enjoy Thai delicacies like pork satay, calamari with lemongrass, and a range of curry dishes. There's a wide selection for vegetarians, including such dishes as Chinese eggplant in a curry-coconut sauce and tofu with cashews. Need plainer fare? Try the pastas. Buon appetito!

Metro: Capitol South

1st Street and Maryland Avenue, NE, facing the Capitol

Open weekdays 9 to 4:30; closed holidays and sometimes for cleaning!

Free lectures when court is not in session, every hour on the half-hour, 9:30 to 3:30

Call 202/479–3211 to learn when arguments will be heard and when opinions are scheduled to be delivered

202/479–3000

www.supremecourtus.gov

National Japanese American Memorial

For All Ages . . . Dedicated in 2000, the beautiful National Japanese American Memorial commemorates the patriotism, heroism, and sacrifice of Japanese-American soldiers in World War II. Although more than 120,000 persons of Japanese ancestry were in-

National
Japanese
American
Memorial

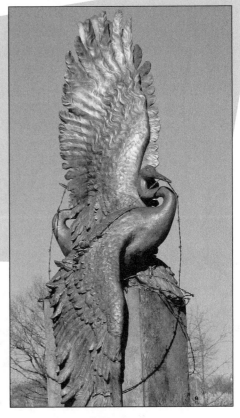

terned in U.S. detention camps, 3,000 served proudly in the military. The Japanese-American 442nd Regimental Combat Team became one of the most decorated military units in the war, earning 18,143 personal decorations, including 9,486 Purple Hearts, 5,200 Bronze Stars, 588 Silver Stars, 52 Distinguished Service Crosses, 22 Legions of Merit, 12 Croix de Guerre, 7 Presidential Unit Citations, 1 Medal of Honor, and 1 Distinguished Service Medal.

Bordered by ornamental cherry trees is a pink granite wall listing the 10 internment camps, their locations, their populations, and the names of the 800 Japanese-American soldiers who lost their lives in the war. Rising 14 feet above a reflecting pool is a green marble column crowned with a bronze statue of two cranes with their left wings extended upward. Their right wings are pinioned to their sides by a strand of barbed wire, the ends of which are held in their beaks. The sculpture symbolizes both individual effort and communal support, while dramatically depicting the attempt of peoples to break free from the bonds of prejudice. (Japanese legend holds that if a person who is ill makes a thousand paper cranes, the gods will grant his or her wish to be well again.) This eloquent statement from the Japanese-American community reminds us that what they endured should never again happen to *any* group.

Some important books have been written about the experiences of people of Japanese ancestry during and after World War II. *Sadako,* by Eleanor Coerr et al., tells the story of a 12-year-old girl who develops leukemia 10 years after the bomb was dropped on her native Hiroshima (tweens). *Last Witnesses: Reflections on the Wartime Internment of Japanese Americans,* edited by Erica Harth, is a moving collection of stories of life in the internment camps (teens). A film about this period, *Come See the Paradise,* is about a soldier who falls in love with a girl whose family is interned in a camp (tweens).

Smart Stuff

For Teens . . . Which U.S. president directed these words to the Japanese-American community? "You fought not only the enemy but you fought prejudice—and you won. Keep up that fight and we will continue to win, to make this great republic stand for what the Constitution says it stands for: the welfare of all of the people all of the time." **(G.)**

Metro: Union Station
In a small triangular park, bounded by New Jersey and
    Louisiana avenues and D Street, NW
Open daily, 24 hours
Lectures every half hour on weekdays 9:30 to 3:30
202/530–0015
www.njamf.com

Victims of Communism Memorial

For Tweens and Teens . . . On a scrap of land a couple of blocks west of Union Station, between Massachusetts and New Jersey avenues and G Street, is an unremarkable (some might say unappealing) statue honoring the estimated 100 million (yes, million)

Smart Stuff

For Tweens and Teens . . . "The Lone Eagle" was the nickname for our country's most famous airmail pilot. Who was he? What made him famous? (H.)

victims of Communism. The 10-foot-high bronze statue is a copy of the papier-mâché Statue of Liberty carried by dissidents in the famous Tiananmen Square protests of 1989. For adults who lived through the Cold War and for students who have studied the horrific reigns of Stalin, Pol Pot, and Mao Tse-tung, this modest marker carries a searing message.

For those interested in some relevant reading, teens will find *The Road to Communism,* by Ted Gottfried, intriguing (though definitely not light reading!). *When the Wall Came Down: The Berlin Wall* and the *Fall of Soviet Communism,* by Serge Schmemann, is history told from a Pulitzer Prize–winning journalist's viewpoint.

> Metro: Union Station
> At the intersection of Massachusetts and New Jersey avenues and G Street, N.W.

The National Guard Memorial Museum

For Tweens and Teens . . . Youngsters whose parents are members of the National Guard or who think only those enlisted in the Army, Navy, Air Force, or Marines go to war will be surprised at the history of the National Guard. Its story is told compellingly in this museum through interactive computer programs, a short film, and many exhibits. From the first militia drills in 1636 to the second war in Iraq, the National Guard has played a significant part in both homeland and overseas defense.

> Metro: Union Station
> 1 Massachusetts Avenue, NW

Open weekdays 10 to 4 or by appointment; groups of more
than 10 people should call two days in advance
202/408–5887
www.ngef.org

Parents/Teachers Take Note

Sometimes you *can* get something for nothing. Mystic
Stamp Company's *free* U.S. stamp catalog is available
online at www.mysticstamp.com.

National Postal Museum

For All Ages . . . With three antique mail planes hanging from the
ceiling, early mail trucks, holographic exhibits, three-dimensional
movies, interactive computers, and laser shows, the National Postal
Museum has something for everyone. Created to display the Smithsonian's collection of stamps and postal history memorabilia, it
houses the world's largest philatelic collection. It's in a beautiful
Beaux Arts building that also serves as the city's main post office
(not to be confused with the Old Post Office Pavilion, closer to the
Mall). Kids enjoy designing a piece of mail and having it "sent" to
themselves. One exhibit takes you on a virtual journey as a Pony
Express rider. The Civil War section chronicles a most extraordinary
piece of mail: a slave named Henry "Box" Brown mailed *himself*
from Richmond, Virginia, to an abolitionist in Pennsylvania in
1856. (This gives new meaning to the term *special delivery.*) Some
exhibits were being updated at this writing, so call ahead if there's a
specific one you want to see. The gift shop has banks made from old
mailboxes, books, and workbooks on stamps and postal history for
children, stamp jewelry, and writing paper and postcards.

Metro: Union Station
2 Massachusetts Avenue, NE
Open daily 10 to 5:30, except December 25; tours for student
groups available weekdays 10 to 3

Library Research Center, weekdays 10–4:30, call ahead for
appointment
202/633–5554
www.postalmuseum.si.edu

★Union Station

For All Ages . . . In a departure from the profusion of government
buildings designed to resemble Greek temples, Union Station was
modeled on the Baths of Diocletian and the Arch of Constantine in
Rome. Clearly this is no small place. When it was completed in
1907, it was the largest train station in the world. This spectacular
building houses not only a bustling train station and subway station, but also two levels of restaurants, two wings of shops, and a
nine-screen movie theater. You can easily spend a day entertaining
yourself here. It's a terrific change of pace when you're suffering
from museum fatigue or need a dry haven from the rain. Younger
travelers will enjoy trying to identify the large figure in front of the
building (Christopher Columbus). Teens will relish trying to figure
out why the statues of 36 Roman legionnaires on the balcony of the
Great Hall all carry shields in the same position. (Since many didn't
wear any other clothing, the powers-that-were thought the shields
were moral necessities.)

This most-visited attraction in Washington (the National Air
and Space Museum is second), Union Station has a long
history of famous travelers. When
General Pershing,
commander of the
Allied Expeditionary
Forces, returned from
World War I in 1918,

Inside Washington's
Union Station

he was welcomed here by President Wilson. Rear Admiral Richard Byrd (the South Pole explorer) had his homecoming here as well. In 1945 thousands of mourners congregated here to meet President Franklin D. Roosevelt's casket, borne on his funeral train. More recently, this grand palace has hosted many presidential inaugural balls.

Shops range from the mall types, including **Foot Locker, Nine West,** and **Structure,** to unique places such as **Made in America,** where you can find government agency baseball caps (CIA, for example) along with "White House" guest towels; **Political Americana,** selling the obvious; and **Flights of Fancy,** offering books, toys, games, and amusements.

Eating choices at Union Station run from the everyday to the truly exotic, from food courts to regular restaurants. On the lower level a large eatery offers everything from Mexican to Japanese cuisine to more traditional American fare. On the first and second floors, restaurants as well as fast-food places give diners a variety of tasty choices.

> Metro: Union Station
> 40 Massachusetts Avenue, NE
> Shops open Monday through Saturday 10 to 9, Sunday 10
>   to 6
> 202/289–1908

Where to Stay in the Capitol Hill Area

Capitol Hill can be pricey, but as in any other real-estate deal, you're paying for location. Here are some suggestions to check out:

> **Capitol Hill Suites**
> 200 C Street, SE
> 202/543–6000
> www.capitolhillsuites.com
> Metro: Capitol South

> **Liaison Capitol Hill Hotel**
> 415 New Jersey Avenue, NW
> 202/638–1616 or 800/638–1116

www.affinia.com
Metro: Union Station

Hyatt Regency Washington on Capitol Hill
400 New Jersey Avenue, NW
202/737–1234 or 800/233–1234
www.washingtonregency.hyatt.com
Metro: Union Station

Answers to Smart Stuff Questions

A. Washington, D.C. Many of the city's license plates now read "Taxation without Representation." (Does this phrase sound familiar?)

B. Fresco is a form of painting in which pigments are applied to fresh mortar, usually on a wall. This technique enables the mortar to absorb the color. The process is repeated in sections until the entire picture is completed. It's found in works of old masters, such as Raphael.

C. A flag flies over the appropriate wing of the Capitol when its occupants are in session. At night a light in the dome indicates which group is burning the midnight oil.

D. The Capitol subway that runs to the Senate and the House office buildings.

E. Will Rogers. His statue represents the state of Oklahoma.

F. The book is *Raising a Successful Child: Discover and Nurture Your Child's Talents,* published by Ulysses Press. The authors' names might sound familiar: Sandra Burt and Linda Perlis. Just seeing if you were paying attention.

G. Harry S. Truman.

H. The "Lone Eagle," Charles A. Lindbergh, flew his plane, the *Spirit of St. Louis,* from Long Island to land at Le Bourget Airfield outside of Paris (May 21, 1927) in 33½ hours, making the first nonstop transatlantic flight, solo.

CHAPTER 3

The National Mall

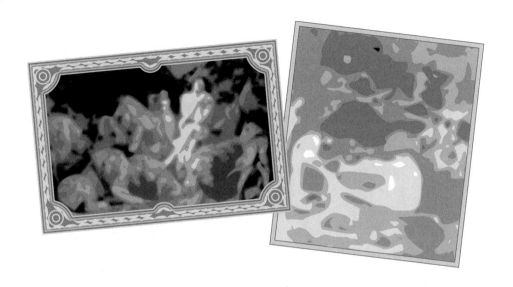

If you were to stand in the middle of the green expanse of the National Mall and look in any direction, you would see some of the most significant and distinguished buildings in the world. Surrounded by Frisbee players, dog walkers, joggers, bikers, skaters, and lunchtime picnickers, you might glimpse the **Lincoln Memorial,** beyond the stark obelisk of the **Washington Monument,** at the west end; the gleaming dome of the **U.S. Capitol** on the east end; or nine buildings of the world-famous **Smithsonian Institution** on the north and south edges. This area is one of the country's oldest federal parks, originally envisioned in Pierre L'Enfant's 1791 plan for the city. It's the center for many special Washington festivals and events, an arrival and departure point for visiting dignitaries and, of course, the location of many of the most famous landmarks in the city. And just think: we all own this wonderful place together!

★Smithsonian Visitor Information Center (the "Castle")

For All Ages . . . Emblematic of America's emphasis on equal opportunity regardless of one's origins, the Smithsonian Institution

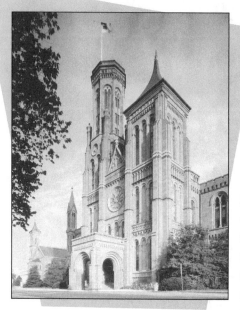

Smithsonian Visitor Information Center (now we can see why it's called the "Castle")

was the gift of an Englishman born out of wedlock. James Smithson (1765–1829) was prevented by his illegitimate birth from entering the clergy, the military, or politics. So he turned to science and eventually became a member of the distinguished body of scientists, the Royal Society. Having no children, he willed his fortune to his nephew, with the provision that if his nephew were also childless, the funds would be used to establish an institution in the city of Washington, D.C., which he had never visited, for the "increase and diffusion of knowledge."

Helpful Hint

Call ahead for a free copy of *Planning Your Smithsonian Visit*.

Standing 9 feet tall in front of the building is the imposing **statue of Joseph Henry,** inventor of the first telegraph, the electric relay, and an electric motor. The standard "unit of inductive resistance," the *henry,* is named in his honor. The sculpture shows him leaning on a pedestal depicting his electromagnet. His family actually lived in this building while he was secretary of the brand-new Smithsonian Institution, where he worked for 29 years.

Interactive touch-screen programs, two electronic wall maps, scale models of the individual museums, and two theaters showing orientation films beckon visitors to stop first at the "Castle," headquarters for the entire Smithsonian Institution. Be sure to ask for the free guide booklet and map of the Smithsonian (available in several languages), the brochure *10 Tips for Visiting the Smithsonian with Children,* and the dining guide listing places to eat within the various buildings. Encompassing numerous museums, galleries, and the National Zoo, the Smithsonian Institution is also among the most outstanding research centers in the world. So extensive is its collection that only 1% of its holdings is ever on display at one time. Some of its numerous facilities are outside Washington, D.C.

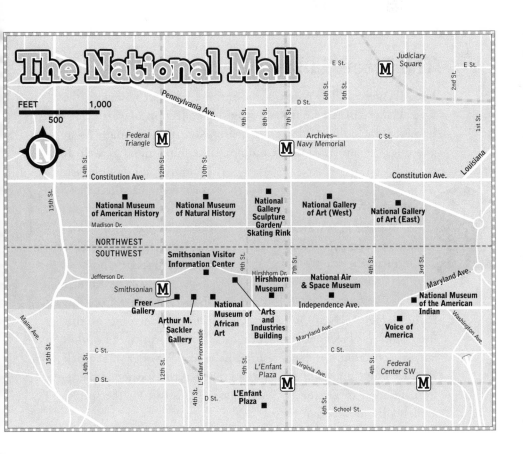

Metro: Smithsonian

1000 Jefferson Drive, SW

Open daily 8:30 to 5:30

All Smithsonian facilities are *free*; fees are charged for some activities.

202/633–1000 for general information

www.si.edu

Even before Earth Day was celebrated, our nation's capital was environmentally sensitive. In 1886 a herd of buffalo (obtained by the then "Department of Living Animals") were housed on the lawn behind the Castle. Evidently, their presence helped stimulate interest in preserving this endangered group (not the bureaucrats!).

The Freer Gallery of Art

For All Ages . . . The oldest of the Smithsonian's art museums, the Freer Gallery of Art houses an extensive collection of Asian masterpieces, including Chinese, Japanese, Korean, and South-Asian paintings, ceramics, jades, sculptures, and miniatures, as well as Buddhist and Islamic art. You'll recognize this gallery by its Renaissance-style facade adorned with colorful banners. Industrialist Charles Freer, who endowed the gallery, learned about Asian art from his friend James McNeill Whistler. One fortunate outcome of this friendship was Freer's accumulation of Whistler's works, the world's largest collection. All ages especially enjoy Whistler's "Peacock Room," a blue-and-gold dining room that was transported in pieces from London to Detroit to Washington, D.C. Ask for the special guidebooks for children.

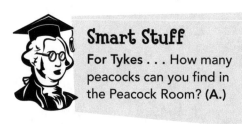

Smart Stuff

For Tykes . . . How many peacocks can you find in the Peacock Room? (A.)

Smart Stuff

For Tweens and Teens . . . What symbol did Whistler use as his signature? How many can you find in this room? (B.)

Metro: Smithsonian
1050 Independence Avenue, SW
Open daily 10 to 5:30
Guided tours available
Group tours must be arranged well in advance
202/633–4880
www.asia.si.edu

The Arthur M. Sackler Gallery

For All Ages . . . Although there are no caverns beneath the National Mall, you can descend 57 feet underground into the Arthur M. Sackler Gallery of Asian and Near Eastern Art through the little kiosk near the Freer Gallery. You can also get here through the underground exhibition passage from the Freer. In contrast to the Freer, the Sackler accommodates visiting exhibits as well as its own collection. From ancient to modern art, the Sackler houses displays of bronze, jade, silver, gold, lacquer, ceramics, paintings, and sculptures from the Mediterranean to Japan. A monthly calendar lists workshops, storytelling events, and other activities. Here, too, ask for the children's guidebook.

The gift shop has beautiful Asian-influenced clothing, scarves, jewelry, pottery, boxes, and notepaper, as well as a large selection of music, posters, postcards, and books (including a special children's section).

Bounded by Independence Avenue and the Castle, the Arts and Industries Building, and the Freer Gallery, the **Enid A. Haupt Garden** sits on the rooftop of the underground museum. In this formal Victorian setting children will particularly enjoy the waterfall, the

Quick Guide to

Attraction	Location
★Smithsonian Visitor Information Center (the "Castle")	1000 Jefferson Drive, SW
The Freer Gallery of Art	1050 Independence Avenue, SW
The Arthur M. Sackler Gallery	1050 Independence Avenue, SW
The National Museum of African Art	950 Independence Avenue, SW
Arts and Industries Building	900 Jefferson Drive, SW
Hirshhorn Museum and Sculpture Garden	Independence Avenue at 7th Street, SW
★National Air and Space Museum	7th Street and Independence Avenue, SW
National Museum of the American Indian	4th Street and Independence Avenue, SW
The Voice of America	330 Independence Avenue, SW (enter on C Street, between 3rd and 4th streets)
★National Gallery of Art	Constitution Avenue between 3rd and 7th streets, NW
National Gallery of Art Sculpture Garden and Ice Skating Rink	Mall at 7th Street and Constitution Avenue, NW
★National Museum of Natural History	10th Street and Constitution Avenue, NW on the Mall
★National Museum of American History	Constitution Avenue between 12th and 14th streets, NW

the National Mall Attractions

Age Range	Hours	Details on
All Ages	8:30 AM–5:30 PM daily	Page 55
All Ages	10 AM–5:30 PM daily	Page 58
All Ages	10 AM–5:30 PM daily	Page 59
All Ages	10 AM–5:30 PM daily	Page 62
All Ages	Closed for renovation	Page 63
All Ages	10 AM–5:30 PM daily	Page 64
All Ages	10 AM–5:30 PM daily	Page 66
All Ages	10 AM–5:30 PM daily	Page 69
Teens	Tours: Mon.–Fri. 11:45 AM	Page 70
All Ages	Mon.–Sat. 10 AM–5 PM; Sun. 11 AM–6 PM	Page 71
All Ages	Daily (hours change seasonally)	Page 75
All Ages	10 AM–5:30 PM daily	Page 76
All Ages	10 AM–5:30 PM daily	Page 78

9-foot-tall moon gates, and the animal-shape topiaries. This is a good rest stop, but not a place for climbing or running. Bring your parasol.

Metro: Smithsonian
1050 Independence Avenue, SW
Open daily 10 to 5:30
Guided tours available
Group tours must be arranged in advance
202/633–4880
www.asia.si.edu

Remember that the "Castle," as well as the other museums on the National Mall, is closed December 25.

The National Museum of African Art

For All Ages . . . Kids love this museum of ancient and contemporary art from sub-Saharan Africa. Be sure to ask for the family guide, which children and adults can use to explore the collection of masks, gongs and other musical instruments, pipes, statues, and stools and other furnishings. Large color photos help explain the purposes of many of the artifacts.

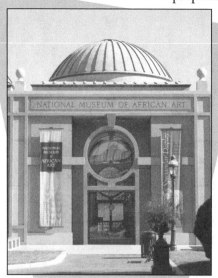

Because the materials used are familiar, including raffia, beads, shells, wood, clay, and fiber, children can readily

The entrance to the National Museum of African Art

picture themselves making
these objects. The many
representations of animals
delight kids of all ages. The
exhibit on the ancient West
African city of Benin is notable for its beautiful metalwork collection. Besides
handmade crafts, the gift
shop stocks CDs, videos,
and tapes of African music.

Smart Stuff

For Tweens and Teens . . .
What exhibit explores the
ancient African city that
flourished long before the
civilizations of Greece or
Rome? (C.)

> Metro: Smithsonian
> 950 Independence Avenue, SW
> Open daily 10 to 5:30
> Hour-long guided tours begin on weekdays at 10:30 and
>   11:45 (occasionally at 1 as well) and at 11 and 1 on week-
>   ends. Arrange group tours at least three weeks in advance
>   by calling 202/633–4646
> For a schedule of family workshops, storytelling sessions, and
>   films, call 202/633–4600
> 202/633–4640
> www.nmafa.si.edu

Arts and Industries Building

For All Ages . . . For the foreseeable future, the Arts and Industries
Building will be closed for renovations. In the meantime, enjoy the
lovely architecture and the beautiful Victorian-style gardens, which
are especially colorful in spring and summer, and the 1940s carousel
in front of the Arts and Industries Building is a clue that this is a
kid-friendly museum. (Yes, you *may* ride on the merry-go-round,
which operates daily 10 to 6, weather permitting.)

Near the Arts and Industries Building, **Discovery Theater**
features performances by singers, dancers, puppeteers, and mimes
most of the year. All the shows are for kids. A large banner marks
the site.

Metro: Smithsonian
900 Jefferson Drive, SW
202/633–1000
www.si.edu/ai

Ready for a snack? Across from the Arts and Industries Building is **L'Enfant Plaza** (Independence Avenue, between 9th Street and 12th Street). Above ground it's a courtyard surrounded by modern office buildings, but below ground there's a complex of restaurants, shops, and movie theaters. There's enough variety here to satisfy almost anyone's hungry tummy: an entire food court where you can find yogurt, cookies, deli sandwiches, pizza, hamburgers, Chinese food, and more. From June through September there are free Wednesday concerts from 11:45 to 1:45; musical offerings include rock, jazz, and pop. The **U.S. Postal Service Headquarters** (475 L'Enfant Plaza, SW) on the ground floor exhibits original artwork created for stamps and rare and unusual postal items. This is open weekdays 9 to 5, but closed on federal holidays.

Hirshhorn Museum and Sculpture Garden

For All Ages . . . Another grateful (and highly successful) immigrant to the United States gave this extraordinary collection to his adopted country. Latvian-born Joseph Hirshhorn began collecting art when he was a teenager, purchasing etchings in New York. In 1974, at the age of 75, he gave a "little gift" to the Smithsonian: 2,000 pieces of sculpture and 4,000 drawings and paintings.

Smart Stuff

For Teens . . . Find the sculpture of a world-famous fictional Spanish hero. Who was the sculptor? How would you describe his artistic style? **(D.)**

Going the Guggenheim one better, the Hirshhorn Museum is not only cylindrical but also stands on sculptured supports 14 feet above ground. American and European art from the late 19th century to the present fills both the unique building and an outdoor sculpture garden. Children who worry that their own artistic creations don't look realistic enough will be delighted to discover the abstract work of grown-up artists on all three floors. Artists in the Hirshhorn collection comprise a roster of important late 19th- and 20th-century painters and sculptors: Calder, de Kooning, Stella, Hopper, O'Keeffe, Pollock, Moore, Rodin, Giacometti, Renoir, Gauguin, Picasso, and Warhol.

Best of all are the sculptures, which exemplify a huge variety of styles, from the delicate dancers of Degas to the enormous wall frieze of Matisse. Surrounding the base of the museum are intriguing outdoor sculptures, including a tall piece that looks like randomly arranged metal rods. Stand underneath and see how they make a familiar pattern. A good place to stretch out when the kids have had enough of standing still and paying attention, the wide-open spaces of the sculpture garden across the street encourage exploration. Colorful koi populate the pond. Just be sure the kids don't climb in and join them.

Begin with the short orientation film in the theater on the museum's lower level. Stop by the information desk to pick up the beautiful free family guide that spotlights works in the collection that kids like and suggests related activities. You can use the cards enclosed to help your kids learn more about the art. Just don't try to win a poker game with these cards.

The gift shop on the lower level carries a wide variety of prints, art books, calendars, posters, note cards, jewelry, and other art-related goods.

From Memorial Day through Labor Day, the Hirshhorn's **Full Circle** out-

Smart Stuff

For Tykes and Tweens . . .
How many sculptures of horses can you find in the Hirshhorn? Talk about the different styles you see; how do they make you feel? (E.)

door café is a good choice for child-friendly dining. With food ranging from hot and cold sandwiches, delicious salads, and personal-size pizzas to child-pleasing desserts such as jumbo chocolate-chip cookies, this self-service eatery is an economical choice. The café is open daily from 11 to 3, weather permitting.

Helpful Hint

Teacher's packets come complete with slides, posters, and information sheets on the works in the collection. Request these well-thought-out materials before you come.

Metro: L'Enfant Plaza or Smithsonian
Independence Avenue at 7th Street, SW
Open daily 10 to 5:30; Sculpture Garden open 7:30 AM
    to dusk
Fee for audiotape tours for special exhibits
Call for information on guided tours and children's programs
202/633–1618
www.hirshhorn.si.edu

★National Air and Space Museum

For All Ages . . . Despite its overwhelming size, this museum is a hands-down favorite with kids. Since its patriotic opening on July 1, 1976, in time for the nation's bicentennial, it has been the most-visited museum in the world. Everywhere you turn, aircraft hover overhead. Most have actually flown, including the Wright brothers' 1903 *Flyer,* Lindbergh's *Spirit of St. Louis,* the Apollo 11 command module *Columbia,* and a Viking Mars lander. Children love to climb into such relics as the American Airlines DC-7 and the Skylab Orbital Workshop, the backup for America's first space station. For many visitors, the most exciting exhibit is something everyone can touch: the famous moon rock.

Arrive when the museum opens, as you'll need plenty of time.

This huge museum will require at least three to four hours, as well as some careful planning, to see everything. A good first stop is the information desk, where you can pick up a floor plan and a list of daily events. An activity board lists times for

Smart Stuff

For Tykes . . . Several exhibits show vehicles used in space. If you were to travel in a spaceship, what would you bring?

activities such as storytelling sessions, paper airplane contests, and special demonstrations. You will need to purchase tickets *immediately* for any film in the **Langley Theater** that fits your group's desires and schedule. Several films are shown each day on an IMAX screen measuring five stories high and seven stories wide. Parents and teachers will approve of these movies, and kids of all ages will enjoy them. At the same time, buy tickets for shows at the **Albert Einstein Planetarium.** The only way to get them *in advance* (up to two weeks) is by going to the box office.

Smart Stuff

For Tweens . . . What was the name of the first animal in space? What kind of animal was it, and what country did it come from? (F.)

Nearly two dozen galleries center on specific themes, including early flight, jet aviation, planetary and lunar exploration, rocketry, military aircraft, space art, computer technology, robotics, aerial imaging, and astronomy. In the "How Things Fly" exhibit, kids can experience numerous interactive activities such as wind and smoke tunnels and control of a full-size Cessna 150 airplane.

You're never far from a gift shop in this museum. Small shops are in many of the display areas, and then there's a much larger one on the first floor, if you haven't already bought enough! Kids can choose from model airplane and rocket kits to books on aeronautics

Parents/Teachers Take Note

Since the National Air and Space Museum is so large, a visit requires advance planning. Let kids work in teams to formulate a blueprint of a tour. The museum's Web site (www.nasm.si.edu) lets them explore the building section by section.

and famous pilots, not to mention souvenirs of all kinds. A favorite with everyone is the freeze-dried "astronaut ice cream," which really does melt in your mouth.

Smart Stuff

For Teens . . . When was the first docking of U.S. and Soviet spacecraft? What is the most recent joint venture in space? How did the Cold War affect such joint operations? Make a prediction for the future of international cooperation in space. **(G.)**

Good reading for tweens includes *Who Was Amelia Earhart?*, by Kate Jerome, et al., and *The Wright Brothers: How They Invented the Airplane,* by Russell Friedman, et al. *The Right Stuff,* by Tom Wolfe, is best for teens, as is *Yeager: The Autobiography of Chuck Yeager. The Spirit of St. Louis,* the story of Charles Lindbergh's famous voyage, is an interesting film for tweens and teens.

Metro: L'Enfant Plaza
7th Street and Independence Avenue, SW
Open daily 10 to 5:30
Guided tours available
Free; fee for theater and planetarium
For school group tours, call 202/633–2563

Time-Saving Tip

Taking a lunch break here is a visual treat. It's also a great time-saver if you're planning to stay a few more hours. The futuristic cafeteria boasts floor-to-ceiling windows with wonderful views of the Capitol, the Mall, and the National Gallery of Art. McDonald's, Boston Market, and Donato's Pizzeria all vie for your fast-food dollars. Prices are reasonable and seating is ample (there's room for 800 people, so you can bring a friend or two). The Mezza Café (202/633–1000), a floor above the cafeteria, serves slightly pricier food, including croissant sandwiches, a variety of soups, and mouthwatering desserts. There are also smoothies and specialty coffees. It's open daily 10 to 5.

For groups of 20 or more, call 202/633–4629
202/633–1000
www.nasm.si.edu

National Museum of the American Indian

For All Ages . . . From impressive displays of traditional crafts (including a full-size canoe and outrigger, each painstakingly built by hand) to interactive exhibits of photos and videos of present-day tribal activities, this museum is a testament to the rich culture of Native Americans. The multilayered red-sandstone building—landscaped to be evocative of the Southwest—is constructed in a kind of spiral, with ramps for easy access to different levels.

A variety of ancient ceremonies takes place in a circular "well" on the main floor. It's a treat for kids of all ages to witness a tribal performance here. In addition to the beautiful artifacts, there's a whole floor devoted to edibles: the food here is exceptional. The cafeteria is divided into sections representing different American Indian nations. The menu in each reflects delicious regional fare. Equally impressive are the two fully stocked gift shops, where you can splurge on beautifully made crafts or on books for all ages.

An animated version of *The Song of Sacajawea,* read by Laura Dern, will appeal to younger viewers. In *A Time for Native Americans,* tweens can learn about 49 significant American Indians from a set of illustrated biographical cards. Tweens will also enjoy *More Than Moccasins,* an activity guide to traditional North American Indian life, with creative ideas and projects. Of particular interest for tweens and teens is *Wounded Knee: An Indian History of the American West,* by Dee Brown. Teens might like to read *The Land Has Memory: Indigenous Knowledge, Native Landscapes, and the National Museum of the American Indian,* by Duane Blue Spruce. *Dances with Wolves* is a movie teens will find poignant.

Metro: L'Enfant Plaza or Federal Center SW
4th Street and Independence Avenue, SW
Open daily 10 to 5:30
202/633–1000
www.nmai.si.edu

The Voice of America

For Older Tweens and Teens . . . Famous since 1942 as a beacon of freedom and information about the United States, the Voice of America (VOA) is near the Mall. Since more than 80 million listeners all over the world tune in regularly, the VOA is of special interest to visitors from other countries who might have listened to it at home. On the free 45-minute tour you can watch broadcasters at work in the radio and television studios and newsroom. Victor Franzusoff, a former broadcaster born in Russia in 1911, describes his own life and his 45 years as a broadcaster, writer, editor, commentator, and chief of the Russian Service for VOA in his book *Talking to the Russian: Glimpses of History by a Voice of America Pioneer* (tweens and teens).

Metro: Federal Center SW

330 Independence Avenue, SW (enter on C Street, between
    3rd and 4th streets)

Tours weekdays at 11:45; make reservations a day in advance

202/203–4990

www.voatour.com

★National Gallery of Art

For All Ages . . . A beautiful blend of past and present, the National Gallery of Art has something for everyone. In two buildings spanning four city blocks, the classical West Building and modern East Building, visitors can see art from the 13th century to the present, one of the finest collections anywhere in the world. Kids will be excited to notice the differences between the reproductions they have seen in books and the real thing.

A welcome addition is the Micro Gallery near the Mall entrance of the West Building, where 13 computer stations with 20-inch color monitors allow visitors to access images and information about the gallery's holdings. If you're computer-comfy, you can create your own personal tour of the museum and print a map showing the locations of specific works of art you want to view.

Built of pink Tennessee marble, the graceful West Building contains long halls of classical sculpture and courtyards adorned with seasonal plants. (If you don't feel cultured in this setting, you never will!) The best of American and European art is represented: Italian, French, British, Dutch, Flemish, German, and Spanish works. Old masters such as Rembrandt, Raphael, Vermeer, Renoir, Monet, Jacques-Louis David, and Leonardo da Vinci are displayed in viewer-friendly-size rooms. This is not a place to rush through, but if museum fatigue sets in, take advantage of any of the small atriums spaced throughout the building, sit down, and relax.

In the hierarchy of gift shops, the one in the West Building is at the top. Filled with posters, prints, postcards, stationery, calendars, a huge collection of art books, silk scarves, jewelry, and even toys and games, here's where to go for high-class souvenirs.

Helpful Hint

Because this is an especially large museum, the temptation is to put on your running shoes and try to race through it all. Resist this urge. Your best bet is to choose exactly what you want to see. A family guide and a floor plan will help you make your selections. See a few things thoroughly and talk about them. Even better, request the services of a docent who can explain all about the works of art.

Below the West and East buildings is a concourse connecting the two, with another gift shop, a cafeteria, and a waterfall (actually, it's a glassed-in wall of water from the fountain outside). The most exciting feature for younger kids will likely be the moving walkway linking the two buildings.

The special excitement of the East Building is in the design of the building itself. The sharp angles and stark exterior hint at the dramatic, light-filled interior. Created in 1978 by architect I. M. Pei, the structure remains the most modern, though not the newest, building downtown.

Smart Stuff

For Teens . . . Find the huge painting entitled *The Dead Toreador,* by Edouard Manet. Kids love the goriness of this piece, but they can also be encouraged to discuss the realism of it and how it makes them feel. What do they think is the artist's opinion of bullfights?

Although the exhibits change frequently, their common denominator is that all represent the masters of modern art, including Picasso, Giacometti, Warhol, Stella, Mondrian, Rothko, Man Ray, Magritte, and Matisse. Children are amazed at the enormous works

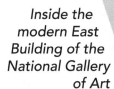

Inside the modern East Building of the National Gallery of Art

hanging high above their heads as they enter. The super-size mobile by Alexander Calder (children love to watch it move) and the giant Joan Miró tapestry are colorful surprises after a visit to the more traditional West Building. The huge elevators (necessarily so for moving large canvasses) and the spiral staircase to the upper level hold particular appeal for younger kids. In this case, getting to the exhibits is half the fun. One dividend for young artists is that many of the objects represented in the works of art do *not* look realistic. This may be some children's first exposure to nonrepresentational styles. Older kids will appreciate the variety of abstract styles, particularly if the artist, like Picasso (who actually began his career with representational painting), embraces a variety of approaches.

Smart Stuff

For Teens . . . One way to combat teens' natural tendencies to plough through an exhibit ("Saw this! Saw that! Yep!") is to have them compare and contrast two works of art. For example, look at two American works from the late 19th century: Winslow Homer's 1876 painting *Breezing Up* and Mary Cassatt's 1893 painting *The Boating Party*. What are the differences in uses of color? Appeal to the senses? Feeling of movement? Ask which painting they prefer, and why. (H.)

Time-Saving Tip

The Cascade Café is among the most popular of the eateries scattered around the Mall. To museumed-out adults and kids, this eatery between the West and East wings of the National Gallery is a welcome and tasty relief. With a large seating capacity (although everyone tries to sit facing the waterfall) and a wide variety of choices ranging from salads to grilled meats, this is an inviting place for all ages and degrees of appetite. The cafeteria is open Monday to Saturday 10 to 3 and Sunday 11 to 4.

Ready for some food? On one of the upper levels in the East Building, high enough for a grand view, is the **Terrace Café.** Upscale in both price and selection, this is not for the burgers and fries gang, but it's a delight for lunch if you're a small, classy few.

Special temporary exhibits at the National Gallery of Art are so popular that many people pick up free "time tickets" (which admit you on a certain day and time) well in advance of their visit. But *all* visitors have access. Go to the ticket counter on the main floor of the West Building early on the day of your visit to pick up tickets. Some are set aside just for this distribution.

Smart Stuff

For Tweens and Teens . . .
Geometry lesson: What geometric shape does the East Building represent? (Hint: It's actually a combination of two interconnected shapes.) (I.)

The gift shops are filled with books of interest, of course. Tykes and tweens might enjoy *Come Look With Me: Exploring Landscape Art with Children,* by Gladys Blizzard. Tweens might enjoy *Girl with a Watering Can,* by Edward Zadrzynska. The *Art for Children* series, by Ernest Raboff, features individual books on such artists as Picasso, Raphael, Chagall, Matisse, and Renoir that are great for tweens.

Metro: Archives

Constitution Avenue between 3rd and 7th streets, NW

Open Monday through Saturday 10 to 5, Sunday 11 to 6; closed January 1 and December 25

Tours of West Building: weekdays at 11:30 and 3:30, Saturday at 10:30 and 12:30, Sunday at 12:30, 2:30, and 4:30. Tours of East Building: weekdays at 10:30 and 1:30, weekends at 11:30, 1:30, and 3:30

For group tours, call one month in advance

Gallery talks Tuesday through Sunday; lectures Sunday at 4, concerts Sunday at 7

Sign language interpretation available with three weeks advance notice

Fee for audiotape tours

202/737–4215

www.nga.gov

Smart Stuff

For Tikes . . . Select an abstract painting and see how many objects you can "find" within it. How does the picture make you feel?

National Gallery of Art Sculpture Garden and Ice Skating Rink

For All Ages . . . Back out in the sunlight, children enjoy wandering through the 6-acre Sculpture Garden, home to a number of modern works by Claes Oldenburg, Roy Lichtenstein, Coosje van Bruggen, Tony Smith, and Magdalena Abakanowicz. Open from late October to mid-March, the circular ice rink is a wonderful spot for skating and socializing. You can even rent skates here. The indoor–

outdoor **Pavilion Café** offers fresh-baked goods, salads, sandwiches, specialty pizzas, desserts, and a welcome cup of hot cocoa or coffee. There's also a children's menu. Keeping your balance on the ice is your job.

> Metro: Archives
> Mall at 7th Street and Constitution Avenue, NW
> Open daily; hours change seasonally
> 202/289–3360
> www.nga.gov/exhibitions/sculptureinfo.shtm

★National Museum of Natural History

For All Ages . . . You know you're not in an art gallery when you're greeted by a huge, hairy, 8-ton African bush elephant in the domed rotunda of the National Museum of Natural History. This tusker is a favorite with children of all ages. From live insects to dead dinosaurs (only the bones, of course), this fossil-filled museum has something special for everyone. Check at the information desk for free, timed admission tickets for the **Discovery Room** and the **Insect Zoo.** Immediately off the rotunda, start with the **Native Cultures of the Americas,** with dioramas of native peoples doing everyday tasks.

For young children, the **Discovery Room,** with its bones, reptile skins, and even a preserved rattlesnake, offers a chance to look *and* touch. The **Dinosaur Hall,** full of skeletons of these colossal creatures, is also a favorite with young visitors. Even without getting wet, your family can have a feeling of total underwater immersion in the newly designed **Sant Ocean Hall.** Overhead hangs Phoenix, a model of a 45-foot-long North Atlantic right whale. Futuristic displays and living and preserved undersea creatures compete with *Ocean Odyssey,* a high-definition underwater film, projected on the wall panels surrounding the center hall. In the Coral Reef section, live sea creatures enjoy their new home: a 1,500-gallon tank. On the second floor, the **O. Orkin Insect Zoo** allows anyone who likes bugs to get up close and personal with cockroaches, centipedes, and tarantulas. You can watch as the tarantulas are fed their meal of live crickets. Chow times are Tuesday through Friday at 10:30, 11:30, and 1:30; weekends at 11:30, 12:30, and 1:30.

For those of us who like our treasures nonmobile, the **Janet Annenberg Hooker Hall of Geology, Gems, and Minerals** has more allure. Kids especially ogle the collection of geodes that glow in the dark. In addition to the famed 45½-karat Hope Diamond, this hall displays earrings worn by Marie Antoinette on her way to the guillotine and features interactive and multimedia activities. Although these offerings are clearly state-of-the-art, they unfortunately do not allow for creation of expensive jewelry of our own.

Helpful Hint
Contact the National Gallery of Art and ask to be sent the packet to help teachers or parents plan ahead.

The museum's jewel is the **Discovery Center,** with its 500-seat IMAX theater featuring movies about the environment and our cultural heritage. Hands-on activities abound here. When kids tire, they can take advantage of the food court in the new 600-seat **Atrium Café** and then drag you through the largest complex of gift shops in the entire Smithsonian.

There are, of course, many books and films about nature, as well as about various cultures around the world. *Jane Goodall and the Chimpanzees*, by Betsy Chessen (tykes), and *Jane Goodall*, by Lola M. Schaefer and Wyatt Schaefer (tweens), explore her life and her work with chimpanzees. *People Around the World*, by Antony Mason (tweens), includes beautiful photos (many with children) about people on every continent. *Sharing Nature with Children*, by Joseph B. Cornell (tweens and teens), is a real classic, and now includes some new nature games. For teens, look at *Wildlife Wars: My Fight to Save Africa's National Treasures*, by Richard Leakey and Virginia Morell.

You can now snack on the same floor as the Ocean Hall! Try the new **Fossil Café.**

Smart Stuff

For Tweens . . . This museum actually has a two-part name. What is the second part? How many native cultures from the Western Hemisphere can you find displayed? (J.)

Metro: Federal Triangle or Smithsonian
10th Street and Constitution Avenue, NW on the Mall
Open daily 10 to 5:30
Free guided tours September to June, daily at 10:30 and 1:30
Fee for audiotape tour
For groups, call 202/633–4629; for group visits to the
        Discovery Room, call 202/357–2747; for group IMAX
        passes, call 866/868–7774
For IMAX film schedule, call 202/633–4629
202/633–1000
www.mnh.si.edu or www.ocean.si.edu

★National Museum of American History

For All Ages . . . Called "the nation's attic" because of the eclectic nature of its contents, the National Museum of American History frustrates those who try to see it all in one visit. Sharing the building with Dorothy's ruby slippers from *The Wizard of Oz* are Thomas Edison's light bulb, jazz king Dizzy Gillespie's trumpet, and the original Star-Spangled Banner.

The mission of the recently renovated and reopened American History Museum is to make American history more user-friendly. To literally shed more light on the subject, the musum's central core has become an atrium with a glass skylight, bathing all three floors in natural light. Main exhibit themes are highlighted by specific artifacts at the entranceways, so visitors can quickly decide where they want to spend their time. From the Greensboro lunch counter exhibit to the 1865 telescope used by America's first female astronomer, there's plenty for kids of all ages to explore.

The museum is organized into East and West Wings on three separate floors. Pick up a map at the Information Booth to plot your visit according to the interests of your group. This eclectic collection includes the exhibits "Transportation and Technology," "Invention at Play," "The Evolution of Families and Communities," "America at War," "The American Presidency," and "Musical Instruments," as well as a giant dollhouse and iconic items from television, movies, and sports.

A special place for 6- to 12-year-olds is Spark! Lab, which has a changing variety of experiments and topics to explore. A relief for parents is a showcase at the rear of the "Invention at Play" room, highlighting the best kinds of toys for kids (from the oldest to the most modern)—those that stimulate kids to be creative.

The Museum's centerpiece is still the fragile Star Spangled Banner, now housed in a special gallery, lighted softly for preservation.

There are plenty of gift shops where you can find Smithsonian-related souvenirs, Star-Spangled Banner mementos, apparel, toys, books, and jewelry.

There's also food available right here at the museum. For lighter fare and the ice cream lovers in your group, try the **Constitution Café** (first floor, by the entrance). For a greater variety, the **Stars and Stripes Café** is organized as a food court, with soups, sandwiches, and salads readily available. Both cafés are open daily 10 to 5).

Smart Stuff

For All Ages . . . Can you find "Stanley," the car that drives itself? How could such a car be used in the future? (K.)

Some materials to enrich a visit to this museum include *Colonial Kids,* an activity book with directions for preparing authentic food, clothing, and other colonial items, as well as hundreds of activity ideas (tweens), and *Dear America: Friend to Friend,* an unusual computer game featuring six girls from different historical periods in American history (tweens).

Amelia and Eleanor Go for a Ride, by Pam M. Ryan, about First Lady Eleanor Roosevelt and aviator Amelia Earhart, is great for tykes. *The Big Book of American Heroes*, by Mike Janulewicz and Richard Widdoves, which profiles people from George Washington to Maya Angelou, appeals to tweens. For teens there's the novel *Ragtime*, by E. L. Doctorow, which was made into a Broadway musical. Tweens and teens can read aloud or even perform Thornton Wilder's classic play *Our Town*.

Metro: Federal Triangle or Smithsonian
Constitution Avenue between 12th and 14th streets, NW
Open daily 10 to 5:30
For guided tours, call 202/357–1481
Fee for audiotape rentals
202/633–1000
www.americanhistory.si.edu

Where to Stay in the National Mall Area

Since none of the Smithsonian buildings has overnight accommodations (alas!), we've tried to locate the next best things. Again, remember to ask for discounts—for any category you can think of (time of year, group, corporate, etc.). Here are a few suggestions to consider:

Hotel Harrington
11th and E streets, NW
202/628–8140 or 800/424–8532
www.hotel-harrington.com
Metro: Metro Center

Who says attorneys aren't creative? The U.S. Attorney for the District of Columbia tried a brief stint at poetry, and the rest is definitely history. His name was Francis Scott Key, and his poem became our national anthem, "The Star-Spangled Banner."

Holiday Inn Washington–Capitol
550 C Street, SW
202/479–4000
www.ichotelsgroup.com
Metro: L'Enfant Plaza

L'Enfant Plaza Hotel
480 L'Enfant Plaza, SW
202/484–1000 or 800/235–6397
www.lenfantplazahotel.com
Metro: L'Enfant Plaza

Answers to Smart Stuff Questions

A. Little ones will have fun searching for the six peacocks in this room.

B. Whistler's trademark was a butterfly. There are four of them in this room.

C. The ancient Nubian city of Kerma, 2500–1500 BC.

D. The sculpture is of Don Quixote, by Giacometti, famous for his elongated realistic figures. Notice the difference between this sculpture and other representational pieces, such as the huge bust of Baudelaire.

E. Of the numerous horse sculptures, children might like to contrast the forceful movement-oriented work of Meissonier, *A Horseman in a Storm,* with the solid, static, almost primitive look of Braque's *Little Horse* and Duchamp-Villon's very abstract *Head of a Horse.*

F. Laika, a dog from the Soviet Union, was the first animal in space. Kids should read about the U.S.–Soviet space race for a better appreciation of the Air and Space Museum's "Space Race" exhibit.

G. The first docking of two spacecraft paired Apollo 18 and Soyuz 19 on July 17, 1975. The joint U.S.–Russian Space Station is the most recent cooperative venture. Teens will enjoy making predictions, but they need to base them on facts about the current scientific and political climates in each country.

H. If the kids are slow getting into this, ask how many different shades of green they can find in Homer's ocean. Contrast this with the water in the Cassatt painting.

I. The building is actually a trapezoid, built of two interconnected triangles. You might have to go up in a helicopter to see this clearly!

J. The second part of the National Museum of Natural History's name is "The Museum of Man." Children will be interested in finding the geographic locations of the many different cultures.

K. "Stanley" can be found in the "Science and Innovation" section of the National Museum of American History. This car was developed to help save the lives of American troops on the battlefield. How do you think this kind of technology would work for turnpike driving in the U.S.?

CHAPTER 4

White House
& Foggy Bottom

Who would have thought that some of the most significant buildings in our country are built on a former swamp stabilized by landfill? The name "Foggy Bottom" comes from the misty, often foul, air that hovered above this swamp on the edge of the Potomac River. A coal depot and gasworks occupied the area that is now home to the **White House,** the **Corcoran Gallery,** the **Kennedy Center,** headquarters for the **Organization of American States,** the **Renwick Gallery,** the mysterious **Octagon House,** and the equally mysterious **Department of State.** These days, "Foggy Bottom" is Washington vernacular for the State Department, whose edicts are sometimes a bit hazy.

★National Aquarium

For All Ages . . . An entire society flourishes underground in the nation's capital. No, it's not the counterculture reappearing. Our nation's oldest public aquarium, scaled just right for children, resides in—of all places—the basement of the **Department of Commerce.** Tanks full of fascinating sea creatures are set low enough to be viewed by even the smallest of small fry. There's a wide variety of undersea life, from eels that can make an electric current (maybe they could help out in an energy crisis) to the strangely shaped hammerhead sharks. One special treat is the 2 PM feeding of the sharks (Monday, Wednesday, and Saturday), piranhas (Tuesday, Thursday, and Sunday), and alligators (Friday)—not a sight for the fainthearted. Younger children especially enjoy getting up close and personal with the marine residents of the Touch Tank. Want to pet a horseshoe crab or handle a starfish? C'mon down!

Metro: Federal Triangle
14th Street, NW, between Pennsylvania Avenue and Constitution Avenue (inside the Department of Commerce)
Open daily 9 to 5; closed Thanksgiving Day and December 25
Fee (cash or check only)
202/482–2825
www.nationalaquarium.com

White House Visitors Center

For Tweens and Teens . . . Since the events of September 11, 2001, most White House tours have been suspended. The White House Visitors Center is the next best thing, offering informative displays and a 30-minute video tour. It's also a comfortable place to sit and relax, with a special activity area for kids to read, write a letter, color, and play puzzle games. You *will* want to see the exterior of the White House, regardless. From Lafayette Square and the pedestrian-only section of Pennsylvania Avenue, you can view this historic and imposing building.

As for breakfast, which will most likely be on your mind if you started out early, you're in luck. On 15th Street, NW, across from the Ellipse, is the **Commerce Department,** which has a cafeteria (202/482–5905) on the lower level, open weekdays from 6:30 to 3. Breakfast here is a bargain. (After all, they *do* know something about commerce.) Just a block from the White House, the **Bread-Line** (1751 Pennsylvania Avenue, NW; 202/822–8900) is open weekdays 7:30 to 3:30. Here you can get made-to-order sandwiches as well as muffins, croissants, and other baked goods, all available to go.

Metro: McPherson Square
1450 Pennsylvania Avenue, NW, between 14th and 15th
    streets (inside the Department of Commerce)
Open daily 7:30 to 4; closed Thanksgiving Day, December 25,
    and January 1.
202/456–7041
www.nps.gov/whho

On Pennsylvania Avenue, in the park bordered by 15th and E
streets, NW, is a massive **equestrian monument** to a larger-than-
life character: William Tecumseh Sherman, famous for his "scorched
earth" march across several southern states during the Civil War. He
was named for the Shawnee Indian chief Tecumseh, admired by his
father. (After his father's death, his foster mother added the more

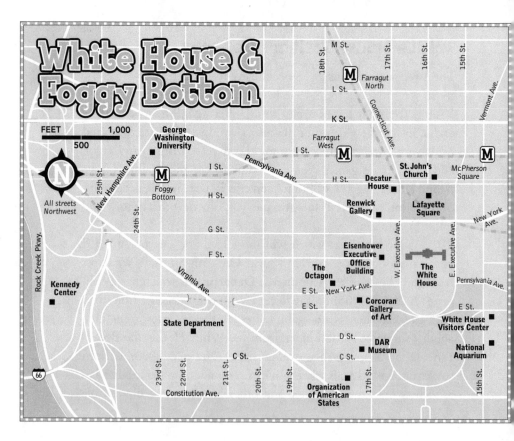

The White House
State Visitors
Entrance

conventional first name.)
This loquacious man, who
loved dancing and pretty
women, was as extro-
verted as his superior, General
Grant, was taciturn. When a movement surfaced to draft him for
the presidency, he answered with the now-famous response, "I will
not accept if nominated and will not serve if elected."

The White House

For Tweens and Teens . . . The White House has been home to
every president except our first. From John Adams's lonely occupation of the unfinished building in 1800 through Franklin D. Roosevelt's tenure when it became known as the "Grand Hotel," to its
setting for scandal in recent years, every administration has put its
own stamp on the president's house. It was Teddy Roosevelt who
had the drab exterior repainted white and officially named the
building the White House, emblazoning it on his presidential stationery. Even children have used the residence in unorthodox ways,

There *was* a time before inaugural balls and affairs of
state. One president took the oath of office and later
walked back to his boarding house and had his dinner
with the other residents. His name was Thomas Jefferson.
His new residence was not yet finished when Jefferson
became president in 1801.

Quick Guide to

Attraction	Location
★National Aquarium	14th Street and Constitution Avenue, NW between Pennsylvania Avenue and Constitution Avenue
White House Visitors Center	1450 Pennsylvania Avenue, NW (inside the Department of Commerce building, between 14th and 15th streets, NW)
The White House	1600 Pennsylvania Avenue, NW
Lafayette Square	Bounded by Pennsylvania Avenue, Madison Place, Jackson Place, and H Street
St. John's Church	16th and H streets, NW (across from Lafayette Square)
Decatur House	748 Jackson Place, NW (entrance at 1610 H Street, NW)
Renwick Gallery	17th Street and Pennsylvania Avenue, NW
Eisenhower Executive Office Building	Pennsylvania Avenue and 17th Street, NW
The Octagon	1799 New York Avenue, NW
Corcoran Gallery of Art	17th and E streets, NW (half block west of the White House)
★DAR (Daughters of the American Revolution) Museum	1776 D Street, NW
Organization of American States Building	17th Street and Constitution Avenue, NW
State Department, Diplomatic Reception Rooms	2201 C Street, NW
George Washington University	2121 I Street, NW
★Kennedy Center for the Performing Arts	2700 F Street, NW (New Hampshire Avenue and Rock Creek Parkway)

White House & Foggy Bottom Attractions

Age Range	Hours	Details on
All Ages	9 AM–5 PM daily	Page 84
Tweens and Teens	7:30 AM–4 PM daily	Page 85
Tweens and Teens	Schedule tours with members of Congress	Page 87
All Ages		Page 93
All Ages	Office Mon.–Sat. 9 AM–3 PM	Page 94
Teens	Mon.–Sat. 10–5; Sun. noon–4	Page 95
Teens	10 AM–5:30 PM daily	Page 95
Teens	No tours at present.	Page 96
Teens	Tues.–Sun. 10 AM–4 PM	Page 96
Tweens and Teens	Closed Mon.–Tues.; Wed. 10–5 ; Th. 10–9; Fri.–Sun. 10–5	Page 97
All Ages	Mon.–Fri. 9:30 AM–4 PM; Sat. 9–5	Page 99
Teens	Mon.–Fri. 9 AM–5:30 PM	Page 101
Teens	Schedule tours in advance	Page 102
Teens		Page 103
All Ages	Tours: Mon.–Fri. 10 AM–5 PM, Sat.–Sun. 10 AM–1 PM	Page 104

like the sons of President Garfield, who used the East Room for their bicycle races.

In this building, members of presidential families, including one president himself, have been married; numerous babies, including several presidential grandchildren and one presidential child, have been born; and seven U.S. presidents have lain in state. Heads of state in other parts of the world live in much larger and more opulent surroundings. This home for the leader of our democracy underscores his title: president, not king.

Smart Stuff

For Tweens . . . There are streets in Washington, D.C., named for every state. On which state's street does the president live? (A.)

Although security concerns have ended most public viewings of the White House, groups of 10 or more can request a tour through their congressional representative up to six months in advance. If you're lucky enough to tour the White House, you'll walk through or past the State Dining Room, the East Room, the Green Room, the Red Room, the Blue Room, the Vermeil Room, and the Library. Secret Service agents are available in each room to answer questions. Antiques, paintings, and other treasures collected over several administrations are on display in these areas and in the hallways. White House staff members, interns, and others are not on display, however; with one notorious exception, they do their work in another part of the building. Outside, if you see the flag flying at the White House, the president is home.

Smart Stuff

For Tweens . . . Which president was married in the White House? (B.)

For some interesting White House digging on your own, we

Smart Stuff

For Teens . . . What Confederate sympathizer, nick-named "the Colonel," lived and died in the White House after the South lost the Civil War? **(C.)**

highly recommend for the youngest readers Anne Denton Blair's *Arthur, the White House Mouse;* Kate Waters's *The Story of the White House;* and *Meet President Barack Obama,* by Laine Falk. Tykes and tweens will enjoy two books by Marge Kennedy: *The Story of the White House* and *See Inside the White House.* For tweens, look at *A Kid's Guide to the White House: Is George Washington Still Upstairs?,* by Betty Denam; *You Are The President,* by Nathan Aaseng; *Ghosts of the White House,* by Cheryl Harness; *Secret of the Missing Teacup,* by Marianne Hering; *The White House: An Historic Guide,* published by the White House Historical Association with the cooperation of the National Geographic Society; and *Mystery at the White House: A President is Missing,* by Nancy Ann Van Wie.

Smart Stuff

For Teens . . . Carved onto the mantle of the State Dining Room is John Adams's hope for future occupants of the White House. What did he wish? Which administration do you feel has most lived up to this expectation? Which the least? **(D.)**

Teens might enjoy *To the Best of My Ability: The American Presidents,* edited by James McPherson and David Rubel; *Theodore Roosevelt: A Life,* by Nathan Miller; and *Abigail Adams: Witness to a Revolution,* by Natalie S. Bober. As for movies, teens can check out *The Candidate, The American President,* and *Dave.* There's a Web site with fun White House facts: *www.whitehouse.gov/about* (take a look at "Whitehouse 101"), and a White House blog: *www.whitehouse.gov/blog.*

Metro: McPherson Square, Metro Center, or Federal Triangle
1600 Pennsylvania Avenue, NW
202/456–7041
www.nps.gov/whho

Which president served the shortest term?
(William Henry Harrison—31 days)
Which president served the longest term?
(Franklin Delano Roosevelt—12 years, I month)

Everyone loves a nice backyard, and presidents get the **Ellipse,** a beautiful green expanse south of the White House. Here you can find a block of granite called the Zero Milestone, the official point used to measure the distance from D.C. to other parts of the United States.

Getting a little hungry as you think about all those lavish state dinners? The **Ellipse Visitor Pavilion** (on the Ellipse, behind the Commerce Department) offers muffins, snacks, and drinks. It's open 8 to 3. Its large selection of pizzas and bottomless salad bowl make **Bertucci's** (2000 Pennsylvania Avenue, NW; 202/296–2600) a favorite of George Washington University students. Reservations

The Oval Office

Smart Stuff

For Tikes . . . Some of the funniest stories about life in the White House describe the antics of Teddy Roosevelt's six children and their pets. If you lived in the White House, what kinds of pets would you like to have there? **(E.)**

are required for groups of eight or more people. It's open Monday to Thursday 11 to 10, Friday and Saturday 11 to 11, and Sunday 11 to 10. **Lindy's Bon Apetit** (2040 I Street, NW; 202/452–0055) serves omelets with home fries and toast—mostly for carry-out—as well as a zillion varieties of burgers, soups, and desserts, all well priced. It's open Monday to Wednesday 7:30 AM to 9 PM, Thursday 7:30 AM to 1 AM, and weekends 11 AM to 2 AM. After you grab your order, head off to enjoy it *alfresco*.

Lafayette Square

For All Ages . . . Directly across from the White House, Lafayette Square is a major landmark with a checkered past. In recent years it has been the site of demonstrations and protests. It was a military encampment site during the War of 1812 and the Civil War, turning it into a muddy pit. Later, President Grant used it for a small zoo. Unfortunately, some of the animals gave off unpleasant odors and had to be removed. In the center of the square, the dominant statue of **Andrew Jackson** includes four guns that were captured by Jackson at the Battle of New Orleans in 1814—an ironic touch, since the war was actually *over* before the battle began. The troops didn't get the message—everyone needed cell phones! A statue of the **Marquis de Lafayette,** a young French nobleman who fought in the Revolutionary War, commands the southeast corner. Nearby stands a statue of scantily clad **Columbia,** who is holding an outstretched sword. Some have suggested that she is shouting, "Give me back my clothes and I'll give you your sword!"

Metro: McPherson Square, Farragut North, Farragut West
Bounded by Pennsylvania Avenue, Madison Place, Jackson
Place, and H Street.

St. John's Church

St. John's Church is called the "Church of the Presidents," because
every president since Madison has attended one or more services
here, all sitting in the same reserved pew. The 1,000-pound bell in
the bell tower was made from a British cannon captured during the
War of 1812.

On July 4, 1917, in a cemetery in Paris, Lieutenant
Colonel Charles E. Stanton stood in front of Lafayette's
tomb. American troops had entered World War I in April,
and General John J. ("Blackjack") Pershing, commander
of the Allied Expeditionary Forces, sent Stanton, a member of his staff, to speak in commemoration of America's
Independence Day. His words would be echoed as American soldiers landed on the shores of France once again in
1944: "What we have of blood and treasure are yours . . .
and now . . . we pledge our hearts and our honor . . .
Lafayette, we are here."

Metro: McPherson Square, Farragut North, Farragut West
16th and H streets, NW, across from Lafayette Square
Metro: McPherson Square
Open Monday through Saturday 9 to 3; Sunday services at
     7:45, 9, and 11. Summer services Sunday at 7:45 and 11.
202/347–8766

For a midday break, stroll over to **Farragut Square** (912 17th
Street, NW), where weekdays bring lunchtime concerts right to the
middle of the business district—a great time and place for a picnic.

Decatur House

For Teens . . . Decatur House, on the northwest corner of Lafayette Park, was home to both a hero and a villain. It was named for Stephen Decatur, the young captain who defeated the Barbary pirates and captured an important British frigate during the War of 1812. He spent only one year in the house before dying in a duel. John Gadsby, a wealthy hotelier, used the house in the 1830s and 1840s to entertain the city's elite while running a slave market in the back. According to contemporary reports, people locked in the attic and an extension along H Street filled the night air with their howls and cries. Fortunately, all that the house contains now is vintage decor. The 40-minute tours, which depart at 15 minutes past the hour, showcase Victorian and Federal styles of furnishings. The museum shop carries books, prints, posters, model ships, and a variety of home accessories.

A film appropriate for teens with a significant story to tell about slavery and human rights is *Amistad*.

Metro: Farragut West or Farragut North
748 Jackson Place, NW (entrance at 1610 H Street, NW)
Monday through Saturday 10 to 5, Sunday noon to 4; closed
    January 1, Thanksgiving Day, and December 25
Tours Friday and Saturday 10 to 5, Sunday noon to 4
Donation
202/842–0920
www.decaturhouse.org

Renwick Gallery

For Teens . . . The Renwick Gallery, a branch of the Smithsonian's National Museum of American Art, focuses on crafts by major artists. Designed in 1859 by James Renwick Jr. (who also designed the Smithsonian Castle), it's a beautiful and opulent setting. The museum shop carries the materials for creating your own artwork, handcrafted items including hand-painted silks, and books for children and adults.

Metro: Farragut West or Farragut North
17th Street and Pennsylvania Avenue, NW
Open daily 10 to 5:30; closed December 25
Guided tours September to June, weekdays at noon, week-
     ends at 1; June to September, Friday at noon, weekends
     at 1.
For school groups, call 202/633–8550
202/633–8530
www.renwickgallery.com

Eisenhower Executive Office Building

For Teens . . . Called by some the "Victorian wedding cake," the
Eisenhower Executive Office Building was erected during President
Grant's administration. When it was completed in 1888 it was the
largest office building in the world. Its Second Empire exterior
more closely resembles a palace than a government building. It
houses the vice president's office, the bulk of the president's staff,
and some interns. At this writing, there were no tours available, but
call ahead; tours will be Saturday mornings when the renovation is
complete.

Metro: Farragut West or Farragut North
Pennsylvania Avenue and 17th Street, NW
202/395–5895
www.whitehouse.gov/history/eeobtour

The Octagon

For Teens . . . Called "Washington's second most famous haunted
house" by one newspaper columnist, the Octagon is a good place to
visit if you like ghost stories. Built by architect William Thornton,
who also designed the Capitol, this building has been home to a
president, a wealthy family, and slaves. President James Madison
signed the Treaty of Ghent, which ended the War of 1812, in an upstairs room. The ghost of a murdered slave girl is said to scream in

the night in this house. The family of Colonel John Tayloe III, the original owner, has contributed its share of ghostly legends as well. The colonel's ghost is believed to ring bells here, and the ghosts of both of his daugh-

Smart Stuff

For Teens . . . Name the only teenager commissioned as a major general in the Continental Army. (F.)

ters are said to appear from time to time. The skeleton of a young girl, found buried in a wall by workers, also contributes to the mystery.

At this writing, the Octagon was undergoing extensive renovations, so call ahead.

Now owned by the American Institute of Architects Foundation, the house displays temporary design and architectural exhibits in the former bedrooms. Downstairs is a permanent exhibit on life in the 1800s—life for the servants, that is. By the way, in keeping with its strangeness, the Octagon is *not* built in the shape of an octagon at all. It was just designed to fit on an awkwardly shaped lot. People still say there are eight angles, even though there are not eight sides. Let us know if you find them.

Metro: Farragut West or Farragut North

1799 New York Avenue, NW

Open Tuesday to Sunday 10 to 4; closed January 1, Thanksgiving Day, and December 25

No walk-in visitors allowed; tours for groups of 10 or more must be arranged in advance

Admission fee

Wheelchair access to first floor only

202/638–3221

www.theoctagon.org

Corcoran Gallery of Art

For Tweens and Teens . . . "The most valuable bequest I can make you is a good name," William Wilson Corcoran wrote to his grandchildren. The father of the Corcoran Gallery of Art gave his own name to one of D.C.'s great art treasures. He was an indefatigable philanthropist, giving money to the District of Columbia, numerous nearby universities, and even individuals who lined up at his office. As a gesture of patriotism after the Civil War (he had been a Confederate sympathizer whose property was seized when he prudently left for Europe during the war years), he put his vast art collection under the governance of a board of trustees and opened it to the public. It's one of the nation's three oldest art museums (along with the Boston Museum of Fine Arts and the Metropolitan Museum of Art in New York).

Smart Stuff

For Tweens . . . What American artist (represented in the Corcoran Gallery) was also a famous inventor? **(G.)**

An expansive Beaux Arts building with a soaring atrium and marble staircases, the Corcoran has an extensive collection of art from the 18th century through the present. Showcasing painters such as Sargent, Bierstadt, and Homer, this museum also features such modern artists as Rothko, Nevelson, and Lichtenstein. Some rooms are devoted to specific European treasures: medieval Renaissance tapestries, Corot landscapes, 19th-century French Impressionist paintings, Delft porcelains, and the Salon Dore (a completely reconstructed Louis XVI–style room from a Parisian hotel).

Smart Stuff

For Teens . . . After viewing one of John Singer Sargent's elegant portraits, find one by modern artist Roy Lichtenstein. Both are representational, yet they are from very different styles. Which appeals to you more? Why? **(H.)**

The temporary exhibits—paintings, prints, and especially photographs—are often worth a special trip. Works of local artists are often hung here as well. The Corcoran, which also houses an art school, offers informative educational materials and special tours.

The museum shop, which is open during museum hours, offers a selection of art books, note cards, jewelry, and other items. As for food, the first-floor **Café at the Corcoran** (202/639–1786) serves light meals and snacks. It's open Monday, Wednesday, Friday, and Saturday 11 to 3, and Thursday 11 to 3 and 5 to 8. Sunday brunch is served 10:30 to 2. Reservations are recommended.

Smart Stuff

For Tweens and Teens . . . Find a painting by 19th-century landscape artist Alfred Bierstadt. What does the painting say about the American West? What elements in his painting reveal his viewpoint? (l.)

Metro: Farragut West or Farragut North
500 17th Street, NW (half block west of the White House)
Open Wednesday 10 to 5, Thursday 10 to 9, and Friday
    through Sunday 10 to 5; closed December 25 and January 1
Suggested donation for visitors over 12
Free 45-minute tours Wednesday to Friday at 10:30, as well as
    Thursday at 7:30
202/639–1700
www.corcoran.org

★DAR (Daughters of the American Revolution) Museum

For All Ages . . . One of the best attics we know of is the third-floor **New Hampshire Period Room/Children's Attic** in the DAR Museum. This imposing building is the headquarters of the Daughters of the American Revolution. Rag dolls, tea sets, tiny cast-iron stoves, and other toys from the 18th through the 20th century remind children that even long ago kids had plenty of ways to pass the time. In the **Touch of Independence** section, kids can dress up in replica colonial clothing and learn about early American trades and materials. And unlike most other attics, this one isn't dusty. A docent must accompany you to this out-of-the-way part of the building. Go to the information desk for details.

For adults and older teens, the lower floors boast 31 period rooms filled with furniture, china, glass, silver, paintings, and even costumes from earlier eras. The gadgets from those times include a foot-controlled toaster, a four-sided guillotine-mousetrap, and a sausage stuffer that looks more like an exercise machine.

Naturally, the DAR Museum focuses on the roles of women in American history. So our friend Sybil Ludington appears here in sculpture and painting. (Remember her? She outrode Paul Revere.)

Smart Stuff

For Teens . . . On December 2, 1823, what U.S. president declared, "The American continents . . . are . . . not to be considered as subjects for future colonization by any European powers" and "We should consider any attempt on their part to extend their system to any portion of this hemisphere as dangerous to our peace and safety"? (J.)

Metro: Farragut West or Farragut North
1776 D Street, NW
Open weekdays 9:30 to 4, Saturday 9 to 5
Tours weekdays 10 to 2:30, Saturday 9 to 4.
for group tours, call 202/879–3341
202/879–3241
www.dar.org/museum

Organization of American States Building

For Teens . . . Part art gallery, part rain forest, and part international offices, this building serves as headquarters for the Organization of American States (OAS). Closely connected to, but not part of, the United Nations, the OAS was chartered in 1948 to provide a system for regional security, economic stability, and social welfare. The richly decorated **Hall of Americas,** the **Hall of Heroes and Flags,** and the **Simón Bolívar Room** deserve a peek. Kids who are too young for a visit to a meeting room will love the main building's tropical entranceway, with palm trees and an Aztec- and Mayan-inspired fountain. The Aztec Garden nearby features a statue of Xochipilli, the Aztec god of flowers.

Amid the beautiful surroundings here are meeting rooms where formal sessions are held in Spanish. Sessions are open to tourists, and translation machines are available. It's a great place for kids to hear and practice their own Spanish. When you're not listening in, you can enjoy the main-floor gallery of 20th-century art from South and Central America. Behind the building is the **Art Museum of the Americas** (201 18th Street, NW; 202/458–6016), filled with works of contemporary artists from Mexico, the Caribbean, and Latin and South America. It's open Tuesday through Sunday 10 to 5.

> Metro: Farragut West or Farragut North
> 17th Street and Constitution Avenue, NW
> Open weekdays 9 to 5:30; closed holidays
> For tour information, call 202/458–3927
> 202/458–3000
> www.oas.org/museum

In this area, you might want to stop in at the **Department of the Interior** (1849 C Street, NW; 202/208–4056) to tour the collection of New Deal-era murals. Reserve in advance for a tour guide (202/208–4743). Browse a collection of authentic Native American

In the category of "your government at work," during the Civil War the Department of Interior's Bureau of Indian Affairs hired a particularly literate clerk. He lost his job, however, when it was found that his desk drawers were filled with his poems rather than government paperwork. His name was Walt Whitman.

pottery, bead work, and turquoise and silver jewelry in the **Indian Craft Shop**. It's open weekdays 8:30 to 4:30, and the third Saturday of the month 10 to 4. Visitors into more consumable goods can appreciate the large cafeteria in the basement, open weekdays 7 to 2:45. Note: this building is two blocks long! Wear your comfortable shoes.

State Department, Diplomatic Reception Rooms

For Teens . . . Although the design for the outside of this building is not particularly creative, the inside contains a surprise missed by many visitors. The diplomatic reception rooms on the eighth floor, which are actually used to welcome visiting dignitaries, also welcome visitors over 12. Along with a distinguished collection of 18th- and early-19th-century American furniture, paintings, and decorative arts are some truly historic pieces. The desk where Thomas Jefferson wrote the Declaration of Independence and the one at which John Adams, Benjamin Franklin, and John Jay signed the Treaty of Paris are displayed.

A book that will appeal to future diplomats is *Talking Peace: A Vision for the Next Generation*, revised ed., written by former president and Nobel Peace Prize–winner Jimmy Carter.

Metro: Foggy Bottom–GWU
2201 C Street, NW

45-minute guided tours must be arranged in advance through
the Web site only
Bring photo ID for admittance; no backpacks, strollers, or
other large items are allowed
202/647–4000
www.state.gov/m/drr
or https://receptiontours.state.gov

George Washington University

For Teens . . . Named for a familiar fellow, this is a renowned university that college-hopeful teens might like to explore. Its hospital, famous for treating President Reagan after his gunshot wound, was featured on the popular television political drama *The West Wing*. And Lisner Auditorium is here; more about that popular concert venue in Appendix I.

The infamous Watergate Hotel is just south of George Washington's campus. At this writing, the hotel was closed for renovation, so check the Web site (www.thewatergatehotel.com) for updates.

Metro: Foggy Bottom–GWU
2121 I Street, NW
202/994–6602
www.gwu.edu

An eye-catching statue stands in the circle at Virginia and New Hampshire avenues, NW, just a few blocks from the Kennedy Center. The sculpture depicts **Benito Juárez,** one of Mexico's greatest leaders. A full-blooded Zapotec Indian who was orphaned at age 3, he went on to become a district attorney, legislator, judge, governor, and representative in Mexico's Congress. Eventually, he served as president of his country, elected twice. One local wag, noting the imperious outstretched arm pointing east, dubbed this "the go-to-your-room statue."

★Kennedy Center for the Performing Arts

For All Ages . . . Talk about the slow pace of government: 200 years ago, George Washington proposed that a national cultural center be located in Washington, D.C. In 1977 the center opened as a headquarters for the performing arts. The enormous and hauntingly realistic bust of John F. Kennedy stands by itself in the **Grand Foyer,** amid oceans of red carpeting and crystal chandeliers. At the information desk, pick up a flag sheet. Kids will especially enjoy craning their necks to identify the flags hanging in the **Hall of States** and the **Hall of Nations.** Gifts from many countries are displayed throughout the building, including sculptures, tapestries, carvings, and Boehm porcelain birds.

The six theaters are home to a variety of performances: plays in the **Eisenhower Theater;** opera, musicals, and ballet in the **Opera House;** symphony concerts, recitals, and popular music events in the **Concert Hall;** drama, chamber music, poetry readings, and modern dance in the **Terrace Theater;** special programs in the **Theater Lab,** and plays and concerts in the **Family Theater.** Although tours are given daily, the best way to enjoy the Kennedy Center is to attend a performance at one of the theaters (see Appendix I), have a meal in one of the restaurants, or ride the elevator up to see the spectacular rooftop views of the Potomac River, Washington, and Virginia.

For theatrical and musical souvenirs, the gift shops here have the most and the best. The large shop near the parking garage level

Smart Stuff

For Tweens . . . Flags have colors and words or symbols that represent something important for a given state or country. Design a flag for your school or family. What colors would you include? What picture, words, or symbols would you choose?

The Kennedy Center for the Performing Arts

carries just about any-
thing you can think of:
prints, posters, jewelry, scarves, mugs, CDs, and DVDs,
just to name a few. The smaller shop, off the plaza entrance, offers a
sampling of what's to be found below.

Dining here, you can be as elegant or as casual as you'd like—
or as your budget permits, from the pricey **Roof Terrace Restaurant & Bar** (202/416–8555; open before major performances),
which serves elegant sit-down meals and a jazz brunch Sundays 11
to 1:45, to the **K. C. Café** (202/416–8576; open daily 11:30 to 8),
where you help yourself cafeteria-style to a range of food from sandwiches to hot entrées. There's coffee and cappuccino, wine by the
glass, and even champagne. Reap the bonus of magnificent views
through a wall of floor-to-ceiling windows, and please your tummy
as well as your pocketbook.

Getting here from the nearest Metro station—Foggy Bottom–
GWU—requires a 15-minute walk. There's also a free shuttle that
runs weekdays 9:45 AM to midnight, Saturday 10 AM to midnight,
and Sunday noon to midnight.

> Metro: Foggy Bottom–GWU
> 2700 F Street, NW
> Free hour-long tours weekdays 10 to 5, Saturday 10 to 1; for
> group tours, call 202/416–8345
> 202/416–8340
> www.kennedy-center.org

Where to Stay in the White House & Foggy Bottom Area

Although many people have stayed overnight at the White House, don't count on getting an invitation. Nearby, and more realistic, possibilities are:

The George Washington University Inn
824 New Hampshire Avenue, NW
202/337–6620 or 800/426–4455
www.gwuinn.com
Metro: Foggy Bottom–GWU

The River Inn
924 25th Street, NW
202/337–7600 or 888/874–0100
www.theriverinn.com
Metro: Foggy Bottom–GWU

Doubletree Guest Suites
801 New Hampshire Avenue, NW
202/785–2000 or 800/222–8733
www.doubletree.com
Metro: Foggy Bottom–GWU

State Plaza Hotel
2117 E Street, NW
202/861–8200 or 800/424–2859
www.stateplaza.com
Metro: Foggy Bottom–GWU

Answers to Smart Stuff Questions

A. The president lives in the White House, at 1600 Pennsylvania Avenue.

B. Grover Cleveland (age 48) married Frances Folsom (age 21) on June 2, 1885, shortly after her college graduation.

C. An elderly and unrepentant Confederate named Frederick Dent had a bedroom close to the North Portico, where he lived out the rest of his life. The former slave owner's coffin rested in the Yankee White House before his burial. How did he merit such treatment? His daughter Julia had married the general of the victorious Union forces, President Ulysses S. Grant.

D. The quote reads, "I Pray Heaven to Bestow the Best of Blessings on THIS HOUSE and on All that shall hereafter Inhabit it. May none but Honest and Wise Men ever rule under this Roof."

E. Funny examples were Alice Roosevelt's blue macaw, named Eli Yale, and her green snake, called Emily Spinach. Quentin Roosevelt's pony, Algonquin, was once smuggled upstairs to his master's room in the White House elevator.

F. The idealistic French nobleman Marie Joseph Paul Yves Roch Gilbert Motier Lafayette (his friends just called him Gilbert) equipped a ship at his own expense and wound up in America as General Washington's aide-de-camp. He secured financial aid, supplies, and volunteers from his home country, fought valiantly in numerous battles, and helped secure Cornwallis's defeat at Yorktown. He was commissioned as a major general one month before his 20th birthday.

G. Samuel F. B. Morse, inventor of the telegraph (and guess what code?).

H. Sargent's soft, muted colors emphasize the three-dimensional realism of his subjects; Lichtenstein's bold colors and strong lines evoke two-dimensional, comic book–style art.

I. Bierstadt romanticized the American West with grand vistas, dramatic use of light and shadow, and a perspective that seems to invite the viewer into his magnificent scenery. Students might want to connect Bierstadt's work with the history of westward expansion.

J. James Monroe, as part of his annual message to Congress, gave his measured response to the eruptions of independent nations in Latin America (1815–22) as they broke away—

often in bloodshed—from their colonial European powers. What became known as the Monroe Doctrine set the precedent for hemispheric solidarity that would take another 125 years to be embodied in a formal organization, the Organization of American States. The wheels of progress grind slowly.

CHAPTER

5

Tidal Basin

From the long slash of black granite in memory of those lost in the Vietnam War to the eerie-looking architecture evoking the concentration camps during the Holocaust, the memorials around the Tidal Basin area are worth a thoughtful, unhurried visit. They include the oldest monument, the landmark obelisk of the **Washington Monument,** and one of the newest, the **National World War II Memorial.** Each tells a distinct story, and each is unique.

Every spring the 3,700 ornamental cherry trees forming a decorative pink necklace around the **Tidal Basin** draw tourists by the thousands. A gift from Japan to the United States in 1912, the trees fell on hard times during World War II, when several "patriots" took buzz saws to some of them. Again in April 1999, some smaller culprits wreaked havoc; a family of beavers was eventually moved to another location by the National Park Service. The major problem these days is people who block your view when you're trying to take a photo.

Vietnam Veterans Memorial

For Tweens and Teens . . . For youngsters to whom the Vietnam War compares in historical remoteness to the War of 1812, a visit to

Parents/Teachers Take Note

First, a word about food. Don't come to this area, which spans Constitution Gardens, the Lincoln Memorial, the Tidal Basin, and the Jefferson Memorial, without bringing some snacks or packing a picnic. Although there are restrooms, there are no real restaurants. Since you'll be doing a lot of walking, wear your most comfortable walking shoes. And bring your water bottle!

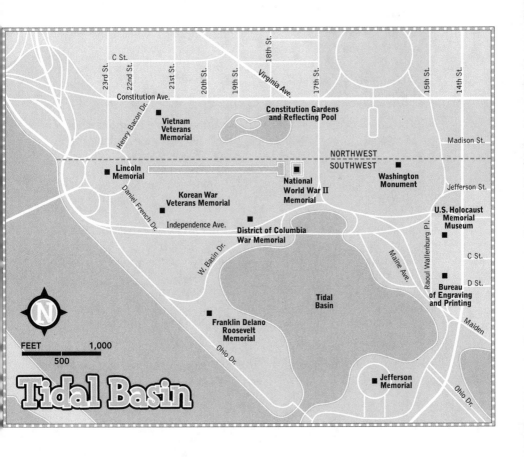

Tidal Basin

Quick Guide to

Attraction	Location
Vietnam Veterans Memorial	23rd St. and Constitution Avenue
Constitution Gardens and Reflecting Pool	17th and 23rd streets, NW (near the Lincoln Memorial)
★Lincoln Memorial	West end of the Mall, at 23rd Street, NW
District of Columbia War Memorial	Independence Avenue and 17th Street, NW
★National World War II Memorial	17th Street, NW (opposite the Lincoln Memorial)
Korean War Veterans Memorial	Near the Lincoln Memorial (between the Reflecting Pool and Independence Avenue, NW)
★Franklin Delano Roosevelt Memorial	West Potomac Park (between Lincoln Memorial and Jefferson Memorial)
★Jefferson Memorial	Southeast side of the Tidal Basin
★Bureau of Engraving and Printing	14th and C streets, SW
U.S. Holocaust Memorial Museum	100 Raoul Wallenberg Place, SW
Washington Monument	15th Street near Constitution Avenue, NW (at west end of Mall)

Tidal Basin Attractions

Age Range	Hours	Details on
Tweens and Teens	24 hours daily	Page 110
All Ages	24 hours daily	Page 116
All Ages	24 hours daily	Page 117
Tweens and Teens	24 hours daily	Page 119
Tweens and Teens	24 hours daily	Page 120
Tweens and Teens	24 hours daily	Page 121
All Ages	24 hours daily	Page 121
All Ages	24 hours daily	Page 124
Tweens and Teens	Mon.–Fri. Sept.–March 8:30 AM–3 PM; April–Aug. 8:30 AM–7:30 PM	Page 126
Tweens and Teens	10–5:30 daily (Tues. and Th. 10–6:30 Apr.–mid-June)	Page 127
All Ages	Memorial Day–Labor Day, daily 9 AM–10 PM (last tour 9:45); Labor Day–Memorial Day, daily 9–5 (last tour 4:45)	Page 131

The Vietnam Veterans Memorial

the Vietnam Veterans Memorial will be an eye-opening experience. Children, spouses, siblings, and friends crowd around the carved names of loved ones killed in this conflict and leave letters, flowers, mementos, and tears. Some of these items are displayed in the National Museum of American History, but most are kept in a government warehouse in Glen Dale, Maryland, which is itself becoming another memorial. Maya Lin, who, as a young Yale senior, designed the monument, described it as a "rift in the earth—a long, polished black stone wall, emerging from and receding into the earth." At each end of the wall, directories help people find the names of loved ones. Park rangers are happy to answer questions. This memorial will pack an unexpected emotional punch with youngsters as yet untouched by war or death.

Two sculptures have been added to this site. *Three Servicemen,* by Frederick Hart, reminds us how young these soldiers were. The *Vietnam Women's Memorial,* by Glenna Goodacre, pays tribute to the women who served.

A good book for tykes is *The Wall,* by Eve Bunting. For tweens look for *Always to Remember: The Story of the Vietnam Veterans Memorial,* by Brent Ashabranner, and for teens there are *A Wall of Names: The Story of the*

Smart Stuff

For Tweens . . . Imagine that you have a sibling or friend fighting in a war far away. Write him or her a letter. What kind of things do you think he or she would want to know?

Vietnam Veterans Memorial, by Judy Donnelly, and *Shrapnel in the Heart: Letters and Remembrance from the Vietnam Veterans Memorial,* by Laura Palmer.

Some movies, although harsh and frequently graphic, are moving testimonies to this traumatic period in our country's history. For tweens and teens, there are *Vietnam, a Television History, Dear America: Letters Home from Vietnam,* and *Guardians of Stone,* featuring James Earl Jones as a guard at Arlington National Cemetery. Teens will relate to *Vietnam: The War at Home; In Country* (about post-traumatic stress disorder); and *1969,* about the reaction to the war here in the United States. There are three we recommend only for older teens: *Born on the Fourth of July,* based on the true story of Ron Kovic; *The Killing Fields*; and *Platoon.*

Smart Stuff

For Teens . . . Imagine that you are a U.S. soldier serving in Vietnam. You are about to participate in a major battle. Write a letter home to your parents, a sibling, or a best friend. What would you want them to remember about you?

Metro: Foggy Bottom–GWU
Constitution Avenue and 21st Street
Open 24 hours; staffed 9:30 AM to 11:30 PM; tours with park
    rangers at 11 AM, 1 PM, 3 PM, and 5 PM.
202/426–6841 or 202/634–1568 for tours
www.nps.gov/vive

Smart Stuff

For Tweens . . . Many people come with paper and pencil and make "rubbings" of names they find on the Wall. You might want to make a rubbing of something you'd like to preserve from a statue or monument.

Constitution Gardens and Reflecting Pool

For All Ages . . . In the middle of this scenic 52-acre park is a lake with an island memorializing the 56 signers of the Declaration of Independence. Cross a wooden bridge and you can see a semicircle of large granite blocks, each carved with the name, signature, place of residence, and occupation of one of the Declaration's signers. (Interestingly, only one listed himself as a politician.) This is a lovely spot for picnicking, biking, or just lolling in the grass.

The Reflecting Pool, modeled on such star attractions as the pools at Versailles and the Taj Mahal, is a pretty good attraction in itself. In summer it's often filled with ducks, and when frozen in winter, with ice skaters.

> Metro: Foggy Bottom–GWU
> Constitution Avenue between 17th and 23rd streets, NW
> Open daily, 24 hours

Parents/Teachers Take Note

If only these stones could talk. When youngsters learn the history of these 56 brave men, they will appreciate the significance of their pledging "[their] lives, fortunes, and sacred honor" to the revolutionary cause. All financially comfortable and well educated, they were not rabble-rousers but rather thoughtful citizens who knew they would have to make personal sacrifices on the new nation's behalf. According to folklore, nine fought and died in the Revolutionary War; five were captured by the British as traitors; two lost sons serving in the Revolutionary Army; two had sons who were captured by the British; one saw his wife die after being thrown into jail; several had to go into hiding, along with their families; and some died in poverty after their property was seized or burned. Freedom always has a price.

202/426–6841
www.nps.gov/coga

★Lincoln Memorial

For All Ages . . . An appropriate memorial to a larger-than-life historical figure is the 19-foot-high marble seated statue of the brooding President Abraham Lincoln. Its home, the elegant rectangular monument, has become, since its dedication in 1922, a symbol of civil rights, justice, and the positive power of our democracy. Ironically, at that ceremony Dr. Robert Moton, then president of Tuskegee Institute (a noted African-American college), and the renowned Booker T. Washington were compelled to sit in the section for nonwhite spectators. Martin Luther King Jr.'s famous "I Have a Dream" speech here in 1963 underscored this site as a place where history is made.

On April 12, 2009, Washington native and opera star Denyse Graves reenacted the historic concert given by opera great Marian Anderson on the steps of the Lincoln Memorial on that date 70 years earlier. Ms. Anderson was barred from performing at the DAR Constitution Hall in 1939 because she was African-American.

Abraham Lincoln, one of Washington, D.C.,'s most visited statues

This tribute was especially moving because three months earlier, on January 20, 2009, the first African-American president, Barack Obama, took the oath of office.

With its 36 columns representing the number of states at the time of Lincoln's death, the memorial is decorated with carved inscriptions from his speeches. The names of 48 states (the number at the time of the monument's dedication) are on a frieze above the colonnade. The sculpture of Lincoln itself, by Daniel Chester French, is a magnet for visitors. It's believed by many that French, father of a deaf child, gave each of Lincoln's hands the American Sign Language position for one of his initials (his left hand forms *A,* and his right, the sign for *L*).

Smart Stuff

For Tweens . . . After re-searching Civil War Washington, D.C., youngsters might like to compile albums of their original "old" letters from Washington to friends or family living far away. Kids especially love trying to make the paper look aged.

In the basement of the memorial is the Legacy of Lincoln Museum, originally proposed by a group of students from Scottsdale, Arizona. Exhibits contain excerpts from some of Lincoln's famous speeches and a photographic history of many of the notable events that have occurred here, and a video tells the building's history. An information booth and bookstore are also on the premises. At night the view from the Lincoln Memorial steps is par-

Smart Stuff

For Tweens and Teens . . . Abraham Lincoln has become an icon, so it's hard to ferret out the fictional from the real. If you can, find out what personality traits he exhibited. Which of these do you think were *helpful* in his capacity as president and commander in chief of the Union forces? Which might have been detrimental?

ticularly moving. To the east is the sparkling dome of the U.S. Capitol, and to the west, across the river in Virginia, you can see the eternal flame at the grave of another slain president, John F. Kennedy.

Any visit to the Lincoln Memorial should provoke discussion. Here are some book suggestions. For tykes: *Abe Lincoln: The Boy Who Loved Books,* by Kay Winter; and *Abe Lincoln Crosses a Creek: A Tall Thin Tale,* by Deborah Hopkinson, et al., For tykes and tweens: *Abe Lincoln's Hat,* by Martha Brenner. A few ideas for tweens are: *Abraham Lincoln,* by Lola M. Schaefer; *Memorial of Mr. Lincoln,* by Brent Ashabranner; *House of Spies: Danger in Civil War Washington,* by Margaret Whitman Blair; *Lincoln: A Photobiography,* by Russell Freedman; *When Marian Sang: The True Recital of Marian Anderson,* by Pam M. Ryan; and *Abe Lincoln Grows Up,* by Carl Sandburg. For teens there are *Lincoln As I Knew Him: Gossip, Tributes and Revelations from His Best Friends and Worst Enemies,* by Harold Holzer; *Lincoln,* by Gore Vidal; and *The Voice That Challenged a Nation: Marian Anderson and the Struggle for Equal Rights,* by Russell Freedman. Two classic movies for tweens and teens are *Young Mr. Lincoln,* starring Henry Fonda, and *Abe Lincoln in Illinois,* with Raymond Massey.

> Metro: Foggy Bottom–GWU or Smithsonian
> West end of the Mall, at 23rd Street, NW
> Open 24 hours; staffed 9:30 AM to 11:30 PM
> 202/426–6841
> www.nps.gov/linc

District of Columbia War Memorial

For Tweens and Teens . . . This miniature Greek temple nestled in the greenery not far from the Lincoln Memorial is usually ignored by busy tourists. Dedicated by President Herbert Hoover on November 11, 1931, it pays tribute to the 26,000 District of Columbia veterans of World War I. Long before the Vietnam Veterans Memorial, this monument honored its soldiers with their names chiseled in the stone around its base.

The memorial was designed for use as a bandstand, and at the opening ceremony John Philip Sousa led the U.S. Marine Band in

"The Stars and Stripes Forever." The more recently opened World War II Memorial has not stimulated interest in its considerably more modest sibling. Lack of upkeep has led to its placement on the D.C. Preservation League's list of the most endangered places; the National Park Service has requested funds for renovation. It's a sad commentary on a sad period in history.

> Metro: Foggy Bottom–GWU
> Independence Avenue and 17th Street, NW
> Open 24 hours
> 202/233–0735 or 202/426–6841

★National World War II Memorial

For Tweens and Teens . . . A mammoth tribute to a mammoth event, the World War II Memorial holds a prominent place on the Mall. Angular stone columns, bronze wreaths, and stone arches are all oversize, emphasizing the overwhelming nature of the conflict that engulfed the globe. Only the large oval pool with multiple fountains softens the starkness of this setting.

The memorial is set up as a giant plaza ringed by 56 granite pillars representing the states and territories that existed during the war. One side is devoted to the war in the Pacific. "Pacific" is carved on an enormous arch. Another arch enshrines the battles of the Atlantic theater. The scenes carved in *bas relief* on the stone retaining walls approaching the plaza chart the period of World War II from our initial involvement (a family gathered around a radio listening to FDR announce the attack on Pearl Harbor as "a day that will live in infamy") to poignant scenes of everyday life from the battlefront to the home front.

Evoking a remarkable period in our nation's and our world's history, this is a powerful site for both grown-ups and youngsters.

> Metro: Foggy Bottom–GWU
> 17th Street, NW, between the Washington Monument and
>   the Lincoln Memorial
> Open daily, 24 hours; staffed 9:30 AM to 11:30 PM

202/426–6841
www.wwiimemorial.com

Korean War Veterans Memorial

For Tweens and Teens . . . West of the Reflecting Pool is the memorial to the "Forgotten War." The Korean War Veterans Memorial, dedicated in 1995 (more than 40 years after the war's end), consists of 19 larger-than-life stainless steel sculptures of soldiers on patrol, a circular Pool of Remembrance, and a 164-foot-long black granite wall etched with the faces of support troops, taken from actual photos of U.S. soldiers, sailors, airmen, and marines. Sixty percent of the $18 million needed for this moving memorial was donated by Korean War veterans; no government funds were used.

Smart Stuff

For Teens . . . What general, who was a major figure in the World War II Pacific theater, was fired by a U.S. president during the Korean War? Why? **(A.)**

Metro: Foggy Bottom–GWU
West end of the Mall at Independence Avenue, NW
Open daily, 24 hours; staffed 9:30 AM to 11:30 PM
202/632–1001 or 202/426–6841
www.nps.gov/kowa

★Franklin Delano Roosevelt Memorial

For All Ages . . . For an entire generation, Franklin Delano Roosevelt symbolized the presidency—for millions, he was the only president they had ever known. His memorial, set on more than 7 acres beside the picturesque Tidal Basin, is unique among the presidential monuments. It's a memorial not only to the man but also to the unsettled times during which he led a nation. The structure pulls us into the story: four outdoor "rooms," one for each of Roosevelt's terms,

President Franklin D. Roosevelt, with his dog, Fala, at the FDR Memorial

evoke those trying times with evocative sculptures, quotes from his speeches, and artistically designed waterfalls over rough-cut granite blocks. At the end is a bronze sculpture of FDR himself, seated in a well-camouflaged wheelchair (find the tiny wheels at the edges of the chair). A new sculpture of FDR was later added after six years of efforts on the part of disability rights advocates. This one shows the president seated in the wheelchair he designed and built from a kitchen chair and bicycle wheels. The contrast of this very human-size statue with the larger-than-life scale of the memorial portrays the vulnerability of Roosevelt's

Smart Stuff

For Tykes and Tweens . . . Do you personally know anyone who uses a wheelchair? Try this experiment: sit on a tricycle and try to open your door and go into your house or apartment without standing up. How would your life be different if you used a wheelchair?

Smart Stuff

For Tweens . . . Interview a neighbor, friend, or family member about World War II. How was life during that period different from your life today? **(B.)**

Smart Stuff

For Teens . . . Interview a relative, family friend, or neighbor about experiences during the Great Depression in the United States. What kinds of social changes occurred as a result of the Depression? (C.)

body as opposed to the invincibility of his spirit, a legacy for us all. An elegant standing likeness of Eleanor Roosevelt is the city's only monument to a first lady.

Children need some advance preparation to understand such an important slice of American history. In addition, a discussion about the status and history of citizens with disabilities would be a logical digression. In a dramatic way, Roosevelt has come to symbolize the triumph of an individual *and* a nation over enormous challenges.

In any library or bookstore you will find many books on FDR. A few suggestions for tweens and teens include *Eleanor Roosevelt* and *Franklin Delano Roosevelt,* both by Russell Freedman. *No Ordinary Time: Franklin and Eleanor Roosevelt,* by Doris Kearns Goodwin, and *Pearl Harbor and the American Spirit: The World War II Generation Remembers the Tragic Event That Transformed a Nation,* by Larry McCabe, are good for teens. Films for tweens and teens include: *Sunrise at Campobello* and *The Grapes of Wrath,* taken from John Steinbeck's classic book. Two DVDs available are: *Eleanor and Franklin: The Early Years* and *Eleanor and Franklin: The White House Years.* For music, try Woody Guthrie's plaintive ballads and the political folk songs of the Weavers.

> Metro: Smithsonian (Independence Avenue exit), plus about
>   a mile walk
> West Potomac Park, between the Lincoln Memorial and the
>   Jefferson Memorial
> Open daily, 24 hours; staffed 8:30 AM to 11:30 PM
> 202/376–6704 or 202/426–6841
> www.nps.gov/frde

★Jefferson Memorial

For All Ages . . . The simple dignity of his memorial belies the complexity of this astonishing man, Thomas Jefferson. An amateur architect (who would have loved the domed rotunda of his memorial), naturalist, inventor, anthropologist, astronomer, musician, and one of his country's leading statesmen, he, along with Benjamin Franklin, exemplified America's version of the "Renaissance man." The man to whom agrarian life was the ideal looks out across a landscape of water and greenery. To his back is the Potomac River, and beyond, the shoreline of his beloved Virginia.

The neoclassical form, with its stately Ionic columns, was a favorite with Jefferson. He used it in designing the Virginia State Capitol, the University of Virginia, and his own home, Monticello. The 19-foot bronze statue of Jefferson is surrounded by quotations from his writings. Inscribed on the frieze over the entrance from the Tidal Basin, depicting Jefferson with other members of the committee selected to draft the Declaration of Independence, is his philosophy: "I have sworn upon the altar of God eternal hostility against every form of tyranny over the mind of man." From the steps, you can look past the Washington Monument to the White House. At night, the illuminated memorial is a spectacle in itself.

Smart Stuff

For Tykes . . . What is the only monument in Washington, D.C., without corners? (D.)

Below the Jefferson Memorial are displays commemorating Jefferson's role in the founding of the country. The gift shop here has reproductions of colonial-style quill pens and other objects from Jefferson's era, as well as postcards and Washington souvenirs. There's also a small bookstore. From spring through fall, a nearby kiosk sells snacks.

Books about Jefferson abound. A few suggestions for tweens are *Meet Thomas Jefferson,* by Marvin Barrett, and *Jefferson's Children: The Story of One American Family,* by Shannon Lanier and Jane Feld-

The Jefferson Memorial in cherry blossom season

man. For tweens and teens there's *Thomas Jefferson: Man on a Mountain,* by Natalie S. Bober. *American Sphinx: The Character of Thomas Jefferson,* by Joseph J. Ellis, and *Jefferson and Monticello: The Biography of a Builder,* by Jack McLaughlin, are great for teens.

Metro: Smithsonian (Independence Avenue exit)
Southeast side of the Tidal Basin
Open daily, 24 hours; staffed 9:30 AM to 11:30 PM
202/426–1852
www.nps.gov/thje

Smart Stuff

For Tykes . . . On the shore opposite the Jefferson Memorial is a **stone lantern** presented by the people of Japan, commemorating friendship between our two countries. It's lighted at the beginning of the Cherry Blossom Festival. You might like to design a statue that will commemorate friendship between the United States and another country.

Smart Stuff

For All Ages . . . Do you have "old" money or "new" money in your pocket? Pull out a $1, $5, $10, or, if you're lucky, $20 bill, and look on the front next to the president's portrait. See if you can find where this bill was printed. Hint: if you have new money, with the jumbo-size portrait, it won't tell the city. But all bills, old and new, tell the date the Department of the Treasury was established. Can you find it? (E.)

At the very tip of East Potomac Park, **Hains Point** marks the convergence of the Washington Channel and the Potomac River. Kids are attracted to the elaborate climbing gym here.

★Bureau of Engraving and Printing

For Tweens and Teens . . . You can't take it with you, but it's still pretty exciting to see. The Bureau of Engraving and Printing produces the most paper money in the world—more than $11.4 billion annually. Even though it's a far cry from their allowance, kids enjoy watching the sheets of money roll off the presses to be cut, sorted, and stacked as familiar bills. Same-day tickets are issued March through August on Raoul Wallenberg Place, SW. Get there early, as the booth opens at 8 and usually gives away the last ticket by 8:30. If you don't want to wait in line, contact your congressional repre-

Why does your homework shred in the washer but your lunch money just gets wrinkled? U.S. "paper" money is actually made of 75% cotton and 25% linen. The average life of a dollar bill is still only 21 months—this probably includes several accidental washings!

sentative about VIP tickets two to three months in advance. No tickets are necessary September through February.

In the gift shop, visitors can buy bags, pens, and paperweights filled with shredded money that didn't pass inspection and postcards of bills with their pictures in the middle but, alas, nothing they can use to pay for these souvenirs. For breakfast, lunch, or snack time, try the cafeteria at the **U.S. Department of Agriculture** (14th Street and Independence Avenue, SW; 202/488–7279). Ten food stations offer an inexpensive and mouthwatering variety. It's open 6:30 to 3:30.

An interesting book on money for tweens and teens is *Money, Money, Money,* by Nancy Winslow Parker. *The Buck Book,* by Anne Akers Johnson, is a fun activity book for older tweens and teens.

Metro: Smithsonian
14th and C Streets, SW
45-minute tours begin every 15 minutes weekdays 9 to 10:45
    and 12:30 to 3 (and 5 to 7 May through August)
Visitor Center: weekdays September through March 8:30
    to 3, April through August 8:30 to 7:30
Visitors over 16 must have valid identification; no strollers
    allowed
Ticket booth opens at 8 AM: first come, first served
202/874–2330
www.moneyfactory.gov

U.S. Holocaust Memorial Museum

For Tweens and Teens . . . Who would have ever guessed that a museum that promises to depress you thoroughly and take a minimum of three hours of your time would be one of the most popular sites in Washington, D.C.? At least 2 million people annually go through this grim monument to one of the darkest periods in human history. In a clever and unnerving combination of styles and materials, the architecture itself evokes the setting of the concentration camps in which 6 million Jews and millions of others, including Gypsies, Poles, political prisoners, homosexuals, Jehovah's Witnesses, and the disabled, were murdered.

Smart Stuff

For Teens . . . As you read the history of the rise of the Nazi party, what signs were there that this was not just another fringe political group? Do you think something like the Holocaust could happen here? Why or why not?

With a fifth-floor library open to researchers of high-school age and older, the museum's permanent exhibitions fill the next three floors. The identity card you are issued on entry gives the history of an actual Holocaust victim. Consult your booklet as you progress through the displays to find out what that person was actually undergoing during each time period. Through oral histories, multimedia presentations, photographs, artifacts, and an actual Polish freight car like those used to transport Jews from the Warsaw Ghetto to the concentration camp Treblinka, visitors participate in an overwhelming experience.

Children under age 11 would find much of the museum overpowering. The exhibit "Daniel's Story: Remember the Children" is designed for youngsters 8 and older. Located on the first floor and available *without* tickets, this exhibition chronicles the story of a fictional but historically accurate German family from their comfort-

Smart Stuff

For Tweens and Teens . . . Suppose you were a friend of Daniel's. What might you have tried to do for him or his family? What risks—if any—would you have been willing to take for them?

able home to a concentration camp. Though it's clear that Daniel survives, his story, told through a child's eyes, packs a significant emotional punch. Children are encouraged to express their feelings in writing or pictures at the end of the exhibit and to post them in a special museum mailbox. The striking Children's Wall, consisting of

3,300 tiles painted by American schoolchildren, memorializes the 1.5 million children murdered in the Holocaust.

The museum shop contains books and videos on the Holocaust and a wide selection of related materials for young readers. Children of all ages should take a look at . . . *I Never Saw Another Butterfly: Children's Drawings and Poems from Terezin Concentration*

Helpful Hint
There's a lot to see here, so allow at least three hours for your visit. *Be sure to wear comfortable shoes.*

Camp 1942–1944. An unusual offering is *The Children We Remember,* by Chana Byers Abells, a very sensitive treatment for the youngest readers, who will need an adult to help them interpret this difficult subject. *The Diary of A Young Girl,* by Anne Frank, is a classic, especially for tweens and teens. *Smoke and Ashes: The Story of the Holocaust,* by Barbara Rogasky, is a thoughtful reader-friendly account of the lives of those touched by the war. *Maus I* and *Maus II,* by Art Spiegelman, especially appeal to young teens because of the allegorical cartoon format.

Another diary, preserved and found after the war, is *Scroll of Agony: The Warsaw Diary of Chaim A. Kaplan,* an eyewitness account that is appropriate for teens. Also for teens are *Night,* by Elie Wiesel, just one of his many moving works, and *Edith's Story,* by Edith Velmans. The latter is based on diaries, reminiscences, and letters, and tells the true story of a young girl during World War II. *Different Voices: Women and the Holocaust,* edited and introduced by Carol Rittner and John K. Roth, and *The Auschwitz Chronicle,* by Danuta Czech, are highly recommended for older teens. Per Anger, who served with this famous Swedish diplomat, wrote *With Raoul Wallenberg in Budapest: Memories of the War Years in Hungary,* interesting reading for older teens. A chronological collection of stories by different writers, *Out of the Whirlwind: A Reader of Holocaust Literature,* edited by Albert H. Friedlander, guides the mature reader

Helpful Hint
Because of its impact on young visitors, it's a good idea to do some reading and discussing *before* visiting the U.S. Holocaust Memorial Museum.

Helpful Hint
To avoid waiting in a long line for same-day, time-specific passes, consider purchasing advance passes to the U.S. Holocaust Memorial Museum. The small service charge is definitely worth it. Call 800/400–9373 or order online at www.tickets.com.

through this time period. No modern collection would be complete without *Schindler's List,* by Thomas Keneally, the book that inspired the Steven Spielberg movie. We also recommend several other films for teens: *Life Is Beautiful, Jakob the Liar, Europa, Europa,* and a recent documentary, *Exodus 1947: The Ship That Launched a Nation.*

If you have an appetite, visit the **Museum Café,** in an annex near the museum. It's open daily 8:30 to 4:30. The vegetarian menu includes sandwiches, soups, salads, and desserts.

Metro: Smithsonian
100 Raoul Wallenberg Place, SW, at 14th Street
Open daily 10 to 5:30 (until 6:30 Tuesday and Thursday from April to mid-June); last admission two hours before closing; closed Yom Kippur and December 25
Get advance tickets by calling 800/400–9373 or by ordering online at www.tickets.com. A limited number of free entrance passes are distributed on a first-come, first-served basis at 10 AM on the 14th Street side of building; limit 10 passes per person.
202/488–0400 or 800/400–9333
www.ushmm.org

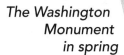
*The Washington
Monument
in spring*

Authorized and erected at the turn of the 20th century, the **statue of John Paul Jones** at Independence Avenue and 17th Street, NW, memorializes a man with a checkered past but an indomitable will at the right historical moment. After some run-ins with fellow colonial merchant mariners, Jones fled to Fredericksburg, Virginia, where he appended the "Jones" to his original last name ("Paul"). His successful exploits as commander of several ships in the Revolution led up to his famous encounter with a British vessel, where, outmanned and outgunned, he outwitted the English captain and boarded the enemy ship as his own ship was sinking. When the enemy captain had asked earlier for Jones's surrender, Jones had replied, "I have not yet begun to fight!" His remains rest appropriately in the chapel of the U.S. Naval Academy in Annapolis.

Washington Monument

For All Ages . . . Measuring more than 555 feet, the world's tallest freestanding masonry structure is visible from nearly everywhere in the city. No cement was used to hold the granite blocks together, but don't worry, the Washington Monument is supposed to be able to withstand even a 145-mile-per-hour tornado. The fact that it sways an eighth of an inch in high winds shouldn't make you seasick—trust us, no one can feel it.

Ride the elevator to the 500-foot level and look out at the amazing views of all of the District of Columbia. When you're ready to descend, there's another interesting choice: you can use the elevator or you can walk down with a guide who will point out memorial stones set into the walls from many different sources. These tours, which include a *very* long walk down, begin at 10:30 and noon. They are limited to the first 25 people who show up, so sign up 30 minutes in advance.

This two-tone memorial is a monument to getting things done in a democracy. It was first discussed as a possibility in 1783; then after many false starts the monument's fund-raising actually began in 1833. At last, on July 4, 1848, the cornerstone was laid. Each state was expected to contribute. Short of funds, Alabama started a new trend by sending a stone instead. Then more than 100 individuals, towns, states, and nations, including the pope and the Cherokee Nation, sent stones to be included in the monument. Construction had stopped by the time of the Civil War, as the project had run out of money. Cattle continued to roam and troops trained on the monument grounds. In 1876 President Grant approved federal funding to complete the memorial. It was dedicated at last in 1885, and opened to the public in 1888. The marble used

Smart Stuff

For Teens . . . Before he left office, President Washington warned against becoming involved in the affairs of other nations. In which wars, if any, do you think he would have approved U.S. involvement? Why?

to complete it was from a different quarry than the original, and is thus a slightly different shade. As the elevator was considered too dangerous for women, only men could ride to the top. Women had to trudge up the 897 steps wearing heavy gowns and petticoats. It must have been hard to be so delicate! One of the mysterious auxiliary benefits of the whole project was the creation of an enormous sculpture of Washington dressed in a toga. It can now be seen guarding the escalators in the National Museum of American History.

Tykes might enjoy *The Washington Monument*, by Kristin L. Nelson, and *Young George Washington: America's First President*, by Janet Woods, while tweens will like *George Washington's Socks*, by Elvira Woodruff, and *George Washington*, by Cheryl Harness. For teens, two good choices are *Washington: The Indispensable Man*, by James Thomas Flexner, and *Citizen Washington*, by William Martin.

> Metro: Smithsonian
>
> 15th Street near Constitution Avenue, NW (at west end of Mall)
>
> Open Memorial Day to Labor Day, daily 9 AM to 10 PM (last tour at 9:45 PM), Labor Day to Memorial Day, daily 9 to 5 (last tour at 4:45); closed July 4 and December 25
>
> For timed tickets, get in line on 15th Street, NW, between Independence and Constitution avenues, NW *before* 7:30 AM. One person may pick up a maximum of six tickets. Get advance tickets by calling 877/444–6777 or by going online at www.recreation.gov.
>
> Fee; same-day tickets free
>
> For security reasons, there are restrictions on what can be brought into the monument; no food or beverages, baby strollers, or large backpacks and suitcases. For a complete list, call 202/225–6827.
>
> 202/426–6841
>
> www.nps.gov/wamo

Where to Stay in the Tidal Basin Area

As for places to stay in this area, we recommend consulting the list at the end of the previous chapter, "White House & Foggy Bottom." The choices there are also the closest ones for touring this part of the city.

Answers to Smart Stuff Questions

A. General Douglas MacArthur felt that he knew better than his commander in chief, President Harry S. Truman, how to carry out the war with North Korea. Seeing the North Korean incursion into South Korea as part of a worldwide communist threat, MacArthur regarded anything less than assault on China (the biggest communist power in the Far East) as appeasement. He repeatedly publicized his *own* views, which included the notion that America should drop "thirty to fifty atomic bombs on Manchuria and the mainland cities of China." He issued his own personal proclamation hinting that the United States *would* invade China, and summed up his philosophy this way: "There is no substitute for victory." The president, secretary of state, vice president, and joint chiefs of staff, among many, decided that there *was a substitute* for an insubordinate general. MacArthur was fired.

B. Examples are rationing, Victory Gardens, war newsreels in movie theaters, and women in what were traditionally men's jobs.

C. Teens might discuss: migration from family farms, shantytowns, the "Bonus Army" (a demonstration to urge Congress to deliver a bonus promised to veterans in 1924), soup kitchens, apple vendors, FDR's election, the influx of professionals and clerical workers to Washington, D.C., to work in newly formed agencies, bread lines, the National Youth Administration (arranging part-time jobs for high-school and college students so they could continue their education), women as their families' main wage earners, or the culture of frugality (just ask a Depression-era survivor!).

D. The Jefferson Memorial.

E. "Old" money notes the city of its printing in the seal to the left of the president's portrait. All bills show the green emblem of the Department of the Treasury to the right side of the president, with the date 1789 at the bottom.

CHAPTER 6

Georgetown & Embassy Row

ashion is fickle. The section of Washington known as **Georgetown** has gone from commercial hub to ramshackle homes and trash-filled alleys to elegant, renovated town houses for the city's movers and shakers. Named for two Georges who had first owned the land (neither King George nor George Washington), George Town was founded by an immigrant Scottish community. Previously a thriving port, it was granted its charter by the Maryland Assembly in 1751. From its official incorporation in 1789 until 1871, George Town had a government separate from its prestigious neighbor, the District of Columbia. At that point, Congress abolished George Town's status as a separate municipality and dubbed the region "Georgetown."

In the middle of the next century a young senator named John F. Kennedy and his family lived here until they moved to a much larger home on Pennsylvania Avenue. Georgetown is still a stylish and pricey area of stately row houses, trendy shops, lively restaurants, and historic buildings. But in some ways it clings to its historic roots: it has no Metro stop and little parking for cars.

Embassy Row is also a class act. The stately mansions lining Massachusetts Avenue make an interesting place to stroll. The British Embassy, with its statue of a victorious Winston Churchill, sits next door to the modern, glass-supported Embassy of Brazil.

The opulent Embassy of Iran made a wonderful spot for State Department functions when that country and the United States severed diplomatic relations following the 1979 Islamic Revolution and the resulting hostage crisis. If you're lucky enough to visit in spring, splurge for a ticket to the Embassy Row House Tour; you can see where other people get to rub important elbows.

★Chesapeake and Ohio Canal National Historical Park

For All Ages . . . Begun in 1828 as the harbinger of an era of more rapid transportation, the C&O Canal has become a site where visitors can enjoy their leisure time. In competition with the more suc-

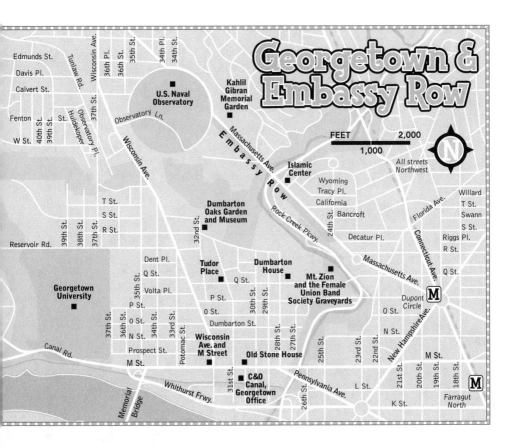

Quick Guide to

Attraction	Location
★Chesapeake and Ohio Canal National Historical Park	Office: 1057 Thomas Jefferson Street, NW
★Old Stone House	3051 M Street, NW
Georgetown University	37th and O streets, NW
Tudor Place	1644 31st Street, NW
Dumbarton Oaks Garden and Museum	1703 32nd Street, NW (between R and S streets)
★Wisconsin Avenue and M Street, NW	
Embassy Row	Dupont Circle; walk north on Massachusetts Avenue, NW
Islamic Center	2551 Massachusetts Avenue, NW
U.S. Naval Observatory	3450 Massachusetts Avenue, NW

Georgetown & Embassy Row Attractions

Age Range	Hours	Details on
All Ages	Park hours vary	Page 137
All Ages	Wed.–Sun. noon–5 PM	Page 141
Teens		Page 142
Teens	Tours: Tues.–Sat. 10 AM, 11, noon, 1 PM, 2:30 PM; Sat. 10 AM–3 PM on the hour; Sun. noon–3 on the hour	Page 143
Tweens and Teens	Gardens 2–6 PM daily (mid-March–Oct.); 2–5 PM daily (Nov.–mid-March)	Page 144
Tweens and Teens		Page 146
Tweens and Teens		Page 148
Tweens and Teens	10 AM–5 PM daily	Page 151
Tweens and Teens	Tours: Mon. 8:30 PM	Page 153

cessful railroads, the canal lost out as a major commercial artery. Today's barges carry people instead of coal, with costumed guides singing folk songs and spinning tales about the history of the canal. Kids will enjoy the locomotion for this replica of a 19th-century canal barge; it's pulled by mules. All ages will wonder at the technology of canal lift locks that regulate the water levels along the way.

Originally designed to connect Washington, D.C., to Pittsburgh, Pennsylvania, the canal stretches a mere 184 miles, from Georgetown into western Maryland. It never reached Pittsburgh. Hikers, bikers, and canoeists travel the canal and its towpath, delighting in the views. Natural rock formations, abundant foliage, and picturesque waterfalls provide spectacular vistas along the way. Famous visitors have included the late Justice William O. Douglas, a committed outdoorsman. When he heard, in 1954, that plans had been approved to *pave* over the canal and turn it into a freeway, he embarked on a protest hike. With 36 other hardy souls, he walked the distance from Cumberland, Maryland, to the canal's end in Georgetown. During the eight days of walking, the protesters were greeted enthusiastically in every town they passed. By the time they arrived in the District, they had sparked a conservation movement. The National Park Service decided to support the canal's preservation as a national historic landmark. Congress officially granted protected status in 1971. The towpath was dedicated in honor of Justice Douglas in 1974.

Refreshments are available at a snack shop on the grounds near the **Great Falls Historic Tavern and Museum** (11710 MacArthur

Helpful Hint

Beginning in Georgetown, this park actually extends all the way to Cumberland, Maryland. To visit the park areas beyond Georgetown, try to take a car. Otherwise, check with Metrobus (202/637-7000; www.metroopensdoors.com).

Helpful Hint

Check with Metrobus (202/637–7000; www.
metroopensdoors.com) for information on getting
around Georgetown. Another operator, Georgetown
Metro Connection, runs six minibuses (every 10 minutes,
7 AM to midnight daily; until 2 AM weekends) on two
routes connecting Georgetown and the waterfront with
the Dupont Circle, Foggy Bottom, and Rosslyn Metro
stations.

Boulevard, Potomac, MD; 301/767–3714). To be sure of satisfying
your hunger, pack a lunch.

> Georgetown Office of the C&O Canal: 1057 Thomas Jeffer-
> son Street, NW; open daily 9 to 4:30
> 202/653–5190 in D.C., 301/767–3714 in Maryland
> Usually dawn to dusk
> Fee for parking and barge rides
> 202/653–5190
> www.nps.gov/choh

★Old Stone House

For All Ages . . . Built in 1765, this is Washington's oldest building. Five rooms hold sturdy furnishings from the 18th century. Costumed guides lead visitors through the house and demonstrate skills
of early-American life, including weaving, candle dipping, quilting,
spinning, and colonial-style cooking. There's also a lovely cottage
garden for picnicking or strolling.

Hungry? Try longtime favorite **Booeymonger** (3265 Prospect
Street, NW; 202/333–4810), open every day 8 AM to midnight. The
creations are as clever as their names: Tuna Turner, Scheherazade, or
Pita Pan, just to name a few. For Vietnamese fare, **Miss Saigon** (3057
M Street, NW; 202/333–5545) has interesting dishes, including veg-
etarian selections. It's open weekdays 11 to 11, weekends noon to 11.

3051 M Street, NW
Open Wednesday to Sunday noon to 5; closed holidays
202/426–6851
www.nps.gov/olst

Georgetown University

For Teens . . . The oldest and largest Jesuit university in the United States, Georgetown University was founded in 1789 by John Carroll, a cousin of one of Maryland's signers of the Declaration of Independence. Unusually tolerant for its time, it was open from the start to students of "every religious profession." After the Civil War, the university changed its school colors to blue and gray, honoring students on both sides who had died in the conflict. From its beginning to the present day, Georgetown has been connected with luminaries. Carroll was friendly with George Washington, Benjamin Franklin, and the Marquis de Lafayette, and Georgetown is the alma mater of a recent president, Bill Clinton. Georgetown University's reputation for scholarship, as well as its beautiful architecture, make it a worthwhile stop, especially for college-bound teens.

A good place to stop is the Leavey Center (3800 Reservoir Road, NW), which houses the university bookstore and food courts.

37th and O streets, NW
202/687–0100
www.georgetown.edu

Shops in Georgetown

With its abundance of green spaces, Washington, D.C., is a refreshing change from many cities. In lovely **Glover Archbold Park** (from MacArthur Boulevard and Canal Road to Van Ness Street and Wisconsin Avenue; 202/895–6000), try the 2-mile nature trail, which starts at 44th Street and Reservoir Road. You can find a bird sanctuary and plenty of picnic areas, too.

Smart Stuff

For Teens . . . Father Patrick Healy has a building named after him on the Georgetown campus. See if you can find out why he was famous. **(A.)**

Tudor Place

For Teens . . . When he wasn't designing the Capitol, Dr. William Thornton turned his talents to this beautiful neoclassical mansion. A home for Georgetown's mayor, Thomas Peter, Tudor Place was completed in 1816. Peter knew a good thing when he saw one. His wife, Martha Custis Peter, was the granddaughter of Martha Washington, and much of the furniture was inherited or purchased from Mount Vernon. There's even a touching letter from George to Martha, written in June 1775, just before he marched off to take command of the fledgling Revolutionary Army. Such other notables as the Marquis de Lafayette, Robert E. Lee, Henry Clay, John Calhoun, and Daniel Webster slept here.

Peter's descendants, Confederate sympathizers, were forced to rent rooms to Union soldiers to keep the house from procurement as a Union hospital. Fortunately, you can tour today without being asked about *your* political sympathies.

A lovely 5-acre, Federal-style garden contains ancient boxwoods, a lily pond, fruit trees, secluded seating alcoves, and a bowling green. But don't bring your bowling ball.

> 1644 31st Street, NW
> 45-minute guided tours Tuesday to Saturday 10, 11, noon, 1, 2, and 3, Sunday hourly noon to 3; closed holidays

Reservations suggested
Fee
202/965–0400
www.tudorplace.org

Dumbarton Oaks Garden and Museum

For Teens . . . The 10 acres of formal gardens at Dumbarton Oaks offer terraced settings for roses, wisteria-covered arbors, an orangery, and gorgeous fall foliage. It's considered one of the finest gardens in the United States. From spring through fall the place is particularly alluring, with seasonal blossoms, fountains, reflecting pools, and interesting pathways. Nearby is **Dumbarton Oaks Park**, 27 acres of woodland. It's accessible only on foot, via Lovers' Lane (honest!), off R Street between Avon Place and 31st Street, NW. The park is open daily 8 AM to dusk.

Dumbarton Oaks houses an unusual art collection spanning many centuries. Pre-Columbian art and artifacts are displayed here in a beautiful series of circular glass pavilions. Included are Olmec jade figures, textiles, jewelry, and funerary pottery. In the renowned Byzantine collection, visitors can see illuminated manuscripts, jewelry, mosaics, and icons.

Smart Stuff

For Teens . . . What is the United Nations, and why was it formed? Of the agencies it has spawned, which ones do you feel have made significant contributions? (B.)

The 1944 Dumbarton Oaks Conversations, held in the music room, with representatives from around the world, led to the founding of the United Nations. Harvard University received the property in 1940 and currently maintains it as a research facility for pre-Columbian, Byzantine, and landscape architecture studies. A fascinating read for teens is *F.D.R. and the Creation of the U.N.*, by Townsend Hoopes and Douglas Brinkley.

Helpful Hint
Older teens and adults are more apt to enjoy this beautiful mansion and its gardens.

1703 32nd Street, NW (between R and S streets)
Museum open Tuesday to Sunday 2 to 5; closed holidays
Gardens open mid-March to October, daily 2 to 6; November
    to mid-March 2 to 5; closed federal holidays and during
    inclement weather
Fee April to October
202/339–6401
www.doaks.org

Completed in 1805, **Dumbarton House** exemplifies Federal-style architecture, with its entire layout exactly symmetrical. The National Society of Colonial Dames of America, headquartered here since 1928, has restored and furnished the house with exquisite period antiques. Featured are children's pieces from museums throughout the United States, as well as documents signed by George Washington, Thomas Jefferson, and Dolley and James Madison. Visits are by guided tour only.

2715 Q Street, NW, in Georgetown
Open September to July, Tuesday to Saturday 10:15 to 12:15;
    closed federal holidays and December 23 to January 2
Fee
202/337–2288

Near 27th and Q streets, NW, are the **Mount Zion** and **Female Union Band Society Graveyards,** the almost forgotten burial places of 6,000 to 10,000 early Washingtonians, mostly African-Americans. Totaling 3 acres just a short distance from Rock Creek Parkway, these burial grounds hold special historic value. There are

Smart Stuff

For Tweens . . . Imagine you were a slave in Civil War times, trying to make the perilous journey from your home plantation near Richmond, Virginia, to the "Free North" across the Mason-Dixon Line. What kinds of signs and symbols would you use to signal the people who would head north after you to show them where it would be safe to stop along the way? (C.)

plans to restore a burial vault that was a hiding place for slaves heading northward on the Underground Railroad.

★ Wisconsin Avenue and M Street, NW

If all this history has made you hungry, you do have more than colonial food at your disposal. American cuisine in an eclectic setting is a hallmark of **Clyde's** (3236 M Street, NW; 202/333–9180). Known for burgers, chili, and crab cakes, Clyde's also serves eggs Benedict with a grilled portobello mushroom in place of the ham. There's a Sunday brunch, too. If you're brave enough to drive, Clyde's will treat you to two hours of parking at the underground garage at Georgetown Park—a genuine bargain. Indian food is offered at **Aditi** (3299 M Street, NW; 202/625–6825). It's open Monday through Saturday 11:30 AM to 2:30 PM and 5:30 to 10 PM, as well as Sunday noon to 2:30 PM. Vegetarians can find lots of options here. Locals recommend the assorted appetizers. Reservations are encouraged for large groups.

Hankerin' for some ribs? Head for **Old Glory** (3139 M Street, NW; 202/337–3406), open Monday through Thursday 11:30 AM to 2 AM, Friday and Saturday 11:30 AM to 3 AM, and Sunday 11 AM to 2 AM. Try the spareribs, barbecued chicken, pit-grilled burgers, and grilled veggies. This is a southern roadhouse-style stop, with live music Tuesday, Thursday, and Saturday nights. Reservations are needed for parties of more than six. If you like to go stargazing, trendy **Café Milano** (3251 Prospect Street, NW; 202/333–6183) is the "in" spot. Regulars from Michael Jordan to Plácido Domingo enjoy the sophisticated Italian fare and fine wines. It's open daily 11:30 AM to midnight.

For Tweens and Teens . . . Fortified for some shopping? From fashionable boutiques to street-corner vendors, aficionados of handcrafted items, antiques, art books and prints, funky or fine jewelry, and vintage or preppy duds can all find something.

Strolling south on Wisconsin Avenue, kids will enjoy **Commander Salamander** (1420 Wisconsin Avenue, NW; 202/337–6610), specializing in offbeat teen fashions; teens and adults will like **Appalachian Spring** (1415 Wisconsin Avenue, NW; 202/337–5780), with its one-of-a-kind handmade American crafts pieces. Just below M Street is **Georgetown Tees** (1075 Wisconsin Avenue, NW; 202/337–4399), where you can find serious and silly designs.

At this point, you have reached the **Shops at Georgetown Park** (3222 M Street, NW; 202/342–8190), where the ornate Victorian interior shelters four stories of restaurants, art galleries, and shops, including **Fire and Ice** (handcrafted jewelry, fossils, and art glass), **Comfort One Shoes** (pricey, but in D.C. you *need* comfy shoes!), **H&M** (for great clothing bargains), **The Hattery** (guess what they sell), **Li'l Thingamajigs**, **Taxco Sterling** (almost like an art gallery, if you like silver), **Le Cadeau** (beautiful and unusual homewares), and, for special treats, **Mrs. Fields Cookies,** and **the Pretzelmaker.** Although this is certainly not a discount shopping center, it's a great place to window-shop. It's a haven on a rainy day. Here you can purchase tickets for the Old Town Trolley Tour Bus, which you take to visit Old Town Alexandria, Virginia (see Chapter 12 and Appendix II).

Now for M Street. Young people will want to check out **Urban Outfitters** (3111 M Street, NW; 202/342–1012) for contemporary clothing and home furnishings; **Steve Madden** (3109 M Street, NW; 202/342–6195), with the clunkiest and chunkiest women's shoe styles; and **Barnes & Noble** (3040 M Street, NW; 202/965–9880), the largest books and music store in the area.

Parking is tough, but at the Shops at Georgetown Park you can park for free in the underground lot if you spend $10 or more. No problem!

Embassy Row

For Tweens and Teens . . . More than 130 countries have embassies in Washington, D.C. Massachusetts Avenue, popularly known as "Embassy Row," is the home for many. Although most are not open to the public, the beautiful exteriors are worth a look. You can take a long, leisurely walk along this appealing route—or this is a nice time to drive the car.

Flags and coats-of-arms outside the embassy doors are not only decorative but also interesting. Kids might enjoy trying to figure out the countries represented before they sneak a peak at the signs by the doors. Some embassies allow public tours. The **Indonesian Embassy** (2020 Massachusetts Avenue, NW; 202/775–5200; www.embassyofindonesia.org) was formerly the home of the Walsh family, whose daughter Evelyn was the last private owner of the Hope Diamond (now in the National Museum of Natural History). Reservations by phone or e-mail are required for weekday visits. The **Finnish Embassy** (3301 Massachusetts Avenue, NW; 202/298–5800; www.finland.org) welcomes visitors for tours by appointment only, 10 to 4 daily. Call regarding the embassy's regular art shows, which are open to the public.

That irrepressible force **Sir Winston Churchill** is beautifully captured in the statue gracing the front lawn of the **British Em-**

Smart Stuff

For Tweens and Teens . . . Washington, D.C., as the nation's capital, is the only city in the country to house foreign embassies. But consulates are found in other U.S. cities. Find out the difference between these terms. Are there any consulates in your city? If so, which ones? **(D.)**

bassy (3100 Massachusetts Avenue, NW; www.britainusa.com). In a metaphor for his intimate connection with the United States, one foot rests on English soil and the other on American soil. (He enjoyed telling Congress, "If my father had been an American, and my mother, British, instead of the other way 'round, I might have got here on my own!") The force of his indomitable will was largely responsible for girding England for the lonely task of defender of the free world while Hitler's armies overran Europe. As British prime minister during history's most widespread conflict, he worked with President Roosevelt to bring Britain the help it needed to survive the onslaught. With characteristic disdain for personal safety, he appeared everywhere, flashing his famous "V" for "victory" sign. His *A History of the English-Speaking Peoples* won him the Nobel Prize for Literature, but clearly the prize he was proudest of was the one that came with the defeat of the Axis powers in 1945. In 1963 the United States made Churchill an honorary citizen.

Tranquil Normanstone Park on Massachusetts Avenue between 30th and 34th streets, NW, is home to the **Kahlil Gibran**

Smart Stuff

For Tykes . . . On the grounds of the British Embassy is a statue of Winston Churchill, the famous British prime minister during World War II. One hand is raised in the sign of the letter V. What do you think that signifies? Make up a hand sign of your own and teach it to your friends. What would it signify?

Memorial Garden. Honoring the famous Lebanese-American poet and philosopher, author of *The Prophet,* the simple footbridge, benches, and fountain provide a wonderful contrast to the trappings of empire in the imposing British Embassy just across the street. The sensitive bronze head, resting on a curved, poolside wall, reminds visitors of Gibran's philosophy. Inscribed on the limestone benches are quotations from his writings. The memorial garden is open daily throughout the year.

Also along Massachusetts Avenue, NW, you can find the embassies of **Brazil** (3006 Massachusetts Avenue, NW; www.brasilemb.org); **South Africa** (3051 Massachusetts Avenue, NW; www.saembassy.org); **Turkey** (2525 Massachusetts Avenue, NW; www.turkishembassy.org); **Japan** (2520 Massachusetts Avenue, NW; www.embjapan.org); **Ireland** (2234 Massachusetts Avenue, NW; www.irelandemb.org); **Greece** (2221 Massachusetts Avenue, NW; www.greekembassy.org); **Togo** (2208 Massachusetts Avenue, NW; www.embassy.org/embassies/tg.html); **Chile** (1732 Massachusetts Avenue, NW; www.chile-usa.org); **The Philippines** (1600 Massachusetts Avenue, NW; www.philippineembassy-usa.org); and **Australia** (1601 Massachusetts Avenue, NW; www.austemb.org).

Other embassies are spread throughout the city, wherever their governments could afford the real estate or felt strategic necessity. One of the newest is the **Embassy of Sweden** (2900 K Street, NW; 202/467–2600; www.swedenabroad.com), which has a dazzling new building on the waterfront in Georgetown. Call ahead for group tours. The **Canadian Embassy** (501 Pennsylvania Avenue, NW; www.canadianembassy.org), a large, modern complex, is near the Capitol. The **French Embassy** (4101 Reservoir Road, NW; www.ambafrance-us.org) is an elegant mansion nestled into a spacious residential neighborhood in the northwest section of the city. The **Embassy of Grenada** (1701 New Hamp-

Kahlil Gibran
Memorial Garden

shire Avenue, NW; www.grenadaembassyusa.org) is in a stately town house near Dupont Circle. (No country is too small to have an embassy in Washington.) The **Embassy of Israel** (3514 International Drive, NW; www.israelemb.org) and the **Embassy of Jordan** (3504 International Drive, NW; www.jordanembassyus.org) make strange neighbors, sitting together on International Drive, NW, in nearly the same kind of proximity their countries occupy in the Middle East.

Books of interest for teens include *In Confidence: Moscow's Ambassador to America's Six Cold War Presidents (1962–1986),* by former Soviet ambassador to Washington Anatoly Dobrynin; *Then, They Were Twelve: The Women of Washington's Embassy Row,* by Marilyn Sephocle; *Black Georgetown Remembered: A History of Its Black Community from the Founding of "the town of George" in 1751 to the Present Day,* by Kathleen M. Lesko, Valerie Babb, and Carroll Gibbs; and *Behind Embassy Walls: The Life and Times of An American Diplomat,* by Brandon Grove.

Movies about our "official" connections with other countries include the hilarious *The Mouse That Roared* (tweens and teens), *The Gods Must Be Crazy* (tweens and teens), and *Wag the Dog* (teens). *The Girl Who Spelled Freedom* (tweens and teens) tells the story of a young Cambodian refugee who becomes a national spelling champion. Teens might enjoy a game called *U.S. Response: The Making of U.S. Foreign Policy.* It involves role-playing of six real-life foreign policy situations.

> Metro: Dupont Circle; walk three full blocks on Massachusetts Avenue, NW

Islamic Center

For Tweens and Teens . . . The jewel of the Islamic Center, and its most conspicuous building, is the sparkling white and delicately spired mosque, adorned by 24 stained-glass windows. Visitors will appreciate the intricate and colorful art on the pillars, walls, and ceilings, and lush carpets underfoot. This is the largest and most ornate mosque in the U.S. Angled on its lot, the mosque was designed to face Mecca.

Helpful Hint
Although this is a very exotic-looking building, the mosque is more exciting for youngsters when viewed from the outside than on a tour.

A strict dress code is enforced—no shorts or short dresses allowed, and all visitors must remove their shoes before entering. Women must wear long sleeves and cover their heads (scarves are available on site).

Surprisingly, the Islamic Center wasn't founded until the middle of the 20th century. After World War II the ambassadors of Egypt, Iran, Turkey, and Afghanistan worked together to establish this religious site. Announced by the mu'azzin from a 160-foot-high minaret, prayers are held five times a day.

Next to the mosque is a small bookstore with souvenirs, books, and some traditional items of clothing. One helpful book for those wishing to learn more about Islam is *Islam: A Very Short Introduction,* by Malise Ruthven (teens and adults).

Smart Stuff
For Tweens . . . Islam is one of several faiths that avoid representations of the human form in art. In Islamic texts and crafts you can notice calligraphy (beautiful and elaborate writing) and repetitious geometric designs that form never-ending patterns. In addition, what familiar shapes and forms from nature can you find in the decorative motifs? **(E.)**

Metro: Dupont Circle
2551 Massachusetts Avenue, NW
Open daily 10 to 5
Call ahead to sign up for a guided tour or to announce that
    you're bringing a large group

202/332–8343
www.theislamiccenter.com

U.S. Naval Observatory

For Tweens and Teens . . . Here's an opportunity to visit the Navy's oldest scientific office (established in 1830) and look through an enormous telescope to see sights even older. On a clear night the 26-inch refractor telescope permits views of the moon, the stars, and even the planets, as far away as 25,000 light-years. (Don't say that nothing new ever comes from Washington.) The *old* U.S. Naval Observatory (located in Foggy Bottom) was the site of an important discovery. Deimos and Phobos, moons of the planet Mars, were detected there in 1877. The 90-minute tours include a 30-minute video, a look at the night sky through an observatory telescope, and a view of the atomic clock that keeps official U.S. time. Some visitors have told us about glow-in-the-dark T-shirts they purchased here.

Helpful Hint

The tour at the Observatory is recommended for *older* tweens and teens and lasts about an hour and a half.

3450 Massachusetts Avenue, NW
Open weekdays 9 to 5, except federal holidays
Tours Monday at 8:30 PM; tickets should be reserved four to
    six weeks in advance
The facility is not well designed for visitors with mobility
    problems
202/762–1467
www.usno.navy.mil

Embassy Row is not famous for its restaurants. But if you get hungry while exploring this area, there are a few spots near the Observatory. **Rocklands** (2418 Wisconsin Avenue, NW; 202/333–2558) is known for its barbecue dinners and selection of hot sauces.

It's open Monday through Saturday 11:30 to 10 and Sunday 11 to 9. Head back down Massachusetts Avenue toward Dupont Circle for other choices (see Chapter 7).

Where to Stay in Georgetown

Yes, there *are* places to stay in Georgetown. Bus service is more convenient than the subway for this area, as you've already discovered. Take a good look at your map in planning where to stay.

Georgetown Suites
1000 29th Street, NW, and 1111 30th Street, NW
202/798–7800 or 800/348–7203
www.georgetownsuites.com
Metro: Foggy Bottom (15-minute walk)

Georgetown Inn
1310 Wisconsin Avenue, NW
888/587–2388
www.georgetowncollection.com

Holiday Inn Georgetown
2101 Wisconsin Avenue, NW
202/338–3120 or 800/315–2621
www.holiday-inn.com

Savoy Suites Georgetown
2505 Wisconsin Avenue, NW
202/905–0019 or 866/589–6276
www.savoysuites.com

Where to Stay Near Embassy Row

If for some reason you really want to rub significant elbows on Embassy Row, just remember: one pays for status.

Hilton Washington Embassy Row
2015 Massachusetts Avenue, NW
202/265–1600 or 800/695–7460

www.hiltonembassyrow.com
Metro: Dupont Circle

Westin Embassy Row
2100 Massachusetts Avenue, NW
202/293–2100 or 800/937–8461
www.westin.com
Metro: Dupont Circle

Answers to Smart Stuff Questions

A. In the era after the Civil War, known as the "Golden Age of Black Washington," African-Americans were given voting rights and many held jobs of responsibility. Some were even elected to Congress. During this time Father Patrick Healy became president of Georgetown University, the first black American to head a major university.

B. An organization of member nations, the United Nations was formed to stimulate conflict resolution through negotiation rather than armed force. Its member agencies include the International Labor Office, the World Health Organization, the Food and Agricultural Organization, and the U.N. Educational, Scientific, and Cultural Organization (UNESCO), among others.

C. The Underground Railroad had a rich set of coded signals, from designs on hanging quilts to the venerable spirituals sung in the fields. The ingenuity of a people officially prevented from learning English as a written language is astounding.

D. *Embassy* denotes the ambassador's residence and any other buildings connected with that country's diplomatic mission, whereas the term *chancery* covers only the diplomatic offices. *Consulates* handle more day-to-day affairs (like visa and passport issues). *Attachés* are diplomats who attend to cultural, scientific, or commercial matters.

E. Tree branches, leaves, flowers, birds, deer, and many other animals.

CHAPTER 7
Dupont Circle
& Adams Morgan

In a section of Washington originally called "the Slashes" (for its unsavory nighttime activities), Dupont Circle is now a safer place. In the 1870s, when Connecticut Avenue was finally paved, this area became an attraction for the wealthy and powerful, whose mansions now serve as private clubs, association headquarters, embassies, office buildings, and art galleries. The circle was renamed in 1882 in honor of Union Admiral Samuel Francis du Pont, a hero of the ironclad ships in the Civil War. In 1884 Congress erected an equestrian statue here that the family found unsatisfactory. They hired Henry Bacon (designer of the Lincoln Memorial) and Daniel Chester French (sculptor of the statue inside) to create the grand neoclassical centerpiece for the small park at the center of the traffic circle.

Dupont Circle today attracts a much different group. You find chess players, brown-bag lunchers, tattered-jeans-clad students, sunbathers, musicians, young lovers (straight and gay), and political demonstrators. This is truly an intersection of major streets and lifestyles.

Anderson House

For Tweens and Teens . . . A wonderful piece of high-class history is the Society of the Cincinnati, headquartered in Anderson House. The Society was founded in 1783 for descendants of American and French officers who fought in the Revolutionary War, and members have met every three years since 1784. The Society is named after the Roman patriot Cincinnatus, who agreed to serve as head of state during an emergency and happily returned to his farm afterward. The example of this citizen-statesman appealed to the founders, one of whom was the great-grandfather of Larz Anderson, owner of Anderson House. In fact, a mural here depicts the Marquis de Lafayette receiving membership in the Society from George Washington, with Anderson's great-grandfather as a witness.

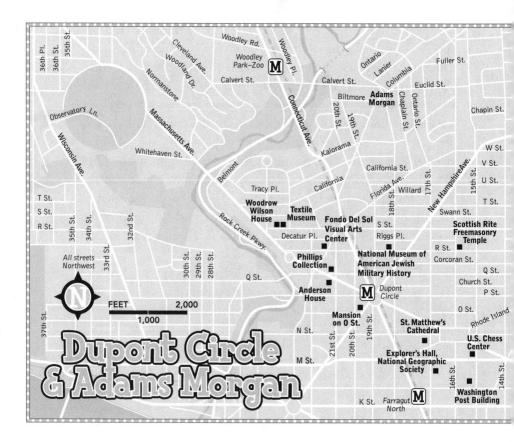

Smart Stuff

For Tweens and Teens . . . As your mother always told you, be kind to your friends. When the fledgling United States took on the powerful Great Britain, it needed all the help it could get. Do you know which three (yes, *three*) countries recognized the United States as a new nation and also declared war on England? Why do you think they would undertake such a course of action? **(A.)**

As befits the home of a former ambassador and his heiress wife, the museum overflows with opulence. In addition to whole rooms decorated with antique furnishings, some ceilings and walls are covered in 23-karat gold leaf. Kids will like the miniature Revolutionary War figurines engaged in "battle." American Revolution displays and George Washington memorabilia will be of particular interest to students studying the country's fight for independence.

Smart Stuff

For Teens . . . History books tell us that perhaps only a third of the colonial populace supported independence at the time of the Revolution, while another third worked for the *British* cause. Assume you were a middle-class colonial merchant with a family to support. Which side would you have chosen and why?

Can't You Make Them Behave, King George? and *Will You Sign Here, John Hancock?*, both by Jean Fritz, will be fun to read for tweens. One popular book for teens about the major players in the American Revolution is *Patriots: The Men Who Started the American Revolution*, by A. J. Langguth. A movie for the entire family to share is *1776*, a musical that truly brings the founding fathers and this historical period alive.

Quick Guide to Dupont Circle &

Attraction	Location
Anderson House	2118 Massachusetts Avenue, NW
The Phillips Collection	1600 21st Street, NW (at Q Street)
Textile Museum	2320 S Street, NW
★Woodrow Wilson House	2340 S Street, NW
Fondo Del Sol Visual Arts Center	2112 R Street, NW (at Florida Avenue)
National Museum of American Jewish Military History	1811 R Street, NW
St. Matthew's Cathedral	1725 Rhode Island Avenue, NW
U.S. Chess Center	1501 M Street, NW
★Explorers Hall, National Geographic Society	17th and M streets, NW
Scottish Rite Freemasonry Temple	1733 16th Street, NW
Mansion on O Street	2020 O Street, NW
★The Washington Post	15th and L streets, NW
Adams Morgan	Area surrounding intersection of 18th Street, NW, and Columbia Road, NW

Adams Morgan Attractions

Age Range	Hours	Details on
Tweens and Teens	Tues.–Sat. 1 PM–4 PM	Page 158
Teens	Tues.–Wed. and Fri.–Sat. 10 AM–5 PM; Thurs. 10 AM–8:30 PM; Sun. 11 AM–6 PM	Page 162
All Ages	Tues.–Sat. 10 AM–5 PM; Sun. 1–5 PM	Page 164
Tweens and Teens	Tues.–Sun. 10 AM–4 PM	Page 165
Tweens and Teens	Wed.–Sat. 1–6:30 PM	Page 167
All Ages	Mon.–Fri. 9 AM–5 PM	Page 168
All Ages	Sun.–Fri. 6:30 AM–6:30 PM; Sat. 7 AM–6:30 PM	Page 170
Tweens and Teens	Mon.–Thurs. 6–9 PM; Fri.–Sat. noon–6 PM	Page 171
All Ages	Mon.–Sat. and holidays 9 AM–5 PM; Sun. 10 AM–5 PM	Page 172
Teens	Mon.–Thurs. 9 AM–4:30 PM	Page 173
Teens	Tours: Sun. 11 AM–2 PM, Mon. noon–2 PM	Page 174
Teens	Tours by reservation only	Page 174
Teens		Page 175

Metro: Dupont Circle
2118 Massachusetts Avenue, NW
Open Tuesday to Saturday 1 to 4; closed major holidays
Library open by appointment weekdays 9 to 5
202/785–2040
www.thesocietyofthecincinnati.addr.com/anderson.htm

The Phillips Collection

For Teens . . . America's first museum of contemporary art, the Phillips Collection was established in 1921 by Duncan Phillips, heir to a steel fortune. The museum is housed in the family's brownstone mansion, giving it an accessible and comfortable feeling. This wonderful collection outgrew its home, so a starkly modern wing now holds some of the treasures. Still, not everything can be displayed at once, so works are rotated regularly. A list of artists represented reads like a "who's who" of modern art: Picasso, Renoir, Bonnard, Van Gogh, Monet, Miró, Klee, Mondrian, Rothko, Kandinsky, O'Keeffe, and Hopper are all featured. Phillips hung his paintings in "peer" groups, looking for ways different paintings would "interact" with each other. He wanted art to come alive for everyone visiting his collection.

Renoir's *Luncheon of the Boating Party,* the most popular work in the Phillips, has a double appeal. Not only does it exemplify the beautiful palette and style of the Impressionists, but it contains portraits of people the artist knew as well.

But art is just one reason to visit this museum. Afternoon concerts, featuring small groups of classical musicians, are a favorite

Helpful Hint

With appropriate preparation, all ages will enjoy this beautiful museum. Call ahead to request the Discovery Pack, a set of self-guide cards for ten specific paintings. A variety of tours is also available for young people.

Smart Stuff

For Teens . . . Duncan Phillips became distressed about the public's lack of knowledge of art when he overheard a college classmate claiming that "Botticelli is a wine, a good deal like Chianti, only lighter," and another, informing the first, that "Botticelli is not a wine, but a cheese." Phillips made it his life's work to acquire and display works of living artists, even amassing a special "encouragement" collection from the work of struggling young painters. Why wouldn't he be likely to have a Botticelli painting? **(B.)**

with locals. They begin on Sunday at 4 between October and May. The cost is included in the price of admission to the museum.

The expanded gift shop is chock-full of wonderful books, cards, games, jewelry, scarves, tapes, and surprises that represent work by the artists in the collection. For anyone craving a snack, a wonderful new café offers light meals and delicious baked goodies.

> Metro: Dupont Circle
> 1600 21st Street, NW, at Q Street
> Open Tuesday, Wednesday, Friday, and Saturday 10 to 5, Thursday 10 to 8:30, Sunday 11 to 6; closed major holidays. Special events are held after 5 PM the first Thursday of each month; call for details.
> Call a month in advance to schedule group tours, 202/387–2151 Ext. 215
> Admission fee; additional fee for special exhibits
> 202/387–2151
> www.phillipscollection.org

Getting hungry? Luckily you're in a neighborhood that is absolutely loaded with restaurants. **Chipotle Mexican Grill** (2600 Connecticut Avenue; 202/299–9111) is open daily 9 AM to 10 PM. You'll find all the usual Mexican favorites here, including tacos and burritos filled with steak, chicken, pork, and vegetarian selections and topped with fresh, healthful ingredients. Smallish **Raku** (1900 Q Street, NW; 202/265–7258) is open Monday through Thursday 11:30 to 10, Friday 11:30 to 11, and Saturday and Sunday noon to 10. It's a good spot for delectable international treats, including such specialties as "Peking duck" in rice-paper pancakes, salads, and sushi. The glass walls open for sidewalk café–style dining. Stop by and pick up a menu, since Raku also delivers. Are you a devotee of Thai food? Try **Thaiphoon** (2011 S Street, NW; 202/667–3505), open Sunday through Thursday 10:30 AM to 11 PM, Friday and Saturday 11 AM to 11:30 PM.

Textile Museum

For All Ages... You will be amazed at the accomplishments of weavers from all over the world when you visit the Textile Museum. Such countries as India, China, Indonesia, Guatemala, Mexico, and Peru are well represented by a lovely variety of offerings. Visitors familiar with Native American cultures will recognize and appreciate the original Navajo rugs. Photographs and videos illuminate the history of the cultures behind the work. Craft demonstrations, interactive displays, and special "please touch" exhibits allow you to get the feel of these creations. Kids can trace the sources for natural dyes, spin wool on a handheld spindle, learn to use a loom, decorate textiles by coloring or stamping patterns on the cloth, and practice various stitching techniques. A computer station has many learning activities.

For beautifully handcrafted scarves, rugs, blankets, and other weavings, visit the gift shop.

Metro: Dupont Circle
2320 S Street, NW

An interesting note, especially for kids who are perfectionists: it's a tradition in many cultures for textile artists to weave an intentional flaw into their work, to remind themselves that humans are imperfect.

Celebration of Textiles Day

Open Tuesday to Saturday 10 to 5, Sunday 1 to 5; closed
    Mondays, federal holidays, and December 25
Docent-led tours weekends at 1:30
For special guided tours, call to schedule at least four weeks in
    advance
Donation
202/667–0441
www.textilemuseum.org

★Woodrow Wilson House

For Tweens and Teens . . . The only presidential museum in Washington, the Woodrow Wilson House was the last home of Woodrow
Wilson, who lived here until his death in 1924. Wilson and his second wife, Edith, remained in the District after his term ended because he wanted to pursue research in the Library of Congress.
Unfortunately, he was already ill when they moved in, and the
house is a tribute to Mrs. Wilson's attention to and concern for his
needs. Mrs. Wilson lived here the rest of her life (she lived long
enough to attend Kennedy's inauguration), lovingly preserving the
home. Visitors will see it as it was during Wilson's life, including his
Victrola with a wooden needle, his movie projector, an ornate

wooden icebox, and even groceries in the lower-level pantry. Some interesting period clothing (including shoes) is displayed in both the closets.

The 45-minute tour follows a half-hour film, narrated by Walter Cronkite, describing the life of our 28th president. Youngsters who have studied the early part of the 20th century, the League of Nations, or the United Nations will find the museum particularly interesting. Idealism isn't just for the young.

Look for the 1944 biographical movie *Wilson*, which delivers a thought-provoking portrait of this intriguing figure. Many Woodrow

Smart Stuff

For Tweens . . . If you were an archaeologist looking at the objects in this house, what could you tell about people's lives in the early 1920s in the United States?

Wilson books are available. The following are a few worth exploring: *Woodrow Wilson,* by Anne Schraff (tweens); *Woodrow Wilson, President,* by Sallie G. Randolph (tweens and teens); *Woodrow Wilson,* by Louis Auchincloss (teens); and *Woodrow Wilson: World Statesman,* by Kendrick A. Clements (older teens).

The tiny gift shop is stocked with books and mementos relating to Wilson and his years in public life.

Smart Stuff

For Teens . . . Edith Bolling Galt Wilson, President Woodrow Wilson's second wife, was roundly criticized for restricting access by even the highest-level officials to her husband during his recovery from a stroke he suffered while president. If the United States were faced with a similar presidential health crisis, what safeguards would you recommend?

Congas on the Outer Circle

Metro: Dupont Circle
2340 S Street, NW
45-minute guided tours Tuesday through Sunday 10 to 4;
    closed major holidays
Call ahead to schedule special tours for school groups
Admission
202/387–4062
www.woodrowwilsonhouse.org

Fondo Del Sol Visual Arts Center

For Tweens and Teens . . . An alternative, artist-operated museum, Fondo Del Sol promotes Hispanic culture through the arts. Washington's only multilingual museum, with programs in Spanish, French, Russian, and English, it has a variety of offerings for children. Con-

Helpful Hint
In addition to all the galleries listed throughout this book, the metropolitan area is filled with *private* art galleries, large and small. You can find a magazine called *Galleries* (301/270–0180; www.artlineplus.com/gallerymagazine/index.php), available at most hotels, very helpful.

temporary and folk art are featured alongside pre-Columbian and religious artifacts. The museum shines during June Walk Week, which features three days of music, videos, and exhibits showcasing the cultures of the Americas.

Metro: Dupont Circle
2112 R Street, NW
Open Wednesday to Saturday 1 to 6:30, or by appointment
Call ahead to schedule special children's programs
Donation
202/483–2777
www.fondodelsol.org:

National Museum of American Jewish Military History

For All Ages . . . Artifacts from the Revolutionary War to the present are found in the National Museum of American Jewish Military History, documenting the contributions of Jewish Americans. Among the many items are bugles, binoculars, weapons, stirrups, flags, posters, and hand-painted maps of troop movements. Young feminists will be especially happy to find an exhibit about Jewish women who served in the U.S. military (they weren't all behind the lines making chicken soup). Guided and self-guided tours are available.

Two books we found of interest are for teens: *Where They Lie,* by Mel Young; and *Hearing a Different Drummer: A Holocaust Survivor's Search for Identity,* by Benjamin Hirsch.

Metro: Dupont Circle
1811 R Street, NW
Open weekdays 9 to 5; closed Jewish and federal holidays
School groups should call in advance
Donation
202/265–6280
www.nmajmh.org

For Tweens and Teens . . . Dupont Circle shopping has a split personality. There are pricey, high-end retailers like **Brooks Brothers** and **Burberry's**, or there are more eclectic shops, bookstores, and galleries. **Ginza,** at 1721 Connecticut Avenue, NW, whisks you away to the folk art of Japan. **Lou Lou,** at 1601 Connecticut Avenue, NW, offers funky jewelry and accessories at sensible prices.

Kramerbooks & Afterwards, at 1517 Connecticut Avenue, NW, is a favorite haunt for locals. Though it's narrow and crowded, don't pass it by unless you're in a big group. Long before the Barnes & Noble folks dreamed of serving cappuccino, Washingtonians were already nestling into the cozy niches here to read and sip.

Head upstairs from Kramerbooks to discover **Gallery 10, Ltd.** for works by exciting artists and varied artistic concepts. **Designer Arts and Crafts USA, Inc.,** at 1709 Connecticut Avenue, NW, is a treat for the artsy and artists in your group—featuring ethnic and unusual jewelry and furniture.

Smart Stuff

For Tweens and Teens . . . Incorporated in the Bill of Rights as the First Amendment is the stipulation that "Congress shall make no law respecting an establishment of religion, or prohibiting the free exercise thereof." Why do you think this particular freedom appears so early in our nation's history? If these provisions were *not* in our Bill of Rights, how do you think our American society would be different? What are some current issues concerning religious freedom in our country?

If you're sleuthing out a good read, real-live detectives will hunt for any out-of-print edition for you at **Second Story Books and Antiques,** at 2000 P Street, NW. You can search through the huge stock of used books yourself if you don't mind a little dust. For a real vintage experience, explore **Red Onion Records and Books** at 1901 18th Street, NW, where the inventory will intrigue tweens, teens, and adults alike. For a fun housewares shopping experience, you can try **Tabletop**, at 1608 20th Street, NW.

This area is full of small art galleries, particularly along R Street west of Connecticut Avenue. While the collections are interesting, including Chinese and Southeast-Asian art and antiques and American and English furnishings, they're generally not geared toward youngsters.

St. Matthew's Cathedral

With vaulted ceiling frescoes and chapels filled with candles, the interior of St. Matthew's Cathedral is a delight. Completed in 1895, after only two years of construction, it's decorated with colorful mosaics and pillars topped with gilded Corinthian capitals. Beneath the 90-foot dome the central altar, a gift from the archbishop of Agra, India, is in the traditional Mogul style of the Taj Mahal.

St. Matthew's has been the site of many memorable events. The funeral for President John F. Kennedy took place here on November 25, 1963, and Pope John Paul II led services here when he visited the city in 1979. Traditionally, a "Red Mass" is celebrated in October, marking the historical opening of the judicial year. (This tradition dates as far back as the Middle Ages, when royal judges wore scarlet robes.) Members of Congress, Supreme Court justices, heads of governmental agencies, members of the diplomatic corps, and, occasionally, the president are in attendance to pray for guidance in their official duties—a good thing to agree on.

Metro: Farragut North or Dupont Circle
1725 Rhode Island Avenue, NW
Open Sunday to Friday 6:30 to 6:30, Saturday 7 to 6:30
Call ahead to arrange a guided tour

202/347–3215
www.stmatthewscathedral.org

There are restaurants, cafés, and take-out stands all over the Dupont
Circle area, so food is plentiful. There's a double-decker treat at 1633
P Street, NW: **Café Luna** (202/387–4005), on the first floor, serves
pizza and pasta, while upstairs at **Skewers** (202/387–7400) you can
find such Middle Eastern fare as grilled eggplant with yogurt, shish
kebabs, and *kufta* (looks like a long hot dog, but it's made of chick-
peas and spices). There's also a variety of vegetable dishes. Both eateries are open Monday through Thursday 11:30 to 10, Friday and
Saturday 11 to midnight, Sunday noon to 10. **Bua** (1635 P Street,
NW; 202/265–0828) serves a variety of Thai dishes, including many
vegetarian entrées. It's open for lunch weekdays 11:30 to 3, weekends noon to 4; dinner Monday to Thursday 5 to 10:30, Friday to
Sunday 5 to 11. For pizza and pastas, visit **Bertucci's** (1218 Connecticut Avenue, NW; 202/463–7733), open Monday to Thursday
11 to 10, Friday and Saturday 11 to 11, and Sunday noon to 10.

U.S. Chess Center

For Tweens and Teens . . . Chess aficionados will enjoy a trip to
this museum. Trophies and photographs document the history of
the game and highlight prominent American players. The center
also teaches chess to local kids, and runs tournaments for all ages
and levels of players.

Metro: Farragut North
1501 M Street, NW
Open Monday to Thursday 6 to 9 PM, weekends noon to
6 PM; closed January 1, July 4, Thanksgiving Day, and
December 25
202/857–4922
www.chessctr.org

Dedicated in 1909, the statue of **Henry Wadsworth Longfellow,**
one of our country's most beloved poets, sits at the corner of Con-

necticut Avenue and M Street, NW. Perhaps it's fitting that the creator of "Paul Revere's Ride," "The Wreck of the Hesperus," "The Song of Hiawatha," and "Evangeline" should sit where he does: in traffic. Maybe he's reminding us all to slow down.

★Explorers Hall, National Geographic Society

For All Ages . . . A real-life *National Geographic* special, this museum is a draw for kids of all ages. Whatever you like in nature—astronomy, biology, geography, weather, space science, and exploration of the planet—you can find it here on the first floor of the society's headquarters. Three-dimensional models of the Grand Canyon, Mount Everest, and the Chesapeake Bay area are featured in the permanent collection. Everyone will enjoy the display of extraordinary photographs from the magazine.

Helpful Hint

Since exhibits change every three to five months, call before your visit. Information about upcoming events is available online about a month prior to their opening.

The most relevant and enjoyable reading materials for a visit to this special place would be any issues of the *National Geographic* magazine, with its familiar yellow-bordered cover, or, for younger children, *National Geographic World*. Subscriptions to either of these magazines make great gifts, either for individuals or schools. Past issues are available at the gift shop.

Metro: Farragut North or Farragut West
17th and M streets, NW
Open Monday to Saturday and holidays 9 to 5, Sunday 10
to 5; closed December 25

Smart Stuff

For Teens . . . In prior centuries, exploration meant discovering new territories or learning about uninhabited areas of the earth. In the latter part of the 20th century, exploration focused on outer space. What do you think our obligations are to the environments we explore?

202/857–7588;202/857–7700 for family programs on
    Saturday
www.nationalgeographic.com

Scottish Rite Freemasonry Temple

For Teens . . . A pyramid-topped building guarded by two sphinxes, the Scottish Rite Freemasonry Temple certainly stands out from the residential building surrounding it. Completed in 1915, it's the headquarters for the Masons of the District of Columbia. Fourteen presidents, from George Washington to Gerald Ford, have been Masons. Dedicated to "spreading the light of knowledge and fraternity," the Masons these days focus on support for children with learning disorders and on literacy training for adults. A tour lasting 1 hour and 45 minutes (not great for most children) gives you the opportunity to see the 1,000-pipe organ, the Hall of Masonic Heroes, and the J. Edgar Hoover Law Enforcement Room. If your teen is a member of DeMolay or Job's Daughters, this site is of special interest.

    Metro: Dupont Circle
    1733 16th Street, NW
    Open Monday to Thursday 9 to 4 and the first Saturday of
        each month 10:30 to 3; tours offered 10 to 4. Library
        open daily 8 to 5.
    202/232–3579
    www.scottishrite.org

Mansion on O Street

For Teens . . . A well-kept Washington secret, this small Victorian-era inn is owned and run by an eccentric dowager, H. H. Leonard. It offers 12 different guest rooms, as well as 88 other rooms on five floors, publicized only by word of mouth and often visited by celebrities. You don't have to stay overnight to visit this unusual mansion, as you can explore the place when it's open for a champagne brunch on Sunday 11 to 2 and "power lunch" on Monday noon to 2. Everything—and we do mean everything—is for sale, from small pieces of jewelry and knickknacks to sculptures and huge paintings. Bring a truck (parking, however, is a real challenge here).

> Metro: Dupont Circle
> 2020 O Street, NW
> Tours Sunday 11 to 2, Monday noon to 2
> Fee
> 202/496–2020
> www.omansion.com

★The Washington Post

For Teens . . . When it broke the Watergate scandal in the early 1970s, the *Washington Post* gained a worldwide reputation for responsible journalism. The diligent reporting and journalistic skills of Bob Woodward and Carl Bernstein eventually resulted in the only resignation of a president, Richard Nixon, in our country's history.

Smart Stuff

For Tweens and Teens . . . Thomas Jefferson once said that given the choice between a democracy with no newspapers and newspapers with no democracy, he'd choose the latter. Why do you think he would make such a choice? Do you agree?

Youngsters interested in news and how a major newspaper is produced will find the *Washington Post*'s downtown headquarters a fascinating place. But they are not likely to see the big presses rolling. Since the *Post* is a morning newspaper, most of it is printed at night. But to see how many people it takes to put out a daily newspaper is indeed a surprise. You will never look at a newspaper in quite the same way again!

Several books of interest to teens who are current-events buffs are *All the President's Men,* by Carl Bernstein and Bob Woodward (also the movie version with Robert Redford, Dustin Hoffman, and Jason Robards); *The Chain Gang: One Newspaper Versus the Gannett Empire,* by Richard McCord; *Our Man in Washington,* by Roy Hoopes; *A Time of Change: A Reporter's Tale of Our Time,* by Harrison E. Salisbury; and *Simon Says: The Best of Roger Simon,* by Roger Simon.

Highly visible when you tour the building is a cutout of a classified ad promotion that reads, "I got my job through the *Washington Post.*" It's signed by President Gerald Ford, who took office after Nixon resigned.

Metro: McPherson Square or Farragut North
1150 15th Street, NW (15th and L streets, NW)
For guided tours for organized groups of 10 to 30 people,
    schedule and reserve two months or more in advance.
    Tours are also given at the paper's printing facility in
    Springfield, Virginia; call to arrange. Children on tours
    must be at least 11 or in 5th grade.
202/334–7969
www.washingtonpost.com

Adams Morgan

For Teens . . . Colorful and exciting, this tiny neighborhood combines international flair and bohemian style. Chock-full of restaurants, cafés, clubs, and shops, Adams Morgan is a mecca for young people and artistic types. The two main streets to explore are 18th Street, NW, running north and south, and Columbia Road, NW, running diagonally northeast and southwest. Originally settled by Native Americans, this area was named Lanier Heights until desegregation (D.C. was the first major U.S. city to voluntarily integrate its schools). The primarily white Adams School merged with the largely African-American Morgan School, and the residents decided to change the name of their neighborhood to reflect this solidarity.

Helpful Hint

This is an area in the midst of change. While adults (and *only* adults) will love its clubs and cafés at night, kids and families enjoy the shops and ambience in the daytime. Come by taxi, as parking is nearly impossible; walking is best in a group. However, it's a very intriguing and educational neighborhood for teens to visit in the daytime.

Many residents of the neighborhood hail from Latin America, the Caribbean, Southeast Asia, and Central Africa, among other places. As a result, the restaurants and stores, packed with handmade items and clothing from all over the world, are adventures to investigate. **Paula's Imports,** at 2405 18th Street, NW, houses an unusual assortment of jewelry, shoes, bedspreads, and other gifts from Africa, India, and Pakistan.

You can find some unusual treasures in Adams Morgan, including architectural details, such as stained- and leaded-glass windows, chandeliers, fireplace mantels, and hardware, which you can discover at the **Brass Knob** (2311 18th Street, NW). Hand-painted furnishings, pillows, and wrought iron fill **Skynear & Co.** (2122 18th Street, NW).

Since locals love secondhand anything, stores with secondhand goods abound. For old books, try **Idle Time Books,** at 2467

18th Street, NW. Like most such places, it's a dusty hunt for treasure here, and politics is the topic of choice.

> **Helpful Hint**
> This neighborhood is a long walk from the Metro stations, so it's a good idea to take a taxi.

In a city where nearly every neighborhood has international cuisine, locals still flock to Adams Morgan. For inexpensive and exotic Ethiopian specialties, visit **Meskerem** (2434 18th Street, NW; 202/462–4100). If you've never had Ethiopian food, be sure to wash your hands before you get started—they're your utensils, along with a spongy form of flat bread called *injera*. Lots of stews are served, often with several on one platter. When ordering, remember that *alicha* indicates the mildly spiced versions, while *watt* refers to the spicier dishes. And they *are* high-wattage, with plenty of green chilies. The eatery is open weekdays noon to 11 and weekends noon to 2 AM. **Banana Leaves** (2020 Florida Avenue, NW; 202/986–1333; www.mybananaleaves.com), an Asian restaurant and sushi bar, offers a wide range of Asian specialties at reasonable prices. From scallion pancakes to tropical or squid salads to spicy seafood hotpot, there's adventuresome eating here. Open Monday through Thursday 11 to 10:15, Friday and Saturday 11 to 10:45, and Sunday 3:30 to 10:30.

> Metro: Dupont Circle (exit at Q Street and head up Connecticut Avenue, NW, to Columbia Road, NW) or Woodley Park–Zoo (walk over the Duke Ellington Bridge to the intersection of Columbia Road and 18th Street)

Where to Stay in the Dupont Circle & Adams Morgan Area

The majority of the hotels in this area are close to Dupont Circle. Adams Morgan has mainly small bed-and-breakfasts. The exception is the Washington Hilton, which has some notoriety of its own (it was outside this hotel that President Reagan was shot).

Carlyle Suites Hotel
1731 New Hampshire Avenue, NW
202/905–0016 or 866/492–0031
www.carlylesuites.com
Metro: Dupont Circle

The Dupont Hotel
1500 New Hampshire Avenue, NW
202/483–6000 or 800/423–6953
www.doylecollection.com
Metro: Dupont Circle

Washington Hilton and Towers
1919 Connecticut Avenue, NW
202/483–3000 or 800/445–8667
www.washington.hilton.com
Metro: Dupont Circle (a long walk)

Answers to Smart Stuff Questions

A. The three countries were France, Holland, and Spain.
B. Botticelli would not have been a "living" painter in Phillips's day. He lived from 1444 to 1510.

CHAPTER

8

Chinatown
& Gallery Place

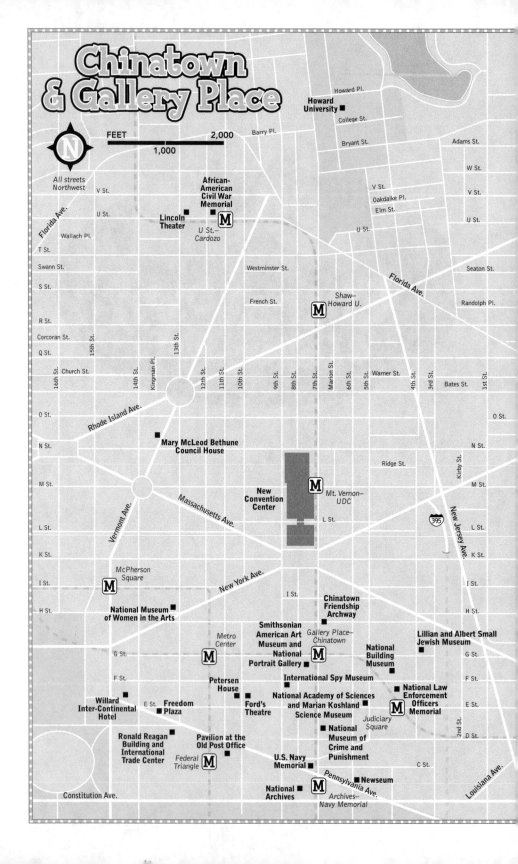

Chinatown & Gallery Place

FEET

1,000   2,000

N

All streets Northwest

Howard Pl.

Howard University ■

College St.

Barry Pl.

Bryant St.

Adams St.

W St.

V St.

V St.

V St.

Oakdale Pl.

Elm St.

U St.

U St.

Florida Ave.

Wallach Pl.

African-American Civil War Memorial

Lincoln Theater ■

U St.– Cardozo

T St.

Swann St.

Westminster St.

Seaton St.

S St.

French St.

Shaw– Howard U.

Randolph Pl.

R St.

Florida Ave.

Corcoran St.

15th St.

13th St.

Q St.

16th St.

Church St.

14th St.

Kingman Pl.

12th St.

11th St.

10th St.

9th St.

8th St.

7th St.

Marion St.

6th St.

5th St.

Warner St.

4th St.

3rd St.

Bates St.

1st St.

O St.

O St.

N St.

Mary McLeod Bethune Council House ■

N St.

Ridge St.

Kirby St.

M St.

New Convention Center

Mt. Vernon– UDC

M St.

L St.

395

New Jersey Ave.

L St.

K St.

K St.

McPherson Square

New York Ave.

I St.

I St.

H St.

National Museum of Women in the Arts ■

I St.

Chinatown Friendship Archway ■

H St.

Metro Center

Smithsonian American Art Museum and National Portrait Gallery ■

Gallery Place– Chinatown

Lillian and Albert Small Jewish Museum ■

G St.

National Building Museum ■

G St.

F St.

Petersen House ■

International Spy Museum ■

F St.

Willard Inter-Continental Hotel ■

E St.

Freedom Plaza ■

Ford's Theatre ■

National Academy of Sciences and Marian Koshland Science Museum ■

National Law Enforcement Officers Memorial ■

E St.

Judiciary Square

2nd St.

Ronald Reagan Building and International Trade Center ■

Pavilion at the Old Post Office ■

National Museum of Crime and Punishment ■

D St.

Federal Triangle

U.S. Navy Memorial ■

C St.

Constitution Ave.

National Archives ■

Pennsylvania Ave.

Newseum ■

Archives– Navy Memorial

Louisiana Ave.

The colorful **Chinatown Friendship Archway** at 7th and H Streets, NW, beckons visitors to the five-block area of D.C.'s Chinatown, a fitting symbol for this section of the city. Filled with art and history, the **Chinatown/Gallery Place** neighborhood has spots that are unique Washington sites. They include the **FBI Building**, the **National Law Enforcement Officers Memorial, the Newseum,** and the **International Spy Museum;** cultural treats like the **National Museum of Women in the Arts,** the **National Museum of American Art,** and the **National Portrait Gallery;** brain food for history buffs like the **National Archives** and **Ford's Theatre;** and ethnic delights for the tummy in Chinatown. Although some of these spots may not be awash with tourists, this area touches a variety of interests and is well worth a visit. You don't have to be an FBI agent to uncover good things to do here.

National Museum of Women in the Arts

For Tweens and Teens . . . Amazing as it may seem, there *were* women artists before the 20th century, and here's the place to see their work. In addition to such relatively recent notables as Georgia

Quick Guide to

Attraction	Location
National Museum of Women in the Arts	1250 New York Avenue (at 13th Street, NW)
Willard Inter-Continental Hotel	1401 Pennsylvania Avenue, NW
Freedom Plaza	Pennsylvania Avenue and 13th, 14th, and T streets, NW
Ronald Reagan Building and International Trade Center	1300 Pennsylvania Avenue, NW
★Pavilion at the Old Post Office	1100 Pennsylvania Avenue, NW
★National Archives	Constitution Avenue at 8th Street, NW
★Newseum	555 Pennsylvania Avenue, NW at 6th Street
U.S. Navy Memorial	701 Pennsylvania Avenue, NW
National Museum of Crime and Punishment	575 7th Street, NW
★Ford's Theatre	511 10th Street, NW

Chinatown & Gallery Place Attractions

Age Range	Hours	Details on
Tweens and Teens	Mon.–Sat. 10 AM–5 PM; Sun. noon–5 PM	Page 181
		Page 187
Tweens and Teens	24 hours	Page 188
All Ages	Visitors Center: Mon.–Sat. 9 AM–6 PM; Sun. noon–5 PM	Page 189
All Ages	Tower: March–Aug., Mon.–Sat. 10–8, Sun. noon–7; Sept.–Feb., Mon.–Sat. 10–7, Sun. noon–6	Page 190
Tweens and Teens	Labor Day–March 14, daily–10–5:30; March 15–Labor Day, daily 10–7	Page 191
Tweens and Teens	9 AM–5 PM daily	Page 194
Tweens and Teens	24 hours, daily. Center: March–Oct., Mon.–Sat. 9:30 AM–5 PM; Nov.–Feb., Tues.–Sat. 9:30 AM–5 PM	Page 195
Tweens and Teens	Mon.–Sat. 9 AM–7 PM (March–Aug.); 10 AM–6 PM (Sept.–Feb.)	Page 196
Tweens and Teens	9 AM–5 PM daily	Page 198

(continues)

Quick Guide to

Attraction	Location
Smithsonian American Art Museum and National Portrait Gallery	8th and F streets, NW
★International Spy Museum	800 F Street, NW
Chinatown Friendship Archway	Bordered by 6th, 7th, H, and I streets, NW
Marian Koshland Science Museum	6th and E Streets, NW
National Law Enforcement Officers Memorial	Between E and F Streets and 4th and 5th Streets, NW
National Building Museum	401 F Street, NW
Lillian and Albert Small Jewish Museum	701 3rd Street, NW (at G Street)
Mary McLeod Bethune Council House	1318 Vermont Avenue, NW
African-American Civil War Memorial	1000 U Street, NW
Howard University	2400 6th Street, NW
Lincoln Theater	1215 U Street, NW

Chinatown & Gallery Place Attractions

Age Range	Hours	Details on
All Ages	10–5 daily	Page 201
Tweens and Teens	Hours vary	Page 203
		Page 204
Tweens and Teens	Wed.–Mon. 10 AM–6 PM	Page 205
All Ages	24 hours, daily.	Page 206
Tweens and Teens	Mon.–Sat. 10 AM–5 PM; Sun. 11–5	Page 207
Teens	By appointment	Page 208
Tweens and Teens	Mon.–Sat. 9 AM–5 PM	Page 209
All Ages	Mon.–Fri. 10 AM–5 PM; Sat. 10 AM–2 PM	Page 210
Teens		Page 211
Teens	Mon.–Fri. 10 AM–6 PM	Page 212

O'Keeffe, Mary Cassatt, Elaine de Kooning, Lila Cabot Perry, Frida Kahlo, and Helen Frankenthaler, you can explore work by artists of much earlier times, including Lavinia Fontana, Rachel Ruysch, and Elizabeth Vigee-Lebrun (painter in the court of Marie Antoinette). Sculptor Camille Claudel, the unhappy mistress and student of Auguste Rodin, is also represented. In addition to the permanent collection on the third floor, the museum hosts a series of changing exhibits.

Ironically, the interior of this Renaissance Revival building, with its pink marble, ornate chandeliers, and grand, sweeping staircase tailor-made for the most elegant of weddings, was originally a Masonic lodge. It's a nice reminder that women belong not only in the halls of Congress, but also in the halls of museums.

Smart Stuff

For Teens . . . Explore the work of two American women artists, one from the 20th century and one from an earlier period. What differences can you find in subject matter and style? How do you think the eras in which they lived influenced their work?

The museum's Education Resource Center can suggest many ways to enjoy the museum, including tours for young people and family-friendly guidebooks to special exhibits. Concerts, films, theatrical and dance performances, workshops, and book signings are some of the other offerings of this national resource.

The gift shop, open during museum hours, is a wonderful place to find something special. From Christmas ornaments to fine jewelry to handmade stuffed animals and toys, there's plenty to see. There are also books for a variety of reading levels on many of the artists whose work is displayed here.

At the **Mezzanine Café** (202/628–1068) you can partake of edible artistic creations weekdays 11:30 to 2:30; reservations are required only for special groups. Choose from hot and cold sand-

> ## Helpful Hint
> Call ahead for a copy of the kid-friendly *Artventure*, a self-guiding tour booklet for the National Museum of Women in the Arts that suggests ways to help 6- to 12-year-olds experience the exhibits.

wiches with artsy names, hot entrées, specialty salads, and desserts, and fortify yourself to move on to your next site. Brunch is offered on the first Sunday of every month from 11 to 3.

Other dining options include **Capital City Brewing Company** (11th and H Streets, NW; 202/628–2222), with a jukebox and a family-friendly menu. The noisy, spacious place is open Sunday to Thursday 11 to 11, weekends 11 to midnight. Choose from full-course meals like grilled salmon and lighter fare like grilled bratwurst sandwiches. Tours of the brewery are available. On the same block, tasty Thai food is found at **Haad Thai** (1100 New York Avenue, NW; 202/682–1111). In this colorful setting you can get crispy appetizers followed by skewers of vegetables or meat. It's open weekdays 11:30 to 2:30 and 5 to 10:30, weekends noon to 11.

> Metro: Metro Center
> 1250 New York Avenue at 13th Street, NW
> Open Monday to Saturday 10 to 5, Sunday noon to 5; closed
>   January 1, Thanksgiving Day, and December 25
> For information on special programs, phone 202/783–7370
> Fee; free first Sunday of each month
> 202/783–5000 or 800/222–7270
> www.nmwa.org

Willard Inter-Continental Hotel

In a city known more for politics than elegance, here's a place that combines the two. A spot to see and be seen, the Willard was where lobbying began. Sam Ward was frequently seen in the lobby with wealthy clients during the mid-1800s. Known as "King of the Lobby," he was Washington's first lobbyist.

The Civil War period was a significant time for the Willard Hotel. Sam's sister, Julia Ward Howe, penned "The Battle Hymn of the Republic" here. The Peace Convention, made up of remnants of the 36th Congress, met here in February 1861, in a vain attempt to avert the Civil War. During the war both Northerners and Southerners stayed here, using separate floors and entrances; but the American flag always flew over the building.

Staying in what is now the Presidential Suite the night before his inauguration, President Abraham Lincoln was asked by owner Henry Willard if there was anything he needed. Lincoln had forgotten his bedroom slippers, so Willard quickly borrowed a pair from his wife's grandfather, who had the biggest feet in town. In the morning, the slippers were returned with a note of thanks, and they are still a Willard family treasure.

The Beaux Arts building, with its heavy crystal chandeliers, Italian marble, and intricate mosaics, recalls a bygone age. And you don't have to lobby for anything!

Metro: Metro Center
1401 Pennsylvania Avenue, NW
202/628–9100 or 888/424–6835
www.interconti.com

Freedom Plaza

For Tweens and Teens . . . One of the numerous benefits of the redevelopment of Pennsylvania Avenue was the dedication of this slice of land. Renamed Freedom Plaza in 1988 in honor of Martin Luther King Jr., it reflects the role the capital city has played from the American Revolution to the present. Standing guard over the plaza is a statue of General Casimir Pulaski, who led Revolutionary troops until he died as a result of battle injuries in 1779. A part of Pierre L'Enfant's original plan for Washington, D.C., it is laid out in stone, surrounded by a variety of historic and contemporary quotations about Washington.

Metro: Federal Triangle or Metro Center
Bounded by Pennsylvania Avenue and 13th, 14th, and E
    streets, NW

Ronald Reagan Building and International Trade Center

For All Ages . . . Named for a president who wanted to *reduce* the size of government, this building is second in size only to the Pentagon. Using an acre's worth of glass in its 125-foot-high atrium, this enormous structure showcases sculptures and a variety of artifacts, including a huge chunk of the Berlin Wall. In addition to a fine restaurant and a café, there's an extensive food court in the concourse level, with 20 individual vendors serving foods from around the world.

The building houses the **D.C. Visitor Information Center** (202/289–8317 or 866/324–7386; www.dcchamber.org) an important first stop on your trip. The 3,200-square-foot center is across the street from the Federal Triangle Metro station, through the Wilson Plaza entrance. Here's *the* place to go for the latest information on where to stay, eat, or shop; cultural opportunities; and services for tourists. There are also plenty of souvenirs for sale. All the maps, brochures, and interactive information kiosks you could dream of are here, as well as stacks and stacks of brochures. Tired of collecting paper? Try this: *talk* with one of the information specialists on hand (you might want to have a pen and paper handy). The center is open daily 9:30 to 5 and closed weekends.

Note: because this is a federal building, there's security at the entrance, and occasionally there are long lines at the metal detectors.

Teens might like to read *The U.S. Role in the Global Economy*, from Close Up Publishing, which focuses on the confusing world of international trade. *The World Is Flat: A Brief History of the Twenty-first Century*, by Thomas Friedman, would be of special interest to teens and adults.

Metro: Federal Triangle
1300 Pennsylvania Avenue, NW
202/312–1300

★Pavilion at the Old Post Office

For All Ages . . . You should stop by the Pavilion at the Old Post Office for two reasons. One is the architecture of this beautifully preserved Washington landmark, especially its grand atrium; the other is the dramatic view from the windows of the clock tower. Lines here are much shorter than at the Washington Monument, and the windows are a whole lot bigger. National Park Service guides take tours up every five to seven minutes. Another treat on your way up is a tour of the **Congress Bells,** a gift from England in honor of the U.S. bicentennial. Resembling the bells of Westminster Abbey, they were cast at London's famed Whitechapel Foundry. The **Washington Ringing Society** holds practice rings on Thursday evenings between 6:30 and 9:30 PM (during which time the tower is closed). If you're lucky enough to be in town at the opening of Congress or on a national holiday, you can hear a phenomenal 90-minute "full peal."

There's a reason why this is called the Pavilion at the Old Post Office, and we bet you can guess it. Built in 1899 as the country's postal headquarters, this Romanesque jewel was repeatedly scheduled for demolition in the late 20th century. It was rescued by concerned citizens who formed a campaign called "Don't Tear It Down." The stunning interior, 10 stories high and topped with a glass ceiling, houses a cluster of shops and a food court. It's a convenient and inexpensive place to grab a delicious lunch or a quick snack, but it can get quite busy when the tour buses arrive. There's a huge variety to choose from, from sandwiches to Indian and Asian cuisine.

Entertainers perform here almost every day—you never know what you'll find. High-school and college groups often give free concerts, as do other musicians. Or you might find clowns, jugglers, dancers, or other creative performers, generally at lunchtime but sometimes around 5 PM as well.

Metro: Federal Triangle
1100 Pennsylvania Avenue, NW
Open March to August, Monday to Saturday 10 to 8, Sunday
    noon to 7; September to February, Monday to Saturday
    10 to 7, Sunday noon to 6

Tower tours: Labor Day to Memorial Day, Monday to Saturday 9 to 4:45, Sunday 10 to 5:45; Memorial Day to
Labor Day, Monday to Wednesday and Friday to Saturday, 9 to 7:45, Thursday 9 to 6:30, Sunday 10 to 5:45.
On all federal holidays tours are 10 to 5:45.
202/289–4224, 202/606–8691 for tower information
www.oldpostofficedc.com

★National Archives

For Tweens and Teens . . . Talk about a firm foundation—this neoclassical building, surrounded by 72 Corinthian columns and topped with a sculpted pediment, rests on 8,500 pilings. It was built atop an old creek bed that ran through the city. (This is *not* the place to have water in the basement!) At the building's Constitution Avenue entrance are two massive bronze doors, each weighing six and a half tons. In the rotunda you can see the three major docu-ments on which the U.S. government was founded: the Declaration of Independence, the Constitution, and the Bill of Rights. Speaking of a democratic heritage, one of only four remaining copies of the Magna Carta of 1297 (purchased and donated by one of democ-racy's most colorful participants, H. Ross Perot) shows how it all began. Just how important these documents are is reflected in their living quarters. By day their helium-filled bronze-and-glass cases are protected by armed guards, and by night the cases do a disappearing act—they sink slowly into an underground vault, reinforced against theft, fire, and even nuclear attack.

Not just a museum, the National Archives is a work-ing center for genealogical research. You can even investi-gate your own heritage. Au-thor Alex Haley found his

Smart Stuff
For Tweens and Teens . . . Going about the business of waging a revolution, the Continental Congress decided to have a written Declaration of Indepen-dence. Why do you think they felt the need for such a document?

The Declaration of Independence at the National Archives

"roots" here, as have thousands of other people. Ask a staff member about researching your family's past.

Custodian of our democracy's valuables, the National Archives building contains 2%–5% of our government's documents. Billions of pieces of paper have to be sorted through each year to select what is to be preserved. The collection includes maps, charts, passport applications, naturalization papers, ship manifests, photographs, passenger lists, reels of film, and some particularly interesting audiotape cassettes (including one with an 18½-minute gap) from the Watergate era. Also included are some surprises, which you can see if you take the tour: President Kennedy's doodles during the Cuban Missile Crisis, a photo of Elvis Presley with President Richard Nixon, and a display of unlabeled presidential baby photos.

Want to go to the movies? A small theater in the building shows free films several days a week (check online for details). These

Smart Stuff

For Teens . . . The United States is one of more than 60 countries in the world to have a *written* constitution. Why do you think our founding fathers considered this necessary? What's your opinion?

may include documentaries, archival footage, and even feature films. You don't need reservations to tour the gift shop, where you can purchase replicas of historic documents, campaign buttons, and books about genealogy.

A book of interest for tykes is *Shhh! We're Writing the Constitution*, by Jean Fritz; for tweens and teens, books include *Johnny Tremain*, by Esther Forbes (it's also a movie) and *The U.S. Constitution and Fascinating Facts About It*, by Terry L. Jordan. For teens there are *The American Reader: Words That Moved a Nation*, edited by Diane Ravitch, and *The Powers That Be*, by David Halberstam. There's also *U.S. History Through the Eyes of Everyday People*; *Words of Ages: Witnessing U.S. History Through Literature*; *The First Amendment: America's Blueprint for Tolerance*; and *The Bill of Rights: A User's Guide*, all from Close Up Publishing.

The film *Yankee Doodle Dandy*, with James Cagney in his Oscar-winning performance, will please everyone. *The Hunt for Red October* is an exciting adventure about the Cold War for tweens and teens, and teens will be challenged by the moral dilemma of using nuclear weapons portrayed in *The Manhattan Project*. Close Up Publishing offers a series of videos, *Ordinary Americans: The Collection*, which includes *Vietnam, The Civil Rights Movement*, and *The Red Scare*. Two other videos for teens are *Profiles of Freedom: A Living Bill of Rights* and *Democracy and Rights: One Citizen's Challenge*.

Smart Stuff

For Tweens and Teens . . . Which famous Revolutionary War figure had a son who was a Tory? (A.)

Anybody want lunch? How about a snack? **The Charters Café** inside the National Archives is open 10 to 4.

Metro: Archives–Navy Memorial

700 Pennsylvania Avenue, NW

Labor Day to March 14, daily 10 to 5, March 15 to Labor Day, daily 10 to 7; closed Thanksgiving Day and December 25; children under 16 must be with an adult

Hour-long behind-the-scenes tours weekdays at 9:45; groups are limited to 30 people; to reserve space, call six weeks ahead.

Visitors must pass through X-ray security to enter

866/272–6272

www.archives.gov

★Newseum

For Tweens and Teens . . . The reemergence of the Newseum is definitely news. The 250,000-square-foot facility built to house the museum sits on Pennsylvania Avenue, between the Capitol and the White House. Visitors will crane their necks to gaze at the panoramic displays that meld journalistic history with the latest interactive technology. Behind-the-scenes looks at what goes on at a newspaper or television studio help explain what goes into "making news."

Seven levels house galleries, theaters, and retail shops. A family-friendly **food court** is complemented by an upscale restaurant headed by legendary chef Wolfgang Puck. The gift shop stocks many items inspired by the museum's collection, and books related to journalism, the media, and the many ways history is recorded. But the 74-foot-high engraving of the First Amendment on the building's facade is perhaps the most impressive thing of all. It's a reminder that a free society is dependent on a free press.

Budding journalists and avid newshounds will enjoy *You Should Have Been Here Yesterday: A Life Story in Television News,* by Garrick Utley (teens), and *World War II On The Air: Edward R. Murrow And The Broadcasts That Riveted A Nation*, by Mark Bernstein and Alex Lubertozzi (teens).

Metro: Archives–Navy Memorial

555 Pennsylvania Avenue, at 6th Street, NW

Open daily 9 to 5; closed January 1, Thanksgiving, and December 25.

Fee

888/639–7386

www.newseum.org

U.S. Navy Memorial

For Tweens and Teens . . . Even if you get seasick in the bathtub, you will appreciate the cascading fountains and naval flags that adorn the U.S. Navy Memorial, across Pennsylvania Avenue from the National Archives. At the center are Stanley Bleifeld's statue *The Lone Sailor* (note: photo op here) and an engraving of "The Navy Hymn." Commemorating all who have served in the U.S. Navy, the sailor watches over fountains and waterfalls (which contain water from the seven seas) and the world's largest stone map of the earth. Summertime weekly concerts by the U.S. Navy Band (Tuesday evening) and drill exercises by the U.S. Navy Ceremonial Guard (Tuesday at 1) entertain visitors on the plaza, weather permitting. Nearly hidden on the northeast corner of the Memorial Plaza is the **Naval Heritage Center,** which, like the hold of a ship, is mostly "below deck." (The main entrance faces Pennsylvania Avenue, with another door on the 8th Street side.) With or without saltwater in your veins, you can find something of interest. *The Homecoming,* another of Bleifeld's evocative sculptures, greets you at the entrance. Interactive videos explain about naval history, ships, and aircraft. In the Navy Memorial Log, check out people you know who have served in the navy. Two centuries of naval history are etched into 13 glass panels on the Wave Wall. On display are myriad paintings and portraits, from the Navy Art Collection to the Presidents' Room (with portraits of presidents who served in the navy). The film *At Sea* is shown at noon daily from Memorial Day to Labor Day.

The Ship's Store offers specifically nautical merchandise. Books to read before or after your visit include *A Boy's Will,* by Erik Christian Haugaard and Troy Howell (tweens); *John Paul Jones:*

Smart Stuff

For Tweens and Teens . . . Six U.S. presidents served in the Navy. Two of them held the post of Assistant Secretary of the Navy. Can you name all of them? (Hint: the two assistant secretaries had the same last name.) **(B.)**

Hero of the Seas, by Keith Brandt (tweens and teens); and *John Paul Jones: A Sailor's Biography,* by Samuel Eliot Morison (teens). As for films, we suggest *Mutiny on the Bounty* (tweens and teens) and *Mr. Roberts* (teens).

Metro: Archives–Navy Memorial
701 Pennsylvania Avenue, NW
U.S. Navy Memorial is open daily 24 hours; Naval Heritage
    Center is open March to October, Monday to Saturday
    9:30 to 5; November to February, Tuesday to Saturday
    9:30 to 5; closed January 1, Thanksgiving Day, and
    December 25.
For concert schedule, call 202/433–4011
202/737–2300 or 800/821–8892
www.lonesailor.org

With the exception of Thomas Jefferson, no American citizen has so exemplified mankind's extraordinary potential as Benjamin Franklin (whose **statue** stands at Pennsylvania Avenue and 10th Street, NW). A statesman, scientist, journalist, and inventor, Franklin lent his ingenuity to much that touched his 18th-century countrymen. His founding of the first lending library and the first volunteer fire department, as well as his invention of the lightning rod, have enriched life in subsequent centuries. When his contemporaries were either retired or deceased, he labored here and abroad as one of America's founding fathers. It's interesting that this statue, portraying him dressed as minister to France, is merely entitled *Printer.* This memorial was the gift of Stilson Hutchins, something of a newspaperman himself. He founded the *Washington Post.*

National Museum of Crime and Punishment

For Tweens and Teens . . . Hard as it is to believe, there is a growing number of interesting museums in Washington, D.C., that actually *charge* admission. One of the newest is the National Museum of Crime and Punishment, a building full of hands-on experiences that should wow even the most blasé teens, and may shock some more sensitive tweens. (Know your customers; some of the material here is pretty graphic, especially for any "tykes" in your brood.)

Exhibits—complete with sound effects and lighting—give visitors a feeling of "total immersion" in their settings. The interactive nature is particularly appealing to kids: they can sit on a police motorcycle, "shoot" on a shooting range, be fingerprinted (and take home this souvenir), sit in a jail cell, and perhaps most exciting, drive in a high-speed police chase simulator. There are lots of artifacts in the history department, ranging from a guillotine, complete with bucket (for catching the victim's head!), to an electric chair to Al Capone's jail cell.

Check online in advance to decide which Crime Scene Investigator (CSI) workshop (1 hour, fee) you'd like to join. Topics are assigned to different days and times. You can learn to read blood spatter patterns and match DNA profiles, investigate a "post-blast" (explosion) scene, identify a criminal through evidence, and learn about messages hidden in ink.

In addition to the fees for several interactive exhibits and the CSI Workshops, you can always drop some more bucks at the Cop Shop—the on-site gift shop. Crime-fighting apparel, books, toys, and games are available for a variety of ages and interests. For this museum, crime *does* pay.

Parents/Teachers Take Note

For Teens . . . There is a movement to give every American (regardless of legal status) a biometric identity device. How do you think this would affect illegal immigration and domestic crime?

A game to try is *Spy Alley,* an award-winning strategy game of suspense and intrigue for tweens and teens. *Spying on America: The FBI's Domestic Counterintelligence Program,* by James Kirkpatrick Davis, is an unusual and interesting book for teens.

Metro: Gallery Place/Chinatown
575 7th Street, NW
Open March to August, daily 9 to 7; September to February,
     daily 10 to 6; closed Thanksgiving and December 25
Fee; additional fees for some activities
202/393–1099; 202/621–5567 for Special Events
www.crimemuseum.org

★Ford's Theatre

For Tweens and Teens . . . The site of one of our country's most
tragic events, Ford's Theatre was where Abraham Lincoln was assassinated on April 14, 1865. Originally a church, it burned to the
ground in 1862, shortly after having been converted into a theater.
Its owner, John Ford, built a larger theater on the site in 1863. Prior
to the fateful night when he was shot, Lincoln had seen a number of
plays here, one of which starred the famous actor John Wilkes
Booth.

The public opposed reopening the building as a theater. The
federal government purchased it in 1866 and used it as an army
medical museum. Among other oddities on exhibit was Lincoln's as-
sassin John Wilkes Booth's spinal column, with its bullet hole. On
July 9, 1893, several floors of the deteriorated building caved in,
killing 22 government workers and wounding more than 100. It
wasn't until the 1960s that the building was restored by the National Park Service. Photographs by Mathew Brady, taken just after
Lincoln's assassination, were used to ensure authenticity. Presidents
since that time have attended the theater here, but no one sits in the
Presidential Box.

In the basement of the building is the **Ford's Theatre Museum.** Depicting the assassination, exhibits here include the gun
used by Booth to kill Lincoln.

After another more recent renovation, Ford's Theatre reopened
in time for Lincoln's bicentennial (February 12, 2009). The theater is
now part of a larger project, the "Tenth Street Campus," focusing on
the life and legacy of our 16th president and the Civil War era. The

Helpful Hint

For Tweens . . . Be sure to ask for the Junior Ranger booklet, with its scavenger hunt for specific Lincoln memorabilia such as the pistol used in the assassination and the clothing he wore. It also contains activities and games. When children complete the booklet, they're awarded Junior Ranger badges.

complex includes the theater, the Petersen House (where Lincoln died), and a new Center for Education and Leadership.

In the wealth of materials about Abraham Lincoln, there are books specifically about the assassination. Several we suggest are *Back to the Day Lincoln Was Shot!*, by Beatrice Gormley (tweens); *Blood on the Moon: The Assassination of Abraham Lincoln*, by Edward Steers, Jr. (older tweens and teens); *Team of Rivals*, by Doris Kearns Goodwin (teens); and *The Day Lincoln Was Shot*, by Jim Bishop (teens). Classic Civil War movies to enjoy include *Friendly Persuasion* (tweens and teens); *Shenandoah* (teens); and *Gone with the Wind* (teens).

Across the street, the **Lincoln House Restaurant and Deli** (504 10th Street, NW; 202/638–4008) can accommodate large groups in its downstairs room. With breakfast options like pancakes and eggs and a variety of deli sandwiches, subs, and gyros, even the biggest appetite can be satisfied. Kids enjoy the all-you-can-eat pizza dinner. It's open weekdays 5:30 AM to 7 PM, weekends 5:30 AM to 3 PM.

A favorite with tweens and teens, **Hard Rock Café** (999 E Street, NW; 202/737–7625) has memorabilia from rock stars hanging from the walls and ceilings. It's a great place for atmosphere, as well as for burgers, steaks, and fajitas. The restaurant, part of the

Smart Stuff

For Tweens . . . If you had been in charge of President Lincoln's Secret Service detail, what provisions would you have made for his safety?

The Presidential Box at Ford's Theatre

international chain, is open Sunday to Thursday 11 to 11, Friday and Saturday 11 to midnight. Specific arrangements for group breakfast events can be made in advance (202/628–6583).

For a little continental flavor, try **Bistro D'Oc** (518 10th Street, NW; 202/393–5444), open Monday through Thursday 11:30 to 2:30 and 5:30 to 10, Friday and Saturday 11:30 to 2:30 and 5:30 to 11, and Sunday 11:30 to 8:30. At this two-story bistro you can indulge in real French cooking or even order a hamburger and fries. On weekends this restaurant is a treat for grown-ups, but you'll need reservations. *Bon appétit!*

Smart Stuff

For Teens . . . If Abraham Lincoln had survived the assassination attempt, what do you think might have been different afterward? (C.)

Metro: Metro Center
511 10th Street, NW
Open daily 9 to 5; closed December 25
Free; requires timed-entry tickets same day or through
Ticketmaster

202/426–6924; 202/397–7328 Ticketmaster box office
www.nps.gov/foth
www.fordstheatre.org

Smithsonian American Art Museum and National Portrait Gallery

For All Ages . . . Before this elegant Greek Revival building was completed in 1867 it was the home of the Patent Office, and had as its top floor the largest room in America—the setting for a raucous party celebrating Abraham Lincoln's second inauguration. Part of the Smithsonian Institution, this recently renovated building melds art and history in a rich series of exhibits (and no wild parties we know of).

Smart Stuff

For Tweens and Teens . . . From the depictions of Native Americans you see, what do you think the artists thought of this ethnic group? How can you tell? Do you think their attitudes were common at the time?

A hit with kids is the fiberglass and epoxy cowboy on a bucking bronco guarding the front of the **Smithsonian American Art Museum.** You can tell them this is definitely a place for "cowboys and Indians," since inside are portraits of American Indians that would

Smart Stuff

For Tykes . . . How about making a collage? After looking at James Hampton's *Throne of the Third Heaven*, made from aluminum foil, younger kids might begin to think about what other materials could be used for art. An enjoyable home or school art project could be assembling a collage from objects collected during their Washington, D.C., trip (string, wrappers, paper cups, safety pins, ticket stubs, etc.).

make Jean-Jacques Rousseau proud. There's a wide variety of work, from the familiar paintings of Winslow Homer to the sparkling piece by James Hampton titled *Throne of the Third Heaven,* giving kids a new appreciation for aluminum foil. Among the 37,500 works of art should be something that will appeal to every age. A good restaurant nearby is **Matchbox** (713 H Street, NW; 202/289–4441), for pizza and burgers. Reservations only accepted for weekdays. It's open weekdays 11 to 10:30, weekends 10 AM to 10:30 PM.

> Metro: Gallery Place–Chinatown
> 8th and F Streets, NW
> Open daily 11:30 to 7; closed December 25
> Tours at 12:30 and 2
> Free
> 202/633–1000
> www.americanart.si.edu

The **National Portrait Gallery** is the place to see paintings of famous Americans, some as you've never seen them before. Portraits range from basketball star Shaquille O'Neal to Secretary of State Hillary Rodham Clinton, and styles encompass everything from newspaper cartoons to full-length likenesses in oil. Some interesting highlights are the diminutive painting of Andrew Jackson wearing one of the first pairs of bifocals, the portrait of Benjamin Franklin that became the model for the $100 bill, and the famed life-size portrait of George Washington by Gilbert Stuart. Also of note are works by the subjects themselves, including the self-portraits of Samuel F. B. Morse, whose likeness truly belongs in this Old Patent Office building.

Smart Stuff

For Tykes . . . After seeing a portrait of P. T. Barnum with the man's head on an insect's body, can you think of other strange combinations that would be interesting or funny? Did you ever see a picture of a mermaid or a minotaur?

Around the corner on 7th Street is Chinatown, where you can find plenty of small ethnic restaurants with noodle dishes, curries, and Szechuan and Cantonese fare. **New Big Wong Restaurant** (610 H Street, NW; 202/628–0491) is family-friendly. It's open Monday through Sunday 10:30 AM to 11 PM.

There are countless books and films about famous Americans portrayed in these museums, including the books *The Story of My Life,* by Helen Keller for tweens and teens; and for teens, *James McNeil Whistler: Beyond the Myth,* by Ronald Anderon and Anne Koval; *America's Old Masters,* by James T. Flexner; and *Edison: Inventing the Century,* by Neil Baldwin. Interesting movies include *Edison: The Man* (tweens and teens) and *The Story of Alexander Graham Bell* (tweens and teens).

Metro: Gallery Place–Chinatown
8th and F streets, NW
Open daily 11:30 to 7; closed December 25
202/633–8300
www.americanart.si.edu

★International Spy Museum

For Older Tweens and Teens . . . Be careful what you say when you visit the International Spy Museum—a hidden microphone, positioned literally in a "fly on the wall," pipes your conversation into another room for others to hear. In the five buildings that were combined to create this big space—located, appropriately enough, a few blocks from the FBI—is the most extensive collection of spy paraphernalia anywhere in the world. Stories of spies from biblical times to the present delight and amaze visitors. From clever gimmicks to serious spy training, an elusive subject is covered—or uncovered—for the wonderment of all. The complex includes a museum, a full-service restaurant, a café, and a gift shop where shoppers can indulge their fantasies of living the life of Agent 007. The password is "FUN."

Reading about spying is *almost* as good as being here—and another way to explore how it is done. The "Nate the Great" series, by Marjorie Weinman Sharmat, is a longtime favorite for tykes and young tweens, as is *Junie B. Jones and Some Sneaky Peeky Spying*, by Barbara Park. Tweens enjoy *Spying for Beginners* (Hotshots series), edited by Lisa Miles. *Spying: The Modern World of Espionage*, by Ron Fridell, is an eye-opener for teens.

Ready to scout out some good eats? Right next door, the **Spy City Café** (800 F Street, NW; 202/654–0995) serves breakfast and lunchtime goodies. There are sandwiches and made-to-order salads, as well as giant Rice Krispies treats and mammoth mouthwatering cookies. The café is open weekdays 8 to 6, weekends 9 to 6.

> Metro: Gallery Place–Chinatown
> 800 F Street, NW
> Hours vary, so call ahead; closed January 1, Thanksgiving
>   Day, December 25.
> Admission fee
> 202/393–7798 or 866/779–6873
> www.spymuseum.org

Chinatown Friendship Archway

The formal entrance to the District's Chinatown—an area roughly bordered by 6th, 7th, H, and I streets—is the Chinatown Friend-ship Archway. Hundreds of dragons in the Ming and Kuing dynasty styles decorate the lavish structure, one of the world's largest single-span archways. The Chinese New Year parade passes under this arch. The mayors of both the District of Columbia and Beijing, China, were present at its dedication in 1986.

A combination of Byzantine, Romanesque, and Moorish ar-chitecture, the **Sixth and I Historic Synagogue** (600 I Street, NW; 202/408–3100; www.sixthandi.org) has stood in the heart of the city for nearly 100 years. Recently renovated—like much of the neighborhood around it—the synagogue is now available for cele-brations and religious services. With its beautiful stained-glass win-dows, vaulted ceilings, and magnificent detailing, this small historic building is a visual treat. It's open Monday to Thursday 9 to 5, and

The Chinatown Friendship Archway welcomes visitors to this part of the city.

Friday 9 to 4:30, and also houses the office and archives of the Jewish Historical Society.

This colorful area is where locals go for delicious Chinese food. One restaurant you might like to try is the very plain **Full Kee** (509 H Street, NW; 202/371–2233). Serving excellent dishes, it's open daily 11 AM to 11:30 PM.

Marian Koshland Science Museum

For Tweens and Teens . . . With its home in the National Academy of Sciences building, the Marian Koshland Science Museum is the perfect vehicle for demystifying the groundbreaking work of the Academy. For example, a fiberglass model of the interior of a cow demonstrates one surprising way methane gas (a cause of global warming) is produced.

The permanent exhibition focuses on some of the seemingly unanswerable questions scientists tackle, such as "What is the universe made of?" and "Why is it rapidly expanding?" Other exhibits, like the applications of DNA technology, employ a variety of interactive displays. In one interesting approach to global warming, you can choose from a list of actions that can reduce this biological hazard. A display then explains how much impact your choice would have. Visitors with a solid interest in science will be amazed by what they find here.

Metro: Gallery Place–Chinatown
6th and E streets, NW
Open Wednesday to Monday 10 to 6
Admission fee
202/334–1201or 888/567–4526
www.koshlandscience.org

National Law Enforcement Officers Memorial

For All Ages . . . A very different kind of memorial to fallen heroes commemorates those who have died protecting us here at home. With two tree-lined "pathways of remembrance," the National Law Enforcement Officers Memorial enshrines the names of officers killed in the line of duty from 1794 to the present. If you're planning a visit in May, you might want to attend the annual candlelight vigil held during National Police Week, when new names are added to the 17,000 already inscribed on blue-gray marble walls. Names are in a random order, but directories are nearby. A bronze statue of an adult lion protecting its cubs guards each entrance, symbolizing the protection, courage, and strength of law enforcement officers. An inscription on the east wall cites the memorial's motto: "In valor there is hope."

Less than two blocks away is the visitor center (a museum is expected to open in 2013), with an interactive video system that highlights biographical information and photographs about each officer, along with the location of their names on the memorial wall. Additional photographs and historical exhibits line the walls. Educators here have done an exceptional job preparing materials for all ages of kids. Individual activity books are available for students from kindergarten through eighth grade. Call and ask for these in advance.

To read about law enforcement officers, try *My Dog Is Lost,* by Ezra Jack Keats (tykes); *Policeman Small,* by Lois Lenski (tykes); *Angie's First Case,* by Donald J. Sobol (tykes and tweens); *Badge of*

Valor, by Brent Ashabranner (tweens); and *A Day in the Life of a Police Cadet,* by John H. Martin (tweens). Movies include *The Great Mouse Detective* (tykes and tweens) and *The Big Sleep* (tweens and teens).

> Metro: Judiciary Square
> Memorial: E Street between 4th and 5th streets, NW
> Visitor Center: 605 E Street, NW
> Memorial open 24 hours; visitor center open weekdays 9 to 5, Saturday 10 to 5, Sunday noon to 5; closed January 1, Thanksgiving Day, and December 25
> Guided tours by appointment
> 202/737–3213
> www.nleomf.com

National Building Museum

For Tweens and Teens . . . Originally called "Meigs' Red Barn," this building was used in the 1880s by clerks processing military pensions. Even today it's often referred to as the Pension Building. Its designer, Army General Montgomery C. Meigs, wanted to provide government workers here with the latest in lighting, ventilation, and safety. The result is an Italian Renaissance–style edifice that is unusual on the outside and breathtaking within.

Taking up a whole city block, the building was constructed of dark red brick, and is encircled by a touching terra-cotta frieze. The work of sculptor Casper Buberl, the frieze depicts the homeward procession of veterans. It's no coincidence that the interior, with its vaulted ceiling and eight massive Corinthian columns (brick, but painted to look like marble—a cost-cutting device), has been the site of inaugural balls since Grover Cleveland's in 1885. The unfinished building at that time lacked only a roof, so a tarp was stretched across the opening. A result was that canaries released to add to the festivities flew to the top, froze in the frigid air, and fell unceremoniously onto the dance floor below.

Two permanent exhibits tell about the building itself and about other landmark buildings. Temporary exhibits, a major crafts fair, and other special programs also make use of the Great Hall's imposing space. The museum's monthly calendar lists hands-on educational activities for the whole family.

The gift shop on the ground floor features books on architecture, as well as crafts and toys. You can find snacks and meals at the **Fire Hook Café** on weekdays from 8:30 to 4, Saturday 10 to 4, and Sunday 11 to 4. Choose from bakery items, salads, and sandwiches.

David Macaulay's internationally renowned books are of special interest for kids of all ages: *City, Pyramid, Castle, Cathedral,* and *Unbuilding* (this one deals with the underground systems that support a modern city). Teens would like *Frank Lloyd Wright: A Biography,* by Meryle Secrest, and *Frank Lloyd Wright's Fallingwater: The House and Its History,* by Donald Hoffman. *Ten Books On Architecture,* by Roman architect and engineer Vitruvius, and *Four Books of Architecture* by Renaissance architect Andrea Palladio are a pair of classic texts by men, renowned in their own time, who have influenced Western architecture ever since.

Metro: Judiciary Square
401 F Street, NW
Open Monday to Saturday 10 to 5, Sunday 11 to 5; closed
     January 1, Thanksgiving Day, and December 25
Docent-led tours begin weekdays at 12:30, weekends at
     11:30, 12:30, and 1:30
Donation suggested
202/272–2448
www.nbm.org

Lillian and Albert Small Jewish Museum

For Teens . . . Dedicated in 1876 as the original Adas Israel Synagogue, this is the oldest synagogue in Washington. The Jewish Historical Society now operates the Lillian and Albert Small Museum here. It includes a restored sanctuary and a permanent exhibit on

Washington's Jewish community, as well as changing temporary exhibits, an archive, and a library.

> Metro: Judiciary Square or Gallery Place–Chinatown
> 701 3rd Street, NW, at G Street
> Open by appointment
> Donation
> 202/789–0900
> www.jhsgw.org

In the middle of Gompers Square (really a little trapezoid of land at Massachusetts Avenue and 10th Street, NW) stands a **memorial** to Samuel Gompers, who immigrated to New York City in 1863 at age 13. Within a year of landing a job as a cigar maker, he formed the Cigar-Maker's International Union. In 1896 he organized the American Federation of Labor (AFL), and served as its president until his death in 1924. He was a strong believer in collective bargaining and a diligent proponent of labor and antitrust laws. The U.S. Department of Labor owes its existence, in part, to his influence. President Franklin D. Roosevelt, a friend to American workers, was present at the statue's dedication in 1933. Behind the seated Gompers are figures representing Industrial Exploitation, the Unity of Unions, Justice, and Home. The base is inscribed with his writings. Youngsters whose parents work in a "union shop" know the value of his legacy.

Mary McLeod Bethune Council House

For Tweens and Teens . . . Near Logan Circle is the former home of educator Mary McLeod Bethune, founder of the National Council of Negro Women. The little girl, the 15th of 17 children, had to walk 10 miles each way to school. She grew up to found Bethune-Cookman College, the first African-American women's college in the United States. The first black woman to become a presidential adviser, Bethune was head of Negro Affairs at the National Youth Administration, appointed to this position by President Franklin D. Roosevelt. Bethune's Victorian town house, now a museum and archives, contains the country's largest collection of original documents chronicling the achievements of African-American women.

Metro: McPherson Square
1318 Vermont Avenue, NW
Open Monday through Saturday 9 to 5
Tours available Monday through Saturday 10 to 4
202/673–2402
www.nps.gov/mamc

African-American Civil War Memorial

For All Ages . . . A memorial to the more than 209,000 African-American soldiers who fought in the Civil War is near the U Street–Cardozo Metro station. At its center is an 11-foot-tall bronze statue called *The Spirit of Freedom.* Names of all African-American Civil War troops are etched into plates of gray steel. A visitor center has computers where you can find details about specific soldiers. Photographs, documents, and artifacts like war medals are included in exhibits.

This neighborhood is called **Shaw,** honoring Robert Gould Shaw. He was the white colonel of the first African-American regiment to fight in the Civil War, the one featured in the film *Glory.*

Many books have been written about the Civil War period. For tykes, try *Follow the Drinking Gourd,* by Jeanette Winter (also an animated movie narrated by Morgan Freeman). For tykes and tweens, check out *Sweet Clara and the Freedom Quilt,* by Deborah Hopkinson. Other suggestions are *Dear Austin: Letters from the Underground Railroad,* by Elvira Woodruff (tweens); *The Last Safe House: A Story of the Underground Railroad,* by Barbara Greenwood (tweens); and *A Different Kind of Christmas,* by Alex Haley (teens).

A wonderful movie about part of the African-American experience in the Civil War is *Glory,* about a heroic black regiment in a fateful battle (tweens and teens). The History Channel's *Underground Railroad* is now available on video. There's also *A House Di-*

vided, by Ken Burns, as well as his landmark miniseries *The Civil War* (teens).

> Metro: U Street–Cardozo (Vermont Street exit)
> 1200 U Street, NW
> Open weekdays 10 to 5, Saturday 10 to 2
> Tours by appointment
> 202/667–2667
> www.afroamcivilwar.org

Howard University

For Teens . . . If you're traveling with high-school students, some may want to take a brief side trip to see this famous university. On one of the capital's highest elevations, Howard offers great views of the city. One of the nation's most prestigious black universities, Howard was founded in 1867 to educate newly freed slaves. It was named for General Oliver Otis Howard, who headed the Freedmen's Bureau after the Civil War. Famous graduates include the late Supreme Court Justice Thurgood Marshall; former New York City Mayor David Dinkins; former Atlanta Mayor Andrew Young; the late Patricia Roberts Harris, secretary of the U.S. Department of Health and Human Services; and novelist Toni Morrison.

Parts of the university library are open to the public. The Moorland-Spingarn Research Center has the largest collection of black literature in the country. Howard University Hospital houses the **Freedmen's Hall Gallery of Art** (2041 Georgia Avenue, NW; 202/865–1471). In addition to describing the hospital's history, the gallery is a permanent educational and cultural site that provides visitors with an opportunity to explore African-American contributions to medicine, health care, and medical research.

> Metro: Shaw–Howard University and walk north along 7th Street, NW (becomes Georgia Avenue).
> 2400 6th Street, NW
> 202/806–6100 or 202/806–6111
> www.howard.edu

Lincoln Theater

For Teens . . . Cab Calloway, Louis Armstrong, Duke Ellington, Count Basie, Ella Fitzgerald, Billie Holiday, and Pearl Bailey were among the black stars who performed at this historic theater. Built in 1920, the Lincoln offered movies, vaudeville, and nightclub acts, and was the first D.C. theater to welcome an integrated audience. It closed in the 1970s but reopened in 1994, restored to its former Georgian Revival elegance. Today it features special events like the D.C. Film Festival, along with jazz, gospel, comedy, and pop shows (see Appendix I for details).

The theater is in the **U Street Corridor,** an area particularly significant in the African-American renaissance of art, music, and entertainment in Washington, D.C. Nightclubs and bars come alive here in the evening. The now famous (after President Obama's visit) **Ben's Chili Bowl** (1213 U St., NW; 202/667–0909) is on the same block as the theater. Featuring chili in every possible variety, it's open Monday to Thursday 6 AM to 2 AM, Friday to Saturday 6 AM to 4 AM, and Sunday 11 to 11.

> Metro: U Street–Cardozo
> 1215 U Street, NW
> Open weekdays 10–6
> Tours by appointment
> 202/328–6000
> www.thelincolntheatre.org

Where to Stay in the Chinatown & Gallery Place Area

Although filled with tourist attractions, this area is limited in its accommodations. It turns out to be a better place to explore in the daytime anyway. We do have a few places you can look into. Be sure to look up these specific locations on your trusty Washington map before you make reservations.

Red Roof Inn
500 H Street, NW
202/289–5959 or 800/733–7663
www.redroof.com
Metro: Gallery Place–Chinatown

Hotel Harrington
436 11th Street, NW, at E Street
202/628–8140 or 800/424–8532
www.hotel-harrington.com
Metro: Metro Center

Grand Hyatt Washington
1000 H Street, NW
202/582–1234 or 800/233–1234
www.grandwashington.hyatt.com
Metro: Metro Center

Answers to Smart Stuff Questions

A. Benjamin Franklin's oldest son was the royal governor of New Jersey, and given the circumstances found it prudent to leave the country.

B. Franklin D. Roosevelt, John F. Kennedy, Richard M. Nixon, Gerald Ford, Jimmy Carter, and George H. W. Bush all served in the Navy. Both Theodore Roosevelt and Franklin D. Roosevelt served as Assistant Secretary of the Navy.

C. It might be instructive to do some reading on the Reconstruction Period and the impeachment of Andrew Johnson (especially since our country has recently lived through another such event). Terms like "carpetbagger" and "Jim Crow laws" are tied to the aftermath of the Civil War and Lincoln's death.

Uptown
& Suburban Maryland

ot all the heavy-duty sites are in the city's center. The area known as **Upper Northwest** or simply **Uptown** is well worth exploring. From high culture to wildlife, treasures of czarist Russia to cuddly looking pandas, from an Amazon rain forest to the world's sixth-largest cathedral, Uptown abounds with variety. A foray into nearby suburban Maryland affords you the opportunity to visit a historic trolley-car museum, walk the campus of a major state university, and delight in the gallery of a world-renowned but homegrown artist.

★National Zoo

For All Ages . . . If you reside in this 163-acre park (along with about 4,999 other animals), it's okay to act wild. (Inhabitants of other notable D.C. addresses don't have the same excuse.) Because of its size, make sure you have a workable "battle plan." For the most enjoyable visit, try to narrow your choices to a few attractions. To help you plan, there are walking-tour maps and animal-feeding schedules available at the visitor center, near the Connecticut Avenue entrance. Clear signs are posted in many strategic spots along the way. *This* is one of the days when you'll need the most comfortable shoes you have ever worn.

One group *not* in need of shoes is the orangutans, making their way on an overhead line from their habitat to the "Think Tank," where they play with computers. Visit the soaring, net-covered aviary and the state-of-the-art Amazonia rain-forest ecosystem, or watch through an underwater window as the graceful sea lions play. From the mischievous, barking prairie dogs in an exhibit close enough for animals and humans to become quite friendly (*don't!*) to the lumbering majesty of the huge Kodiak bears (imagine *their* summers in the capital's heat), there's something for everyone. There are delightful pandas named Mei Xiang and Tian Tian to ooh and aah over in their own custom-designed quarters. In July 2005 Mei Xiang gave birth to a tiny baby boy panda.

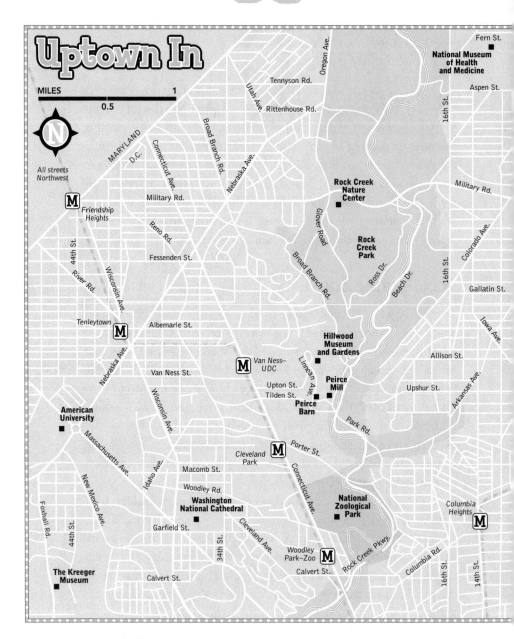

If all that oohing and aahing has made your gang ravenous, the zoo has remedies. In addition to the ice-cream stands and snack bars throughout the grounds, there are two restaurants: the fast-food-oriented **Panda Café** (guess where you can find it?) and, down

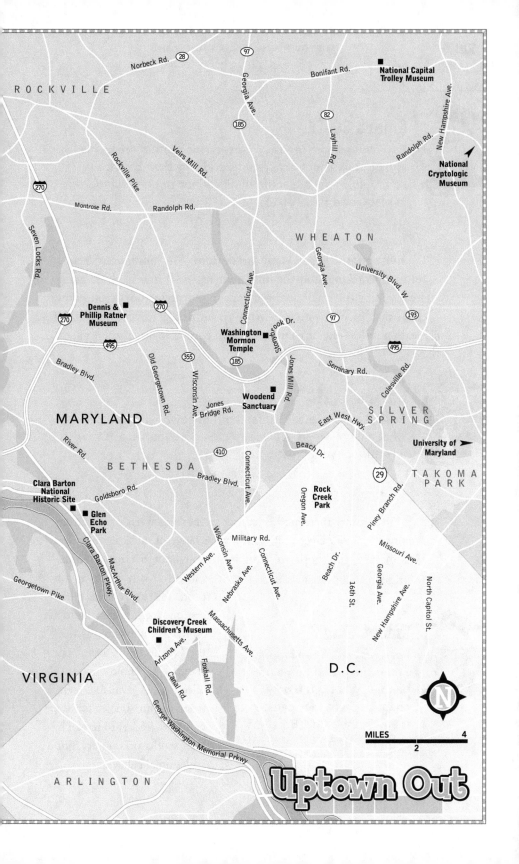

Smart Stuff

For Tweens and Teens . . . After a visit to the Amazonia exhibit, talk about ecosystems and why their balance is so fragile. What are some ramifications of deforestation in places like Brazil? **(A.)**

the hill a bit, the larger **Mane Restaurant.** The grounds are beautiful for picnicking, and the only animals you'll find in those grassy areas will be the small buzzing, crawling, or flying ones (you know, the usual picnic "guests"). Keep your drinks covered in warm weather unless one of your group is an entomologist-in-training.

Smart Stuff

For Tykes . . . Since Batman has already been invented, what animal would you use to create a superhero? Draw a picture of your creation.

In summer there are free sunset serenade concerts on Thursday evenings on Lion/Tiger Hill, with a wide range of musical selections. Well-marked gift shops are scattered throughout the zoo grounds. Here you can stock up on postcards, key chains, posters, and yet another stuffed animal. A bookstore is near the Connecticut Avenue entrance. A whole range of selections is available here, from picture books for the youngest readers to research-level works on conservation and animal behavior.

Smart Stuff

For Tykes . . . The National Zoo is the proud home of pandas. What is the only country where they can be found in the wild? **(B.)**

Looking for a "group rate" at the National Zoo

Metro: Woodley Park–Zoo

Connecticut Avenue bus lines L2 and L4 stop at the main entrance

3000 block of Connecticut Avenue, NW (entrances also on Harvard Street, NW, and Beach Drive, NW)

Grounds open April to October, daily 6 to 8; November to March, 6 to 6; closed December 25

Friends of the National Zoo conducts tours on weekends; for reservations up to two months ahead, call 202/633–3025

Free

202/633–4800

http://nationalzoo.si.edu

★Washington National Cathedral

For All Ages . . . The Cathedral Church of St. Peter and St. Paul (better known as the Washington National Cathedral) has seen its share of historic events. Services for the endings of both World Wars took place here, as did the funerals of Presidents Wilson and Eisenhower. Many famous people have spoken from its pulpit, including the Reverend Martin Luther King Jr., Archbishop Desmond Tutu, and the Dalai Lama. Perhaps one of the most moving moments occurred when Colonel Thomas Schaefer, one of the Iranian hostages released from captivity in 1981, greeted the congregation: "Good

Quick Guide to

Attraction	Location
★National Zoo	3000 block of Connecticut Avenue, NW (entrances also on Harvard Street, NW, and Beach Drive)
★Washington National Cathedral	Mount St. Alban at Massachusetts and Wisconsin avenues, NW
American University	4400 Massachusetts Avenue, NW (between Ward and Wesley circles)
Hillwood Museum and Gardens	4155 Linnean Avenue, NW
Rock Creek Nature Center	5200 Glover Road, NW
Peirce Mill	3545 Williamsburg Lane, NW (at the corner of Tilden Street and Beach Drive, NW)
Peirce Barn	2401 Tilden Street, NW
National Museum of Health and Medicine	6900 Georgia Avenue, NW (Building 54)
The Kreeger Museum	2401 Foxhall Road, NW
Glen Echo Park	7300 MacArthur Blvd, Glen Echo, Maryland

Uptown & Suburban Maryland Attractions

Age Range	Hours	Details on
All Ages	6 AM–8 PM (April–Oct.), 6 AM–6 PM (Nov.–Mar.) Open every day except Dec. 25	Page 215
All Ages	Mon.–Fri. 10 AM–5 PM; Sat. 10 AM–4:30 PM; Sun. 8 AM–5 PM	Page 219
Teens		Page 226
Teens	Tues.–Sat. 10 AM–5 PM	Page 227
All Ages	Wed.–Sun. 9 AM–5 PM	Page 228
All Ages	Closed for renovations	Page 231
Tweens and Teens	Sat.–Sun. noon–6 PM	Page 232
Tweens and Teens	10 AM–5:30 PM daily	Page 232
Teens	Sat. 10–4; Tues.–Fri. by appointment	Page 233
All Ages	Mon.–Thurs. 10 AM–dusk; Fri.–Sat. 9 AM–midnight; Sun. 9 AM–dusk	Page 234

(continues)

Quick Guide to

Attraction	Location
Discovery Creek Children's Museum	4954 MacArthur Boulevard, NW
Clara Barton National Historic Site	5801 Oxford Road, Glen Echo, Maryland
Woodend Sanctuary	8940 Jones Mill Road, Chevy Chase, Maryland
The Washington Temple and Visitors Center of the Church of Jesus Christ of Latter-Day Saints	Stoneybrook Drive in Kensington, Maryland, off Beach Drive
The Dennis & Phillip Ratner Museum	10001 Old Georgetown Road, Bethesda, Maryland
National Capital Trolley Museum	1313 Bonifant Road, Silver Spring, Maryland
University of Maryland	College Park, Maryland
National Cryptologic Museum	9800 Savage Road, Fort Meade, Maryland

morning, my fellow Americans. You don't know how long I've been waiting to say those words."

As far back as 1701, Pierre L'Enfant had planned for the city to have its own cathedral, but as in most federal undertakings, a great deal of time elapsed before the deed was under way. Taking a

Uptown & Suburban Maryland Attractions

Age Range	Hours	Details on
Tykes and Tweens	Sat.–Sun. 10 AM–3 PM	Page 236
All Ages	10 AM–5 PM daily	Page 237
All Ages	Mon.–Fri. 9 AM–5 PM Grounds: Dawn to dusk daily	Page 238
All Ages	Visitor center: 10 AM–9 PM daily	Page 239
All Ages	Mon.–Thurs. noon–4; Sun. 10 AM–4:30 PM	Page 240
All Ages	Hours vary	Page 242
Teens		Page 243
Tweens and Teens	Weekdays 9 AM–4 PM	Page 243

mere 83 years from President Theodore Roosevelt's laying of the cornerstone until its completion in 1990, the "Cathedral," as it's affectionately called in D.C., is a beautiful place to explore. This Gothic-style church, the sixth largest in the world (and one of the few in the world to have both heat and air-conditioning), is built in

Helpful Hint

All ages are welcome here. It's a house of worship, so reminders about quiet behavior are essential. Children under 5 might find touring here difficult.

the shape of a cross. The building contains no steel framework; only the stone flying buttresses support the vaulted ceilings. All the artwork, both interior and exterior, was made by hand. Of particular note are the stone carvings—children especially love discovering the gargoyles perched high above their heads. Kids also appreciate the **Children's Chapel,** complete with pint-size chairs and pipe organ.

The **Gloria in Excelsis Central Tower,** the highest point in Washington (its address is officially Mount St. Alban), is said to be among the last towers in the world to contain both a carillon and a 10-bell peal. Push the seventh-floor button in the elevator to get to the **Pilgrim Observation Gallery,** where you can see a film about the cathedral's history and enjoy extraordinary panoramic views from 70 windows that overlook Washington and Virginia.

Also sharing the Cathedral's landscaped acreage are two attractive gardens, one of which is the medieval-style **Bishop's Garden** (complete with a maze). Its herbs, teas, and jellies, along with books and gifts, are sold in the adjacent **Herb Cottage.** At the greenhouse you can buy growing plants. The Cathedral also has a

Smart Stuff

For Tykes and Tweens . . . Look at David Macaulay's book *Cathedral.* Medieval buildings frequently had gargoyles (strange-looking creatures often used as water spouts) decorating the eaves. How many can you find? Draw a picture of one you'd like to put on the roof of your school. (C.)

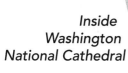

*Inside
Washington
National Cathedral*

gift shop, in which you can even purchase snacks to enjoy on the grounds.

The Gargoyle's Den, for ages 6 to 12, focuses on crafts used to build a cathedral, from making stained glass to carving gargoyles. It's held on Saturday from 10 to 2. Family Saturday, held once a month, is for parents with kids ages 4 to 8. Make reservations at 202/537–2934. A treat for the more refined in your group would be the tour followed by afternoon tea at 1:30 on Tuesday and Wednesday. Make reservations weeks or even months in advance by calling 202/537–8993.

Several restaurants are within easy walking distance. **Cactus Cantina** (3300 Wisconsin Avenue, NW; 202/686–7222) dishes up Mexican food in colorful surroundings. **Café Deluxe** (3228 Wisconsin Avenue, NW; 202/686–2233) serves excellent American food,

Smart Stuff

For Tweens and Teens . . . The Washington National Cathedral was begun in 1907 and completed in 1990. Medieval cathedrals frequently took a century or more to construct. A project so massive usually involved the entire community. What kinds of skills do you think were needed for this undertaking? **(D.)**

Smart Stuff

For Tweens and Teens . . .
Who is the only president
buried in the Washington
National Cathedral? (E.)

including some vegetarian offerings. **American City Diner** (5532 Connecticut Avenue, NW; 202/244–1949) is a short drive away. With lots of comfort food and a long list of floats, malts, and milkshakes, it's a fun stop for the whole family. It's open 7 AM to 11 PM Sunday to Thursday, and 24 hours Friday and Saturday.

> Metro: Tenleytown (it's a 20-minute walk south along Connecticut Avenue)
>
> Take any N bus up Massachusetts Avenue, NW, from Dupont Circle, or a 30-series bus on Wisconsin Avenue, from Georgetown or Tenleytown or Friendship Heights
>
> Massachusetts and Wisconsin avenues, NW
>
> Open weekdays 10 to 5:30; Saturday 10 to 4:30; Sunday 8 to 5
>
> For guided tours, call 202/537–6207
>
> Pipe organ demonstrations Monday and Wednesday at 12:30; carillon recitals Saturday at 12:30
>
> Donation
>
> 202/537–6200
>
> www.nationalcathedral.org

American University

For Teens . . . Set on a 75-acre campus that was a Civil War army post, American University draws students from all over the country and around the world. Its suburban-style campus is within Washington's city limits, with access to downtown and Georgetown (a favorite student haunt). Many come here to take advantage of the government internship programs nearby. The school has connections with nearly 1,000 private, nonprofit, or government institutions. Although it was founded under Methodist auspices, by an

1893 act of Congress American University is a comfortable environment for students of all faiths and cultures.

Providing space for performances, concerts, and exhibits, the imposing new Katzen Arts Center sits at the corner of Massachusetts and Nebraska avenues, NW. Its galleries house the university's own collections as well as contemporary art from around the world. A 6,000-square-foot sculpture garden complements the building's modern design.

> Metro: Tenleytown
> 4400 Massachusetts Avenue, NW, between Ward and Wesley
>   circles
> 202/885–6000
> www.american.edu

Hillwood Museum and Gardens

For Teens . . . Not only did Battle Creek, Michigan, bring us some of our most famous cereals, but it also gave us the redoubtable General Foods heiress, Marjorie Merriweather Post. Hillwood Museum, the 41-room mansion that houses her incredible collection of decorative arts, was her home until she died in 1973. Filled with priceless objets d'art, primarily from France and Russia, Hillwood is perhaps best known for its treasures from the

Helpful Hint
Adults, of course, will especially enjoy this lovely museum and its grounds. Children under 12 are not admitted.

czarist era, purchased when Post's husband, Joseph Davies, was ambassador to Russia in the 1930s. Her youngest daughter, film star Dina Merrill, described how these unwanted remnants from royalty were stacked in warehouses and how Marjorie climbed through the piles to select her choices. Collections of china place settings, tapestries, French Sevres porcelain, masterpieces by Carl Fabergé, oil paintings and furniture from Catherine the Great, and gilded French provincial furniture fill this Rock Creek Park mansion.

The 25 acres of elegant grounds include an assortment of lovely gardens and a cabin that holds artifacts from Ms. Post's home in the Adirondacks. This collection includes baskets, beaded items, moccasins, pottery, and blankets from the Navajo, Hopi, Acoma, and Santa Clara tribes.

Helpful Hint

Hillwood also has a gift shop, but don't expect to scoop up deals on pricey antiques.

In the old stables is a café that serves Russian specialties and English afternoon tea. The lunch menu changes during the year, but Russian delicacies such as blintzes, borscht, and stuffed cabbage are usually offered. It's open Tuesday to Saturday, 11 to 4:30.

Books and movies provide background for all the beautiful and interesting objects seen at Hillwood. For example, the classic movie *Dr. Zhivago,* from the bestseller by Boris Pasternak, is still unparalleled in its user-friendly portrayal of a turbulent time in Russia (teens). *Reds,* with Warren Beatty, gives more of a political view (teens).

> Metro: Van Ness–UDC (it's a 20-minute walk from the station)
> Take the L1 or L2 bus from the Van Ness–UDC Metro station to the corner of Connecticut Avenue and Tilden Street
> 4155 Linnean Avenue, NW
> Open Tuesday to Saturday 10 to 5, and on select Sundays throughout the year; closed January and most federal holidays
> Admission
> 202/686–5807
> www.hillwoodmuseum.org

Rock Creek Nature Center

For All Ages . . . Rock Creek Park, 2,100 acres of parkland running through the center of Washington, has something for everyone. At

Rock Creek Nature Center kids can handle animal pelts, feathers, and bones and watch a beehive in action. The reptiles, amphibians, and fish are fed daily at 4— you can help feed them on Friday. Ranger-led programs

Helpful Hint

Rock Creek Park is less accessible by public transportation, so it's a good idea to bring a car.

include nature talks, forest hikes, and craft demonstrations. The Discovery Room has hands-on activities for youngsters from ages 2 to 5.

The 75-seat planetarium offers free weekend and Wednesday afternoon shows (children over age 4 are welcome). Once a month between April and November the National Capital Astronomers pair up with the National Park Service to present "Exploring the Sky," an evening program that lets young people explore the night sky with powerful telescopes.

Smart Stuff

For Tykes . . . Look for the live lizards and frogs. Do you know what a chameleon is? If you had a lizard of your own, what would you name it? Where would it live? What would it need from you?

For the Daniel Boone in some of us, there are self-guided nature trails. Make sure to sign out a Discovery Pack at the front desk for each child in your group. The binoculars, field microscope, and magnifying lens included in the kit will make the walk more interesting. For more enterprising youngsters between 5 and 12, ask for the "Junior Ranger Activity Book." When children complete five of the eight activities, they earn Junior Ranger certificates and patches.

There's much more to do in Rock Creek Park. There's an especially nice playground at the edge of D.C. in Chevy Chase, Maryland, that's been a family favorite for several generations. **Meadowbrook Recreation Center** (7901 Meadowbrook Lane;

301/650–2600), just off East-West Highway, has beautiful picnic areas, as well as swinging, climbing, and sliding equipment for the little ones and tennis and basketball courts and ball fields for the older kids and adults. A welcome reprieve when the kids—or the adults!—need a break.

Smart Stuff

For Tweens . . . Animals, plants, and people lived in this area of what is now the city of Washington, D.C., long before European colonists came to America. Ask the ranger about the Native American civilization here. Can you find some stone arrowheads by the nature trail?

Two nature books we like for tykes are *Kids Camp!: Activities for the Backyard or Wilderness,* by Laurie Carlson, and *Nibble, Nibble: Poems for Children,* by Margaret Wise Brown. For tweens there's *Backyard Birds,* by Jonathan P. Latimer; *Backyard Stars: A Guide for Home and the Road; Glow-in-the-Dark Constellations: A Field Guide for Young Stargazers,* by C. E. Thompson and Randy Chewning; and *The Insect Book: A Basic Guide to the Collection and Care of Common Insects for Young Children,* by Connie Zakowski. For everyone there's *Talking to Fireflies, Shrinking the Moon: Nature Activities for All Ages,* by Edward Duensing; and *The Lorax,* by Dr. Seuss. (All ages *need* this one.)

As for movies, tweens should check out the animated version of *Johnny Appleseed,* read by Garrison Keillor, and *Willy the Sparrow. Bambi* is good for tykes and tweens—but prepare them for the sad parts. Kids' reactions can really surprise you. We know of one instance when a young child was totally distraught during *Bambi* because she thought the young deer had disappeared, when in fact he had merely grown up.

No Metro stop
5200 Glover Road, NW

Open Wednesday to Sunday 9 to 5; closed January 1, July 4,
     Thanksgiving, and December 25
Call ahead or check online for a calendar of special events
202/895–6070
www.nps.gov/rocr

Peirce Mill

For All Ages . . . Take a trip back in time to see the best thing since
before sliced bread: how corn and wheat become the flour that kids
are used to seeing in the bakery. The restored 19th-century stone
building houses a gristmill, complete with an enormous waterwheel
outside and a ponderous millstone inside. Peirce Mill presents a
real-life example of the way an important agricultural process
worked in the 1820s. At this writing, this historic building was
closed for restoration. Call ahead to make sure it is open.

Smart Stuff

For Tweens . . . Colonial mills like Peirce Mill depended
on waterpower to grind their grain. What other power
sources can you think of for this job? **(F.)**

No Metro stop
3545 Williamsburg Lane, NW, at the corner of Tilden Street
     and Beach Drive
Wednesday to Friday 202/895–6070 or weekends 202/
     282–0927
www.nps.gov/pimi

Smart Stuff

For Teens . . . Areas of the United States were developed specifically because of their proximity to power
sources. Can you single out some places where economic progress has come on the heels of the development of an industrial power source? **(G.)**

*Historic
Peirce Mill in
Rock Creek Park*

Peirce Barn

For Tweens and Teens . . . Formerly the carriage house belonging to Isaac Peirce, who built Peirce Mill, this gallery is now home to the works of local artists. Exhibits include photographs, paintings, prints, sculptures, and ceramics.

No Metro stop
2401 Tilden Street, NW
Open weekends noon to 5
202/895–6070
www.nps.gov/pimi

National Museum of Health and Medicine

For Older Tweens and Teens . . . During the Civil War, diseases killed more soldiers than did bullets. This museum, housed at Walter Reed Army Medical Center, was established in 1862 to explore the causes. Antique diagnostic and surgical instruments and an extensive microscope collection share space with a bone from Abraham Lincoln's skull and one from President Garfield's spine, diseased organs, and body parts, and an exhibit focusing on biology and anatomy.

The modern world is not exempt from troubles: an exhibit to educate visitors about HIV is called "Living in a World with AIDS."

A few books of interest here are: *An American Plague*, by Jim Murphy (tweens and teens); *Pox Americana: The Great Smallpox Epidemic of 1775–1782*, by Elizabeth Fenn (teens); and *Year of Wonder* (a novel), by Geraldine Brooks (teens).

A classroom film on the circulatory system, *Hemo the Magnificent*, was written and directed by Oscar-winning director Frank Capra (tweens and teens). *Fantastic Voyage* is another classic that focuses on the human body and how it works—it *is* fantastic (tweens and teens).

Smart Stuff

For Teens . . . It's widely acknowledged that more Civil War soldiers died of disease than were killed on battlefields. If you were a doctor on staff in a Civil War hospital, what medical breakthrough do you think you would have wanted most?

Metro: Takoma Park or Silver Spring, then a short taxi ride
6900 Georgia Avenue, NW (Building 54) inside the grounds
    of the Walter Reed Army Medical Center
Open daily 10 to 5:30; closed December 25
Call for tour arrangements
Donation
202/782–2200
nmhm.washingtondc.museum

The Kreeger Museum

For Teens . . . Set among the mansions on Foxhall Road is this contemporary house-turned-museum, filled with modern art. Carmen and David Lloyd Kreeger built this as their home, though they always intended it to become a museum to hold their collection. The building consists of 22-foot-square marble modules that contain works by van Gogh, Chagall, Monet, Cézanne, and Picasso. Every

Smart Stuff

For Teens . . . This museum was originally a family home. If you were the curator, what guidelines would you use for the kinds of art to be placed in each room? What kinds of art would you want in your bedroom if you could choose anything you wanted?

room in the building (including the bathrooms) is filled with original art. Out back is a wonderful sculpture terrace.

For yummy eating nearby, a popular choice is **Chef Geoff's** (3201 New Mexico Avenue, NW; 202/237–7800), a neighborhood bistro that serves hamburgers and pizzas along with more upscale fare. It's open Monday to Thursday 11:30 to 10, Friday and Saturday 11:30 to 10:30, and Sunday 10 to 10.

> No Metro station
> 2401 Foxhall Road, NW
> Saturday 10 to 4, Tuesday to Friday by appointment; closed in August, and January 1, Thanksgiving and the day after, and December 25
> Tours Tuesday through Friday at 10:30 and 1:30; reservations required; tours Saturday 10:30, 12, and 2 (reservations not necessary on Saturday)
> Fee
> Children under 12 are not permitted
> 202/337–3050 or 202/338–3552
> www.kreegermuseum.org

Glen Echo Park

For All Ages . . . Offering more than 100 different classes in art, dance, music, and theater, Glen Echo Park emphasizes the arts and cultural education. Housed here are art studios—some in primitive-looking, thatched-roof huts called yurts—for pottery, glassmaking, quilting, jewelry-making, painting, and metalwork. Beautiful handmade pieces are for sale. The **Spanish Ballroom,** breathtakingly renovated, is a treat. An old stone tower houses the **Glen Echo Gallery,** with original artwork, books, postcards, and souvenirs.

Since 1921 the beautiful antique Dentzel **carousel** has entertained kids. It's one of only 27 of the craftsman's creations remaining in North America. (If you're coming *just* for the carousel, call ahead to make sure it's running.) Park rangers can tell you more about this restored ride.

Glen Echo has quite a history, as native Washingtonians will remember. What began as a cultural and educational center in the 1800s (by the National Chautauqua Assembly) later metamorphosed into a colorful amusement park, complete with swimming pool and ballroom. Closed in 1968, it was turned over to the National Park Service in 1970.

No Metro station

7300 MacArthur Boulevard, Glen Echo, Maryland

Open Monday through Thursday 10 to dusk, Friday and Saturday 9 to midnight, Sunday 9 to dusk; closed January 1, Thanksgiving Day, and December 25

Tours with rangers weekends at 2; call to arrange other days or times.

Free; admission fees for carousel, puppet shows, theater

301/492–6229

www.glenechopark.org

Residential neighborhoods hide small parks and playgrounds in many areas of the city. **Battery-Kemble Park** (Chain Bridge

Helpful Hint

You can do a lot of walking here, some uphill, so wear comfortable shoes and take your time.

The **Snack Bar** (open when the carousel runs) sells ice cream, and other snacks. The nearby picnic grove is a great place to enjoy your lunch alfresco.

Road, between Nebraska Avenue and MacArthur Boulevard, NW; 202/895–6000) is colorful in any season. There are lots of hills for youngsters to climb up and roll or sled down. Open spaces invite kite flying and ball playing.

Discovery Creek Children's Museum

For Tykes and Tweens . . . A real discovery on the museum scene is a place with two campuses, the Discovery Creek Children's Museum, now a part of the Living Classroom Foundation. A dedicated staff and many volunteers, including teenagers, make it possible for groups of kids to have an incredible variety of hands-on experiences. They can produce rainstorms (complete with clouds), enter a volcano, and crawl through a mineshaft to view a cross-section of the earth. They come face-to-face with live animals, hike to a local creek to learn about the water cycle, and create crafts. A small climbing wall is available for ages 4 to 11 the first weekend of each month. The list of activities is more impressive than any other nature program we've seen. Beautiful educational materials are available in advance.

Helpful Hint

Get in touch with Discovery Creek Children's Museum before your visit to get a list of special activities.

Along MacArthur Boulevard the pickings are slim, but there are a few restaurants worth a visit. One old favorite is **Listrani's** (5100 MacArthur Boulevard, NW; 202/363–0619). A kid-friendly neighborhood favorite, Listrani's serves pizza, pasta, and other Italian dishes. For a picnic in the park, try **Glen Echo Pizza and Subs** (7307 MacArthur Boulevard; 301/263–0414). It's a carry-out with pizzas and subs that are sure to fill up hungry tummies.

No Metro station

Museum at 4954 MacArthur Boulevard, NW, and Old Stable Building at Glen Echo Park, 7300 MacArthur Boulevard, Glen Echo, Maryland

Open weekends 10 to 3, weekdays for prearranged groups

Admission
202/488–0627
www.livingclassroomsdc.org

Clara Barton National Historic Site

For All Ages . . . Adjacent to Glen Echo Park is Clara Barton National Historic Site, the last home of the founder of the American Red Cross. Known as the "angel of the battlefield," Clara Barton left her government job during the Civil War to bring supplies and medical care to soldiers on the battlefield. Although she had no formal training as a nurse, she had natural ability and a great deal of bravery. She was soon asked to supervise all the Union Army's nurses. Following the Civil War she gave lectures on her experiences. During this time she learned about the Red Cross that had been founded in Switzerland in 1864. She spent years lobbying for federal government support to found an American chapter, which was finally accomplished in 1881. From 1897 to 1904 the building served as the headquarters for the organization.

Smart Stuff

For Tykes . . . Pretend you were a nurse during wartime. Draw pictures of the kinds of supplies you think you would need.

Humanity, impartiality, neutrality, independence, voluntary service, unity, and universality are the seven guiding beliefs of the American Red Cross. It helps victims of natural disasters, including earthquakes, floods, and storms, as well as medical disasters. Clara Barton didn't retire until she was 83. Her life is an example of selfless public service.

Some of the books about Clara Barton focus on different aspects of her life. We recommend *Clara Barton: Red Cross Pioneer*, by Matthew G. Grant, for tykes and tweens; and *The Story of Clara Barton*, by Zachary Kent, and *Clara Barton: Angel of the Battlefield*, by Rae Bains, for tweens.

Smart Stuff

For Tweens and Teens . . . The Red Cross has chapters all over the world. What health issues do you see worldwide today? What kinds of remedies would you suggest?

No Metro station
5801 Oxford Road, Glen Echo, Maryland
Open daily 10 to 5; closed January 1, Thanksgiving Day, and
    December 25
Guided tours every hour until 4; call ahead for groups of 10
    or more
301/320–1410
www.nps.gov/clba

Woodend Sanctuary

For All Ages . . . The Audubon Naturalist Society's peaceful 40-acre estate Woodend serves as a wildlife sanctuary. Explore the meadows and woods and follow a self-guided nature trail. Inside the main building, formerly a private residence, visit the **Wilbur Fisk Banks Memorial Collection of Birds,** with 594 different kinds of bird specimens on display. The bookstore has animal-friendly gifts, such as birdfeeders and animal treats, as well as a wide selection of nature books and educational toys. Picnicking is allowed, but in the true spirit of conservation, visitors are responsible for taking their trash with them when they leave.

Many books on related subjects are available here and in other bookstores and libraries. *Stokes Beginner's Guide to Birds,* a "flip book" by Donald and Lillian Stokes, is good for very young visitors. Two very effective guides for tweens are the *Pocket Guide to Song-birds,* by the National Audubon Society, and *National Geographic Garden Birds: My First Pocket Guide,* by David Lindsey. Tweens and teens might find *The National Audubon Society Field Guide to North American Weather,* by David M. Ludlum, of interest; they are usually especially interested in snow (and "snow days"). *The Audubon Backyard Birdwatcher: Birdfeeders and Bird Gardens,* by Robert Burton, appeals to teens and adults who hope to lure more varieties of birds to their own turf.

A few minutes west of Woodend—and just south of the Capital Beltway—is a friendly shopping strip featuring **Einstein Brothers Bagels** (8542 Connecticut Avenue, Chevy Chase, MD; 301/656–0766), a good stop for yummy sandwiches, soups, and salads. It's open weekdays 5 AM to 7 PM, weekends 6 AM to 6 PM. If you want some snacks to take along "just in case," you can always visit the **Chevy Chase Supermarket** (8531 Connecticut Avenue, Chevy Chase, MD; 301/656–5133), a family-owned, neighborhood grocery store directly across the street.

> No Metro station
> 8940 Jones Mill Road, Chevy Chase, Maryland
> Grounds open daily dawn to dusk; main building open weekdays 9 to 5
> Call ahead for information on special programs and events for families
> 301/652–9188 or 301/652–3606
> www.audubonnaturalist.org

The Washington Temple and Visitors Center of the Church of Jesus Christ of Latter-Day Saints

For All Ages . . . Like the spires of a faraway castle, the striking white marble steeples of the Washington Temple of Jesus Christ of Latter-day Saints serve as a special landmark in the Washington suburbs. The building is just off Exit 33 on the Washington Beltway, about a 30-minute drive from the center of the city. It offers a glimpse into one of a handful of non–Native American religions founded in America. With a missionary component of worldwide volunteers, the Church of Jesus Christ of Latter-day Saints has become truly international.

The visitor center has multimedia presentations and hands-on displays, as well as seasonal events and programs, including a festival of lights for Christmas. Books and videos are available for young children, teens, and adults. The temple itself is not open to the public, but the grounds provide lovely walks.

In preparation for or to follow up a visit here, an explanatory book might be helpful. *What Do Mormons Believe?*, by Rex E. Lee, is a good source for teens. A very old but informative film about the history of the Mormons in the United States is *Brigham Young, Frontiersman*.

No Metro station
On Stoneybrook Drive in Kensington, Maryland
Visitor center open daily 10 to 9
301/587–0144 for visitor center

The Dennis & Phillip Ratner Museum

For All Ages . . . This jewel of a museum sits unobtrusively—except for an enormous new steel archway called "Genesis"—near an upscale shopping strip in Bethesda, Maryland. Phillip Ratner, a local sculptor, built this museum to house part of his world-renowned collection. Here you can also find moving images of immigrants to Ellis Island, a model for his work at Ellis Island. In the galleries on the first level are temporary exhibits of the works of emerging artists. On the second floor are more than 100 of the works on permanent exhibit, most of them scenes from the Bible. In an adjacent building, the carriage house, kids will especially enjoy discovering the colorful, whimsical sculptures from children's stories (including some of Ratner's own tales).

More good news: you're in an area where there are several good choices for snacks and meals. Take advantage! Just down the block from the Ratner Museum is **Geppetto's** (10257 Old Georgetown Road; 301/493–9230), complete with Pinocchio decorations. At this local favorite, in the Wildwood Shopping Center, you can choose from a wide variety of pizzas and your favorite Italian dishes. Across the street, in the Georgetown Square Shopping Center, you can find two different choices. **Hamburger Hamlet** (10400 Old Georgetown Road; 301/897–5350), a link in this national chain, is especially known for its many kinds of delicious hamburgers and scrumptious desserts. The menu is lengthy, and we can vouch for almost any choice. Sometimes there can be a long wait at suppertime, so come early. **Bradley's Ice Cream Shoppe** (10400 Old Georgetown Road; 301/530–7766) has more than ice cream (though that's delicious, of course!). It offers gourmet sandwiches on all kinds of fresh breads.

Smart Stuff

For Tweens and Teens . . . Pick a sculpture to study. What is distinctive about Ratner's use of the human form? What elements of the sculpture convey the emotional impact of the story represented?

And as long as you're here, there's a nearby remedy for all those with worn-out shoes. Just beyond the above-named restaurants is **DSW Designer Shoe Warehouse** (10400 Old Georgetown Road). There's an expansive selection of discounted shoes (and socks) for everyone in the family. It's a treat for both your wallet and your feet.

As long as you're in Bethesda, here are two more suggestions. They are not within walking distance of the Ratner Museum, but are worth the trip. The old-fashioned **Tastee Diner** (7731 Woodmont Avenue; 301/642–3970) is a longtime local favorite. It's as common to see teens hanging out here as their parents, though not necessarily at the same time of day. The menu is extensive, the food satisfying, and it's open 24 hours.

There's also a free bus, the **Bethesda Circulator** (301/215–6661; www.bethesda.org), that travels all over the area, passing many restaurants, galleries, and shops along the way. It runs Monday through Thursday 7 AM to midnight, Friday 7 AM to 2 AM, and Saturday 6 PM to 2 AM. You can pick it up at the Bethesda Metro station, or anywhere along the well-marked route. The "trolley" is accessible for the disabled as well. Kids love it!

> Metro: Grosvenor, then a short ride by bus or taxi
> 10001 Old Georgetown Road, Bethesda, Maryland
> Open Monday through Thursday noon to 4, Sunday 10 to
>   4:30; closed holidays (call first)
> Tours by appointment
> Free
> 301/897–1518
> www.ratnermuseum.com

National Capital Trolley Museum

For All Ages . . . To return to an era when getting there was half the fun—and twice the time—we recommend the National Capital Trolley Museum. This museum in suburban Maryland houses historic trolleys from the D.C. area and around the world.

You can tour exhibits, watch a slide show or a 10-minute historical film, and marvel at a working-model trolley of the old Chevy Chase line from the 1930s, complete with miniature people and scenery. But the highlight of a visit is definitely the trolley ride, now through the woods on tracks laid lovingly by museum volunteers. It's a bumpy journey, but kids will enjoy the bouncy seats and the colorful period advertisements plastered overhead. Remnants of Washington's old trolley tracks can still be found in Georgetown, making a car ride there a bumpy experience. Adults might wonder what we grew up with that will one day be seen as antiques—besides ourselves.

Because the Trolley Museum is on parkland, this is a wonderful place for a picnic. There are tables right behind the museum.

> Metro: Twinbrook or Glenmont, then a short ride by bus or
>   taxi
> 1313 Bonifant Road, Silver Spring, Maryland
> Open January to mid-March, weekends noon to 5; mid-
>   March to mid-May and October to mid-November,

Thursday and Friday 10 to 2, weekends noon to 5; mid-June to mid-August, Thursday and Friday 11 to 3, weekends noon to 5; December, weekends 5 to 9; closed December 24, 25, 31, and January 1
Trolley rides every half hour; last ride half hour before closing
Call ahead for free summer programs for groups of 10 or more
Admission fee
301/384–6088
www.dctrolley.org

University of Maryland

For Teens . . . Big big big! The University of Maryland in College Park, on a beautiful sprawling site, is the flagship campus of the public research university for the state of Maryland. A center of research and graduate and undergraduate education in myriad fields, the university is worth a visit for teens interested in a large, diverse suburban college environment. Stop at the Dairy for a cone. Founded with an agricultural focus in 1862, this place still produces great ice cream from its own herd of Holsteins. It's open weekdays 10 to 4.

Metro: College Park, then a 10-minute walk to campus
Visitor center Room 1201 in Turner Hall on Baltimore Avenue
Visitor center open during school year weekdays 8 to 5, Saturday 9 to 3
301/314–7777
www.umd.edu

National Cryptologic Museum

For Tweens and Teens . . . A peek behind the secret curtain surrounding our intelligence community, the National Cryptologic Museum has thousands of artifacts on display. The craft of code making and code breaking will fascinate youngsters. Teens and adults will enjoy the revelations of cryptology's impact on historic events.

Next door to this museum is National Vigilance Park, housing two reconnaissance airplanes used for clandestine missions. Kids will be wowed.

A book for tweens is *Top Secret: A Handbook of Codes, Ciphers, and Secret Writing*, by Paul Janeczko.

No Metro station
Savage Road, Fort Meade, Maryland
Open weekdays 9 to 4; first and third Saturday of the month
    10 to 2; closed federal holidays
Schedule group tours in advance
301/688–5849
www.nsa.gov/about/cryptologic_heritage/museum/

Where to Stay in the Uptown Area

The good news is that this is generally a safe area, with restaurants and shops and easily accessible subway stops. The bad news is that it can be a little pricey. Do your arithmetic as you plan.

Days Inn Connecticut Avenue
4400 Connecticut Avenue, NW
202/244–5600 or 800/329–7466
www.daysinn.com
Metro: Van Ness–UDC

Embassy Suites at the Chevy Chase Pavilion
4300 Military Road, NW
202/362–9300 or 800/362–2779
www.embassysuitesdc.com
Metro: Friendship Heights

Marriott Wardman Park Hotel
2660 Woodley Road, NW
202/328–2000
www.marriott.com
Metro: Woodley Park–Zoo

Where to Stay in Suburban Maryland

Convenience and sometimes better bargains can be had in some of the suburban Maryland areas. Here are a few suggestions:

Hyatt Regency Bethesda
One Bethesda Metro Center
Bethesda, Maryland 20814
301/657–1234 or 800/233–1234
www.hyattregencybethesda.com
Metro: Bethesda

Crowne Plaza
8777 Georgia Avenue
Silver Spring, Maryland 20910
301/589–0800 or 800/227–6963
www.crowneplaza.com
Metro: Silver Spring

Quality Inn & Suites
7200 Baltimore Avenue
College Park, Maryland 20740
301/864–5820 or 800/228–5151
www.choicehotels.com
Metro: College Park

Answers to Smart Stuff Questions

A. Kids might be surprised to learn that many everyday products (such as rubber and medicines) have their origins in the rain forest. A debate between the "industrialists" and the "conservationists" might be fun. Changes in climate, natural resources, and living or working patterns of indigenous peoples have all resulted from deforestation. Exploring these issues would make a good research project.

B. China.

C. Some especially amusing gargoyles found on the Cathedral are a bearded hippie with a protest sign, Darth Vader (from *Star*

Wars), a weeping sea turtle (it's too cold up there?), and the eerie-looking skeleton of a horse (no hay up there, either).

D. Included in a community-wide effort would have been church officials, architects, builders, stonecutters, painters, calligraphers, sculptors, patrons, and even serfs to do the manual labor. Instead of unions, there were craft-based guilds for artisans. Frequently, those who began such a project did not live long enough to see its completion, and that wasn't due to labor negotiations.

E. Woodrow Wilson.

F. Some other power sources are mules, horses, or oxen; air–wind (windmill); electricity or batteries.

G. For example, New England mill towns, Hoover Dam, and the Tennessee Valley Authority.

CHAPTER

10

Northeast
& Southeast

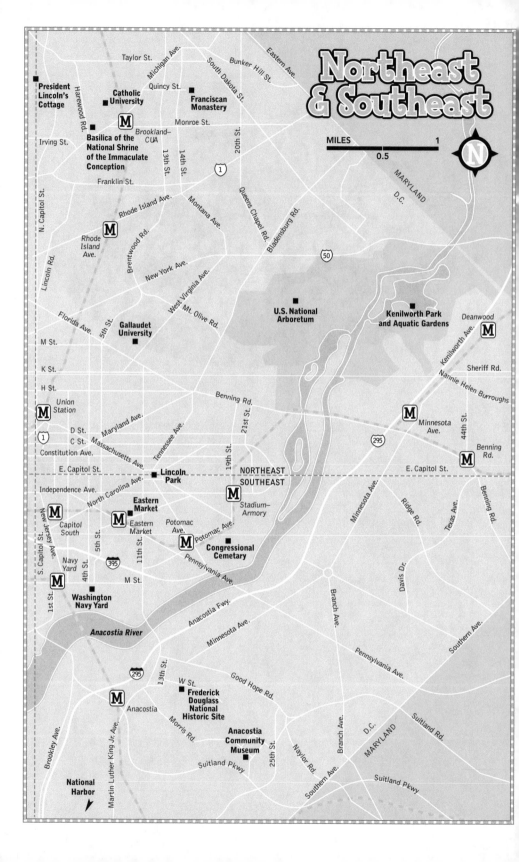

From the beauty of nature to the beauty of the spirit, Northeast and Southeast Washington have treasures to discover. The **National Arboretum** and **Kenilworth Aquatic Gardens** overflow with color and fragrance in the warmer months. From the **Basilica of the National Shrine of the Immaculate Conception** to the **Emancipation Statue** in **Lincoln Park,** this section of the city commemorates the strivings of man's spirit.

Catholic University

For Teens . . . Talk about a campus with a landmark! **The Basilica of the National Shrine of the Immaculate Conception** is the eye-catching centerpiece of Catholic University. Known for its outstanding drama and music departments (the training ground for some famous stage and film stars), Catholic University is the only U.S. university operating under specific papal authority. The Gothic buildings, set on a lush green campus, make an interesting stop for college-bound young people.

A favorite hangout for Catholic U. folks is **Colonel Brooks Tavern** (901 Monroe Street, NE; 202/529–4002). The friendly staff can guide you through a menu filled with enormous and mouthwa-

Quick Guide to

Attraction	Location
Catholic University	620 Michigan Avenue, NE
★Basilica of the National Shrine of the Immaculate Conception	Michigan Avenue at 4th Street, NE (on the campus of Catholic University)
Franciscan Monastery	1400 Quincy Street, NE
President Lincoln's Cottage	3700 North Capitol Street, NW
Gallaudet University	800 Florida Avenue, NE
U.S. National Arboretum	3501 New York Avenue, NE (another entrance on R Street, NE)
Lincoln Park	E. Capitol Street between 11th and 13th streets, NE
Eastern Market	7th Street (between North Carolina and C streets, SE)
Washington Navy Yard	6th and M streets, SE
Anacostia Community Museum	1901 Fort Place, SE
★Frederick Douglass National Historic Site	1411 W Street, SE
National Harbor	Waterfront Street, just off Routes 95 and 210
Kenilworth Park and Aquatic Gardens	Anacostia Avenue and Douglass Street, NE; ⅛ mi south of Jct. U.S. 50

Northeast & Southeast Attractions

Age Range	Hours	Details on
Teens	Tours: Mon.–Fri. 10:30 AM–2 PM	Page 249
Tweens and Teens	Open daily. April–Oct., 7 AM–7 PM; Nov.–March, 7 AM–6 PM	Page 252
Tweens and Teens	Daily 9 AM–5 PM	Page 254
Tweens and Teens	Visitor Center Mon.–Sat. 9:30 AM–4:30 PM; Sun. 11:30 AM–5:30 PM	Page 255
Teens	Vistor center Mon.–Fri. 9 AM–4:30 PM	Page 255
All Ages	8 AM–5 PM daily	Page 256
All Ages	24 hours daily	Page 258
All Ages	Tues.–Fri. 8 AM–5 PM; Sat. 6 AM–6 PM; Sun. 9 AM–4 PM	Page 260
All Ages	Mon.–Fri. 9 AM–5 PM; Sat.–Sun. 10 AM–5 PM	Page 260
All Ages	10 AM–5 PM daily	Page 262
Tweens and Teens	Mid-Oct.–mid-Apr. 9 AM–4 PM; mid-Apr.–mid-Oct. 9 AM–5 PM	Page 264
All Ages		Page 265
All Ages	7 AM–4 PM daily	Page 266

tering sandwiches, such as "The Colonel's Favorite," a triple-decker affair of turkey, cheese, pastrami, and coleslaw. Grilled vegetable enchiladas make a tasty appetizer. It's open Sunday to Friday 11 AM to 1 AM, Saturday 11:30 AM to 1 AM.

> Metro: Brookland–CUA
> 620 Michigan Avenue, NE
> Tours during the school year, weekdays at 10:30 and 2;
>   summer tours at 10:30; sign up at Web site
> 202/319–5305 or 800/673–2772
> www.cua.edu

★Basilica of the National Shrine of the Immaculate Conception

For Tweens and Teens . . . The blue, red, and gold-leaf mosaic dome atop the Basilica of the National Shrine of the Immaculate Conception is a local landmark. The largest Catholic church in the Western Hemisphere, it was built without a steel frame. Architecturally, Byzantine and Romanesque styles (of 1,500 and 1,000 years ago) are quite different from the Gothic so frequently used in the United States.

Helpful Hint

This might be a difficult place for younger children because all visitors are expected to be quiet and respectful. Pick up a map at the crypt-level information desk.

You can explore 60 chapels throughout the building. Altars in 32 chapels are devoted to veneration of the Virgin Mary, who, by papal decree, became the patron saint of America. Two hundred stained-glass windows provide brilliant color. The 329-foot-high Knights' Bell Tower, topped with a large gilded cross, holds a 56-bell carillon. A striking mosaic, *Christ in Majesty,* adorns the main altar.

The Descent of the Holy Spirit, the largest mosaic, is in the dome. In 1999 a local artist's 38-ton marble relief, *The Universal Call to Holiness,* was installed on the basilica wall. The artist, George Carr, used local residents as his models for the 750-square-foot carving.

Whereas the upper building with its vaulted ceilings gives a feeling of spaciousness and serenity, the crypt is constructed in the spirit of the Roman catacombs. A gallery in the crypt displays the crown of Pope Paul VI from his coronation.

Snack alert: there's a cafeteria on the crypt level that is open daily 8 to 2. Hot meals, sandwiches, and desserts are served.

Smart Stuff

For Tweens and Teens . . . Who is the only American to be made a saint by the Catholic Church? (A.)

Daytime visits are recommended to allow visitors to better appreciate the beauty of the facility, *as well as for personal safety.* You have to walk through Catholic University to get to the Shrine, so wear comfortable shoes.

For general information about Catholicism, look at *American Catholicism,* by John Tracy Ellis (teens). There are some interesting films to learn from as well. *A Man for All Seasons* (tweens and teens) is one example. *The Scarlet and the Black* deals with one aspect of the Catholic Church during World War II (tweens and teens). Also enjoyable is *The Nun's Story,* starring the young Audrey Hepburn (teens); and *Heaven Knows, Mr. Allison,* starring Robert Mitchum and Deborah Kerr (teens). And a few more for teens: *The Messenger: The story of Joan of Arc* and *Entertaining Angels: The Dorothy Day Story* of the spiritual journey of an "American Mother Teresa."

> Metro: Brookland–CUA
> Michigan Avenue at 4th Street, NE, on the campus of
>   Catholic University
> Open April to October, daily 7 to 7; November to March,
>   daily 7 to 6

Guided tours Monday to Saturday 9 to 3, Sunday 1:30 to 4;
　　no tours Thanksgiving or December 25
Carillon recitals in summer, Sunday at 5:30; guest recitals
　　Sunday at 6
202/526–8300
www.nationalshrine.com

Franciscan Monastery

For Tweens and Teens . . . It's not every day you get an opportunity to wander around a working monastery (unless you live there, of course). On the grounds are famed rose gardens, among the largest in the country; some of the roses here even bloom in early winter. The church is modeled after the famous Hagia Sophia in Istanbul. Surrounding it are representations of the Stations of the Cross, the Garden of Gethsemane, and the Holy Sepulcher. Below are the catacombs, which replicate those used in Rome by early Christians who hid there to avoid persecution. The dark passageways with their steep stairs evoke some of the harrowing stories of early martyrs. If you're lucky, you will have a guide who relishes sharing some of these tales.

Metro: Brookland–CUA
1400 Quincy Street, NE
Church and gardens open daily 9 to 5
Guided tours Monday to Saturday at 10, 11, 1, 2, and 3;
　　Sunday at 1, 2, and 3.

Donation suggested
202/526–6800
www.myfranciscan.com

The Franciscan Monastery is an intriguing stop for visitors.

President Lincoln's Cottage

For Tweens and Teens . . . At one time a home for retired veterans, the Lincoln Cottage (the second most important site of Lincoln's presidency) and adjacent visitor center and grounds have undergone a complete "green" renovation. This was originally a place of respite for President Lincoln and his family, but government business was also accomplished here. The cottage was the setting for cabinet meetings, war strategy reviews, and the deliberations that led to the Emancipation Proclamation. This house provided its famous resident privacy, but not release from the burdens of the nation's most horrific war.

A small, guided group tour is available, with imagery relating stories of Lincoln and his family. One highlight for older tweens and teens is the award-winning "Lincoln's Toughest Decisions Gallery"; participants gather at a large wooden table reminiscent of Lincoln's Cabinet table, and try to decide how they might have advised the president on various issues.

> No Metro access; H8 Metrobus stops across from Eagle Gate; it's easier to come by car or taxi
>
> Entrance at "Eagle Gate," at the intersection of Rock Creek Church Road, NW, and Upshur Street, NW
>
> Visitor Center open Monday to Saturday 9:30 to 4:30, Sunday 11:30 to 5:30; closed January 1, Thanksgiving, and December 25
>
> Tours Monday to Saturday 10 to 3, Sunday noon to 4; reservations needed
>
> Fee; advance tickets (available online) recommended; photo ID required
>
> 202/829–0436 or 800/514–3849
>
> www.lincolncottage.org

Gallaudet University

For Teens . . . The world's *only* university for the deaf was established in 1864. It sits on a 99-acre campus with buildings in Victorian Gothic– and Queen Anne–style architecture. Gallaudet's 2,200 students made big news in 1988 by insisting that the school be headed by a deaf person. Dr. I. King Jordan became the first non-hearing president of Gallaudet University.

Gallaudet is especially recognized for its unique drama department. Three shows are produced annually in American Sign Language, with voice interpretation available for the hearing.

Because of the specialized nature of this university, it's the perfect stop if a member of your group is hearing impaired.

> No Metro station
> 800 Florida Avenue, NE
> Visitor center open weekdays 9 to 4:30
> Tours conducted in American Sign Language at 10 and 2; if an interpreter is needed, call 202/651–5199 two weeks in advance
> 202/651–5000
> www.gallaudet.edu

U.S. National Arboretum

For All Ages . . . A world-class collection of trees, bushes, and flowering annuals and perennials, this 444-acre site was established in 1927 for research and educational purposes. Trails lead visitors through various gardens filled with specialty plants. Teak benches invite rest and contemplation. The **National Bonsai and Penjing Museum Collection** showcases American, Chinese, and Japanese artistically dwarfed trees set amid miniature landscapes. The **National Herb Garden** is not only delightful to your nose but practical as well (no, you may not pick the herbs here to take home). From medicines to fuel, from dyes to beverages, from the delicious scents of licorice and English lavender to the unmistakable pungency of ginger, kids can learn how useful plants can be. In the **National Grove of State Trees**, hunt for your state's official tree (ask for a list at the Administration Building).

From the R Street entrance you can access the Information Center and the Administration Building, which has restrooms, public phones, and water fountains. In this same area is the aquatic garden, with pond lilies and large koi (colorful Japanese carp). These interesting fish are fed from the back terrace from April to November at 12:30, if requested ahead of time by a visiting group. Be sure kids do not feed them *anything* except the special food provided.

Smart Stuff

For Tykes . . . Look for the fish in the aquatic garden. What are these fish called? Draw a picture of your favorite.

Money jangling in your pockets? The **Arbor House Gift Shop** has souvenirs, soap, stuffed animals, postcards, books about plants and their care, and a complete guidebook for the gardens. The shop is open March through December, daily 10 to 3:30. There's nothing for the tummy except drinks, so bring a picnic and enjoy it in the Arboretum's beautiful settings.

If you don't mind a little walk, a block and a half north is the reasonably priced **Deli City** (2200 Bladensburg Road, NE; 202/526–1800), renowned for its corned beef. It's open weekdays 6 AM to 5 PM.

Smart Stuff

For Tweens and Teens . . . Find your state tree in the National Grove of State Trees. Why do you think this particular kind of tree was chosen? What is it usually used for? What are the state trees of Alaska and Hawaii? Could they be grown where *you* live? How about in each other's climates? **(B.)**

Books that might be of interest to tweens are *Tom Brown's Field Guide to Nature and Survival for Children,* by Tom Brown; and *Nature's Wonders: For the Young at Art: Creative Activities for Ages Six and Up Using the Please Touch Philosophy,* by Susan Striker and Sally Schaedler. For teens, there are *Silent Spring,* by Rachel Carson; *My*

First Summer in the Sierra, by John Muir; and *Walden,* by Henry David Thoreau.

> No Metro station
>
> 3501 New York Avenue, NE (another entrance on R Street, NE)
>
> Grounds open daily 8 to 5; closed December 25; check Web site for additional closings
>
> National Bonsai and Penjing Museum Collection open daily 10 to 3:30
>
> 40-minute tram tours mid-April to mid-October, weekends at 10:30, 11:30, 1, 2, 3, and 4
>
> Free
>
> 202/245–2726
>
> www.usna.usda.gov

The *Franklinia altamaha* is an interesting tree. Named for Benjamin Franklin, a man who seemed to have an interest in everything, it now grows nowhere else.

Lincoln Park

For All Ages . . . Memorializing the abolition of slavery, Lincoln Park is home to two historic statues. Dedicated in 1876, **Freedom's Memorial** was funded by former slaves, some of whom also served in the Union Army during the Civil War. It shows a life-size Abraham Lincoln holding a copy of the Emancipation Proclamation. At his feet is the likeness of Archer Alexander, the last man to be captured under the Fugitive Slave Law.

Also here is the **Mary McLeod Bethune Memorial,** the city's first statue to honor an African-American woman.

Helpful Hint

Call 202/619–7222 to request the National Park Service's brochure about the African American Heritage Trail.

The National Council of Negro Women, founded by Bethune in 1935, erected this statue in her honor in 1974. This 12-foot-tall monument features an elderly Bethune, complete with cane, reaching out to black children, exemplifying her focus on learning and self-respect for African-Americans.

Smart Stuff

For Tykes . . . If you were a slave, you would have to do just what your master or mistress told you to do *every* day. Try this with a friend: have your friend boss you around for one hour; then change places and you be the boss. Suppose your master or mistress told you to do a really *bad* thing—what would you do? **(C.)**

Several movies and books are worth investigating. Books we suggest for tweens and teens include *A Picture of Freedom: The Diary of Clotee, A Slave Girl,* by Patricia McKissack; and *To Be A Slave,* by Julius Lester. For teens there's *Uncle Tom's Cabin,* by Harriet Beecher Stowe; and *Black Like Me,* by John H. Griffin. Movies include *Malcolm X* and *King: A Filmed Record . . . Montgomery to Memphis.*

Metro: Eastern Market
East Capitol Street between 11th and 13th streets, NE

Set on a 30-acre hillside by the Anacostia River, **Congressional Cemetery** is the final resting place for a variety of celebrities. Founded in 1807, this spot is where Civil War photographer Mathew Brady, "March King" John Philip Sousa, former FBI director J. Edgar

It wasn't until 1977 that an African-American woman served as a cabinet secretary. President Jimmy Carter named Patricia Roberts Harris to be secretary of Housing and Urban Development.

Hoover, and the lesser-known former vice president Eldridge Gerry (who left us "gerrymandering" as his legacy) are all buried. The cemetery is at 1801 E Street, SE. It's not near a Metro station, so take a taxi.

Eastern Market

For All Ages . . . Despite a huge fire that damaged much of the building in 2007, the butcher, the baker, and the candlestick maker are still selling their wares at Eastern Market, seven blocks from the U.S. Capitol. Built in 1871 and rebuilt and renovated in 2009, Eastern Market is the city's last remaining public market. Children love the colorful array of clothing, toys, arts, produce, and flowers. On Saturday extra vendors set up shop, selling products from all over the world. Here you *can* get a snack.

There are plenty of shops surrounding Eastern Market, so allow time to explore the neighborhood. Nearby is the **Fairy Godmother** (319 7th Street, SE), a bookstore for families, filled with children's books and toys. Known for its wonderful selection of secondhand reads, **Capitol Hill Books** (657 C Street, SE) is another find. Interested in something to wear? Try **Clothes Encounters of A Second Kind** (202 7th Street, SE), where you can probably rub elbows with Capitol Hill staffers vying for the same outfits you like.

> Metro: Eastern Market
> 7th and C streets, SE
> Open Tuesday to Friday 8 to 5, Saturday 6 to 6; Sunday flea
>   market 9 to 4
> 202/543–7293
> www.market5gallery.org

Washington Navy Yard

For All Ages . . . Some *yard*! The oldest naval installation still in use in the United States, the Washington Navy Yard opened in 1799 as a shipyard for the Navy. Later it was a plant for manufacturing weapons and munitions. Today it houses, among other things, the

U.S. Navy Museum and the Navy Art Collection. The outdoor military history park has cannons and naval artifacts to discover.

In a refreshing hands-on style, kids can peek through real submarine periscopes, operate the controls of antiaircraft weapons, and perch on a real cannon at the **Navy Museum.** The exhibits in Building 76 include a hand-propelled submarine, called the *Intelligent Whale,* from 1869.

Smart Stuff

For Tykes . . . How many kinds of ships can you find in this museum? Can you find one that carries airplanes? What is it called? **(D.)**

If your youngster spends a few minutes exploring, he or she will be awed by the fully rigged foremast and the gun deck from the frigate USS *Constitution* (better known as "Old Ironsides"). The film *In Harm's Way* highlights the Navy's role in World War II. Videos, a Corsair fighter plane, and an interactive game are all part of this exhibit. All hands on deck!

A retired navy destroyer, the USS *Barry* (in service from 1956 to 1982, used in the Cuban Missile Crisis and in the Vietnam War) is at Pier 2. Tours of the USS *Barry* are available by reservation only. Call 202/433–6897 by 2 PM the day before you plan to visit.

Smart Stuff

For Tweens . . . Who is considered "the father of the U.S. Navy"? What is his famous quote? **(E.)**

There are a number of books that provide background here. For tykes, there's the *Coming Home Series: Navy Dad,* by Sandy Loren Zana. Teens will enjoy *Six Frigates: The Epic History of the Founding of the U.S. Navy,* by Ian W. Tell, *and Decision at Sea: Five Naval Battles That Shaped American History,* by Craig L. Symonds.

You and your landlubbers might (or might not!) be happy to

In Building 67, the **Navy Art Collection** features paintings of military scenes.

know that **McDonald's, Subway,** and **Dunkin' Donuts** are all open in the Navy Yard on weekdays. (On weekends your only option is McDonald's). There's also a food court with Au Bon Pain, Sbarro's, and Coyote Jack's that is open for breakfast and lunch.

> Metro: Navy Yard or Eastern Market
> Visitors enter at 11th and O streets, SE, on weekdays, and at
>   6th and M streets, SE, on weekends
> Open weekdays 9 to 5, weekends and holidays 10 to 5
> Reservations at least a day in advance required due to in-
>   creased security; call 202/433–6897
> 202/433–4882
> www.history.navy.mil

Helpful Hint

Although the Navy Yard itself is perfectly fine to explore during the daytime, the surrounding neighborhood is *not*. Take a taxi or your own car. Inside the gates there's plenty of free parking, especially on weekends.

Anacostia Community Museum

For All Ages . . . The Smithsonian Institution established the Anacostia Community Museum in 1967 to concentrate on the richness of African-American history. The goal of its founder, John Kinard, was to help young people build pride in their own culture. Changing exhibits focus on painting, photography, and sculpture. A small shop offers postcards, posters, and books by and about African-Americans. Lectures, workshops, and educational programs, as well as concerts, poetry readings, and dance programs, all take place here. Call for details.

Tour the museum grounds on the **George Washington Carver Nature Trail,** less than ⅓ mile long (doable even for young museumgoers). Take the trail *only* with a guide, however; the neighborhood is not a safe place to explore on your own.

Named for its original inhabitants, recorded as Nacothtant or Anaquashtank, the name of this area became Anacostia. Home to a large free black community before the Civil War, Anacostia developed into a middle-class African-American community by the early 1900s. After years of decline, the city is trying to revitalize this area by bringing in government offices, improving roads, and creating affordable housing.

Many books and films can enrich the experience of visiting the Anacostia Community Museum. *The Drinking Gourd,* by F. N. Monjo, is a good title for tykes; as is *Harriet and the Promised Land,* by Jacob Lawrence, a beautifully illustrated story of Harriet Tubman. Worthwhile choices for tweens include *Benjamin Banneker: Astronomer and Mathematician,* by Laura Baskes Litwin and Benjamin Banneker; and *Dear Benjamin Banneker,* by Andrea Davis Pinkney.

For tweens and teens there's *The Black Washingtonians: The Anacostia Museum Illustrated Chronology,* foreword by D. C. Delegate Eleanor Holmes Norton; *Story Painter: The Life of Jacob Lawrence,* by John Duggleby; *Roll of Thunder, Hear My Cry,* by Mildred D. Taylor; and *The Selected Poems of Langston Hughes*—or any Langston Hughes poetry. For teens, President Barack Obama has written a memoir of his youth called *Dreams from My Father.* Also check out *The Negro in the Making of America,* by Benjamin Quarles; *Manchild in the Promised Land,* by Claude Brown; *Native Son,* by Richard Wright (now a classic); and *The Future of Race,* by Henry Louis Gates, Jr. and Cornel West.

Movies for tweens and teens include *Perfect Harmony* and *A Raisin in the Sun.* For teens there are *Home of the Brave; A Soldier's Story;* and *In the Heat of the Night.*

Metro: For safety and convenience, come by car or taxi
1901 Fort Place, SE

Open daily 10 to 5; closed December 25
For tour information, call 202/633–4870
202/633–4820
www.anacostia.si.edu

★Frederick Douglass National Historic Site

For Tweens and Teens . . . Opened to the public in 1972, Cedar Hill was the last home of Frederick Douglass, former slave, statesman, and activist for human rights. It still contains many of the original Victorian furnishings. To this day, it still has no electricity. Douglass's life is portrayed in exhibits and a film in the visitor center.

Named for the cedar trees that graced the 9-acre lot, Cedar Hill was originally part of a 237-acre plot being subdivided for development. When Douglass purchased it in 1877, the real-estate deed restriction, in addition to preventing "soap-boiling, piggeries, and slaughterhouses," forbade ownership except by "white persons only." After his first wife, Anna, died in 1882, he brought his second wife, Helen Pitts, to live there. She was white.

Having taught himself to read and write while still a slave, Douglass escaped from his captivity in 1838, at the age of 21. A tall, handsome man and an excellent speaker, he published his first autobiography, *The Narrative of the Life of Frederick Douglass: An American Slave,* in 1845. In it, he identified his former master, effectively jeopardizing his own life. He fled to England, and friends purchased his freedom. Returning to the United States, he published his own newspaper, *The North Star,* in Rochester, New York, and was a stationmaster for the Underground Railroad there. A well-known abolitionist, he recruited black soldiers for the Union Army, and after the war he supported Reconstruction.

In addition to other federal appointments, Douglass served as secretary of the Santo Domingo Commission, marshal and recorder of deeds of the District of Columbia, and minister of the United States to Haiti. His house was dedicated as a memorial to Douglass in 1922, to serve, as his wife Helen wished, as a "Mount Vernon to the black community."

Among the many books about this famous man and his times are *Frederick Douglass: Portrait of a Freedom Fighter,* by Sheila Keenan (tykes); *Escape from Slavery: The Boyhood of Frederick Douglass in His Own Words,* edited by Michael McCurdy (tweens); and his three autobiographies, *The Narrative of the Life of Frederick Douglass: An American Slave, My Bondage and My Freedom,* and *Life and Times of Frederick Douglass* (teens). A wonderful book (and movie) about this period in our history is *Having Our Say: The Delany Sisters' First 100 Years,* by Sarah Louise Delany and Annie Elizabeth Delany (tweens and teens).

Smart Stuff

For Tweens and Teens . . . What do you think enabled Frederick Douglass to be such a powerful advocate for abolition? Do you think it helped or hurt his cause that he was a former slave?

Metro: For safety and convenience, come by car or taxi

1411 W Street, SE

Open mid-October to mid-April, daily 9 to 4; mid-April to mid-October, daily 9 to 5; closed January 1, Thanksgiving Day, and December 25

Tours available at 9, 12:15, 1:45, 3:30; tours for large groups available at 9:30, 10:45, and 2; advance reservations required

202/426–5961

www.nps.gov/frdo

National Harbor

For All Ages . . . The hottest new Washington area vacation spot is National Harbor. Technically in Oxon Hill, MD, it covers 300 acres, and is across the Potomac River from Old Town, Alexandria (Virginia).

The waterfront setting provides a pleasing backdrop for numerous shops, restaurants, and hotels, but the developers have not neglected entertainment. Cirque du Soleil has its D.C. home in National Harbor, and there are free after-sunset kid-friendly movies on the Plaza's "Big Screen" from spring to fall.

The locally famous sculpture *The Awakening* is a delight to children, who climb its partially exposed giant limbs.

Watercraft of all kinds connect National Harbor to such sites as Old Town, Alexandria, and historic Mt. Vernon, VA, in addition to Georgetown and downtown Washington. You can choose a water taxi or a river cruise, or sign up for a rented canoe or a guided fishing expedition.

At this writing, sites are still being developed in the National Harbor, so check the Web site when your trip planning begins.

No Metro station; come by car, bus, or boat
Oxon Hill, Maryland
www.nationalharbor.com

Kenilworth Park and Aquatic Gardens

For All Ages . . . The last natural marsh in the city, Kenilworth Park and Aquatic Gardens has the largest group of water lilies and aquatic plants in the world. Water lilies, lotuses, water hyacinths, and other exotic varieties of water plants flourish in this 14-acre sanctuary. These ponds and marshes, along with the Anacostia estuary, provide natural habitats for waterfowl, turtles, frogs, and small mammals, in-

Smart Stuff

For Tykes . . . There are lots of stories of make-believe people so small they can fit into tiny spaces. Make up a story about a person or an animal that lives inside a lotus flower. What happens to the flower at night?

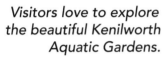

Visitors love to explore the beautiful Kenilworth Aquatic Gardens.

cluding muskrats, raccoons, and opossums. A ¾-mile trail leads past the marshland to an outlook across the Anacostia River.

Begun inauspiciously on his property, the gardens were a hobby of Walter B. Shaw, a Civil War veteran. In 1882 he planted water lilies from his original home in Maine near his new house by the Anacostia River. His water plants multiplied so rapidly that a hobby became a commercial venture. The gardens became a popular spot for Washingtonians' Sunday outings in the 1920s.

There are plenty of rare blooms here. Possibly the oldest flower seeds ever cultivated, those from the stunning pink East Indian lotus, were transported from a Manchurian lakebed in 1951. They are believed to have been between 350 and 960 years old! This gives a whole new meaning to the term "late bloomer"!

The visitor center has a map of the park, as well as

Helpful Hint

Most plants are in bloom May through September; go before 1 PM for the best view.

pamphlets and brochures, an aquarium exhibit, and a display on the gardens' history. Picnic tables are available, and National Park Service naturalists lead nature walks in the gardens on summer weekends.

Metro: For safety and convenience, come by car or taxi
1550 Anacostia Avenue, NE
Open daily 7 to 4; closed January 1, Thanksgiving Day, and
    December 25
202/426–6905
www.nps.gov

Smart Stuff

For Tweens and Teens . . . What ancient civilization depicted the lotus flower as a crown for its kings and queens? (F.)

Where to Stay in Northeast & Southeast D.C.

There are places to stay in these areas, some with restaurants and pools, and even group-rate bargains to be found. But for safety's sake, *use* the free shuttle services, if available.

Capitol Hill Suites
200 C Street, SE
202/543–6000 or 800/537–8483
www.capitolhillsuites.com
Metro: Capitol South

Gallaudet University Kellogg Conference Center
800 Florida Avenue, NE (93 rooms on Gallaudet University
    campus)
202/651–6000
www.gukcc.com

Metro: Union Station or Gallaudet/New York Avenue (via free shuttle bus)

Hampton Inn and Suites
250 Waterfront Street (National Harbor)
301/567–3531
www.nationalharboroxonhillsuites.hamptoninn.com

Residence Inn Marriott
192 Waterfront Street (National Harbor)
301/749–4755 or 800/331–3131
www.marriott.com/nationalharbor

Answers to Smart Stuff Questions

A. Saint Elizabeth Ann Bayley Seton was born in 1774 to a Protestant family and was both a wife and mother before she turned to Catholicism. Entering the novitiate as a widow, she rose to become mother superior of her convent. After her death she was credited with the miraculous healing of several people with incurable diseases. This native-born American woman was canonized in 1975.

B. The state tree of Alaska is the Sitka spruce. The state tree of Hawaii is the kukui tree.

C. If a child brings up the idea of running away, you might talk a bit about the Underground Railroad.

D. A ship that can carry planes on its decks is called an aircraft carrier.

E. Often considered the "father of the U.S. Navy," John Paul Jones refused to surrender to the British during the Revolutionary War, declaring, "I have not yet begun to fight!"

F. The lotus flower was pictured by the ancient Egyptians in its closed, or nighttime, form, as the tall white crown for royalty. In both India and ancient Egypt, the lotus played an important role in religion. In one legend, it was said to be the birthplace and residence of the sun god, Atum or Ra. Closing at night, the flower's petals hid the sunlight from the earth.

CHAPTER 11

Northern Virginia

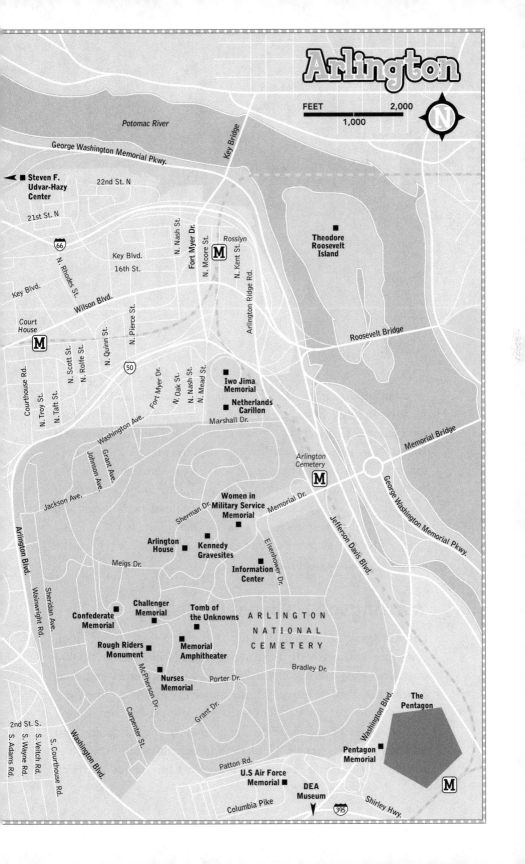

I f you like sightseeing outdoors, here's an opportunity to spend time in some beautiful and meaningful surroundings. From the monuments and memorials of **Arlington National Cemetery** to the idyllic setting of **Theodore Roosevelt Island**, Northern Virginia offers opportunities for enjoyment of nature and reflection on history. If you're lucky enough to be in a group selected to tour the **Pentagon,** you'll have an opportunity to appreciate the vastness of our military headquarters. You can also admire the tall steel spires arching skyward in tribute to the U.S. Air Force. Whatever stops are of interest to you, it's worth a trip, as the natives say, "across the bridge."

★Arlington National Cemetery

For All Ages . . . Set high on hills overlooking the city, Arlington National Cemetery is the final resting place of more than 230,000 of our nation's veterans, statesmen, and national heroes and their dependents. Participants in all our nation's wars, even some from the Confederacy, can be identified by clearly marked headstones. Sections of the cemetery are dedicated to astronauts, chaplains, and nurses who were veterans. Until 1948 interment locations were determined by race and rank. Now, however, a private and a general might lie side by side. In addition to the Tomb of the Unknowns from our four major wars, the cemetery has poignant memorials to those who have served the United States from the battlefield to spaceflight to the White House. The sound of "Taps," gracing even the most standard funeral here, can be overwhelming.

Everyone can visit here, but not all of the people you see are tourists; many are family and friends visiting gravesites of loved ones. Every week there are 90 to 100 burials.

Helpful Hint

Arlington National Cemetery can get pretty hot in the middle of a summer day, so plan to make your cemetery visit *early* or *late* in the day.

Metro: Arlington Cemetery

Directly across Memorial Bridge from the Lincoln Memorial, just off Memorial Drive

Open April through September, daily 8 to 7; October to March, daily 8 to 5

Parking fee

No cars are allowed in the cemetery; relatives visiting gravesites may request temporary passes

The *only* guided tours are through Tourmobile; to contact the company, call 202/554–5100

703/607–8000

www.arlingtoncemetery.org

Information Center

A visit to Arlington National Cemetery involves a great deal of walking, whether you're heading for a specific gravesite or wandering among many. Tourmobile offers guided tours throughout the cemetery, leaving the information center every 15 to 20 minutes. You can get on and off at various points along the way. These are the last restrooms you'll see until you reach the Arlington House, so take advantage of the facilities.

Quick Guide to

Attraction	Location
★Arlington National Cemetery	Directly across Memorial Bridge from the Lincoln Memorial, just off Memorial Drive
U.S. Air Force Memorial	One Air Force Memorial Drive; Arlington, VA at Columbia Pike just off 395S
Iwo Jima Memorial	Fort Myer Drive, just outside Arlington National Cemetery, near the Netherlands Carillon
Netherlands Carillon	Off U.S. Route 50, just outside Arlington National Cemetery, near the Iwo Jima Memorial
Theodore Roosevelt Island	Between the District and Virginia, on the Potomac River, just north of the Theodore Roosevelt Bridge
DEA Museum	700 Army Drive
The Pentagon	In northern Virginia, across the Potomac River from Washington, D.C.
National Weather Service	44087 Weather Service Road; approximately 4 miles NE of Dulles Airport
Steven F. Udvar-Hazy Center	14390 Air and Space Museum Parkway, near Dulles Airport

Northern Virginia Attractions

Age Range	Hours	Details on
All Ages	Open daily. April–Sept., 8 AM–7 PM; Oct.–March, 8 AM–5 PM	Page 272
All Ages	Call 703/247–5808 for information	Page 291
All Ages	Sunset Parade the first Tues. in June through third Tues. in August, 7 PM	Page 291
All Ages	Call for bell schedule	Page 292
All Ages	Dawn to dusk, daily	Page 294
Teens	Tues.–Fri. 10 AM–4 PM	Page 296
Teens	Call for information	Page 296
Tweens and Teens	Tours Mon.–Fri. 10 AM–1:00 PM and 5 PM–7:00 PM	Page 298
All Ages	Open daily Sept.–March 10 AM–5:30 PM; April–Aug., 10 AM–6:30 PM	Page 299

Helpful Hint

Don't come here without eating first. You cannot purchase food anywhere in the cemetery, and, while you're on the grounds you're not allowed to eat snacks you might have hidden in your pockets.

First, pick up a map at the information center so that you can plan which part of the cemetery you would like to visit. Exhibits clarify what there is to see. Informative brochures, as well as books and videos, are all available. If you're looking for the burial site of a particular person, the staff can help you locate it.

Arlington House

On a June day in 1831 a young couple got married in the front parlor of this house and was destined to live in it for 30 years. Mary Anna Randolph Custis, great-granddaughter of Martha Washington, married her teenage love, a dashing young military officer named Robert E. Lee. They lived in the house with her parents and inherited the estate. Six of their seven children were born here. As a colonel in the U.S. Army, Lee wrote one of his sons as late as January 1861, "Secession is nothing but revolution." Yet, in the end, he felt obligated to fight with his region. On April 22, 1861, U.S. Army Colonel Robert E. Lee accepted the command of the Confederate forces when his home state of Virginia joined the Confederacy. One month later Union troops quartered officers in the house and soldiers on the surrounding property. Lee's longtime friend, fellow Southerner and Quartermaster General Montgomery Meigs, retali-

Smart Stuff

For Tykes . . . Can you find a picture of a Civil War soldier? Can you tell by the uniform's color which army he fought in? Why do you think neither side chose red, yellow, or orange?

Robert E. Lee's family home, Arlington House, is a fascinating place to tour, along with the National Cemetery that became its backyard.

ated for Lee's desertion of the Union Army and chose Lee's estate as the home for the National Cemetery. With war dead buried in their yard, the Lee family never returned to live in this home and sold it to the U.S. government in 1882.

Interestingly, Lee's own family mirrored the upheaval that confounded even the closest of ties. His cousin, also named Robert E. Lee, was a Union officer. Still revered in the South as a man of integrity and valor, Robert E. Lee is commemorated here on the grounds he once called home.

Smart Stuff

For Tweens . . . What was the name of General Lee's famous horse? (It never shied away from battle and even had bullets whiz beneath its belly.) (A.)

In one of history's ironies, Congress dedicated Arlington House in Robert E. Lee's honor in 1925, making it a permanent memorial in 1955. Today park rangers in period costumes answer questions and assist visitors on self-guided tours. Some of the furnishings are original. Lee's bedroom upstairs is where he signed his resignation from the U.S. Army. Slave quarters adjoin the main house. Both Mrs. Lee and her mother, Mrs. Custis, taught their

Smart Stuff

For Tweens and Teens . . .
Who was called the "soldiers' soldier"? Why? (B.)

slaves to read and write in this building, and Robert E. Lee officially freed all his slaves at Arlington House in 1863, even though the Confederacy was still fighting to preserve the institution of slavery.

Two interesting books for teens are *The Lady of Arlington: The Life of Mrs. Robert E. Lee*, by John Perry; and *Robert E. Lee: A Biography*, by Emory M. Thomas.

At this writing, renovations were underway and due to be completed in 2010. The first floor of the house is still open to visitors, but call first.

Open daily 9:30 to 4:30; closed January 1 and December 25
703/235–1530
www.nps.gov/arho

Gravesite of General Omar Bradley

The last American five-star general, Omar Bradley commanded the 12th Army Group in World War II, the largest single command ever held by an American officer. He is one of only five people ever to hold that rank.

Challenger Memorial

This memorial honors the crew of the space shuttle *Challenger,* which exploded just after its liftoff in 1986. The vertical monument depicts the crew on the front and the poem "High Flight," by John G. Magee Jr. (quoted by President Ronald Reagan), on the reverse. The remains of crew members are buried in the cemetery.

Challenger was the first spaceflight to have a private citizen aboard, the public school teacher Christa McAuliffe. The crew—Mission Commander Dick Scobee, Mike Smith, Greg Jarvis, Ron McNair, Judy Resnik, and Ellison Onizuka—was also representative of some American minorities; McNair was African-American, Resnik was Jewish, and Onizuka was Asian-American. The *Challenger* explosion marked the only American space shuttle disaster in the 20th century. Unfortunately the 21st century began with another loss: the shuttle *Columbia,* along with its crew.

The Confederate Memorial

Confederate soldiers are also buried in Arlington National Cemetery. Life-size figures of soldiers (both white and black), sweethearts separating, parents and children, Roman goddesses, and women representing Bible verses are featured in the Confederate Memorial. A statue of a warlike goddess supports a wounded woman clinging to a shield, the sculptor's emotional portrayal of his region's losses. The frieze in bronze at the base depicts Southern troops departing for battle and then returning in defeat. The monument's designer, Moses Jacob Ezekiel, himself a Confederate veteran, is buried at its base.

Commissioned in 1900 to commemorate the sacrifices of the Confederate forces, the monument was erected in 1914 on the birthday of Jefferson Davis, the only Confederate president. It was dedicated by President Woodrow Wilson, a native of Virginia, who said, "Turn your faces to the future . . . as we have shed our blood upon opposite sides, we now face and admire one another."

Arranged in concentric circles around the monument, the gravestones of the Confederate soldiers have pointed tops. Some say it's to keep Yankees from sitting on them.

An interesting view of the Confederacy is presented in the book *Military Memoirs of a Confederate: A Critical Narrative,* by General Edward Porter Alexander (teens).

Gravesite of Justice William O. Douglas

Appointed to the Supreme Court by Franklin D. Roosevelt in 1939 at the extraordinarily young age of 41, Justice William O. Douglas was an outspoken advocate for individual rights. He served for 36 years. A native of Washington State, he was also a staunch conservationist, and made a lasting contribution to Washington, D.C., by helping preserve the historic C&O Canal (now a popular recreation site) from destruction by developers. (See Chapter 6.)

It's interesting to read about complex people like Justice Douglas. Two books Douglas wrote are about different aspects of his life:

Go East, Young Man: The Early Years (autobiography; teens) and *Nature's Justice: Writings of William O. Douglas*, edited by James O'Fallon (teens).

Gravesite of Medgar Evers

A towering figure in the American civil rights struggle, Medgar Evers was assassinated for his efforts. But his dream of equal rights for African-Americans continued. A year after his death Congress enacted the Civil Rights Act of 1964, prohibiting public, employment, and union discrimination.

The movie story about Medgar Evers, *Ghosts of Mississippi* (teens), is also told in a book, *The Ghosts of Medgar Evers: A Tale of Race, Murder, Mississippi, and Hollywood,* by Willie Morris (teens). The film *Mississippi Burning* portrays, in graphic detail, the racism prevalent at the time (teens).

Gravesites of President John F. Kennedy and Jacqueline Kennedy Onassis

When President Kennedy visited Arlington 12 days before his assassination, in November 1963, he was heard to remark, "It's so peaceful here, I could stay here forever." This president, long on grace and ideals but short on time to accomplish his goals, left a nation and a generation in mourning at his death. A young husband, father, and charismatic leader, Kennedy strode onto the national stage as the personification of a dynamic, progressive era in America. An entire generation gauged their dreams by his, and many chose their life's work as a result of his call to public service. His death punctuated a time of turbulence seared into the consciousness of all who lived through it, one barely believable to later generations.

Marked by an eternal flame, President Kennedy's marble, slate, and Cape Cod fieldstone gravesite also includes a low wall with quotes from his speeches. How apt that the torch he spoke of being "passed to a new generation" is echoed in the flame above his grave, and can be seen at night from many points around the city. Next to him lie his wife, former first lady Jacqueline Bouvier Kennedy Onassis, and two of their children who died in infancy.

In any season, tourists make pilgrimages to the Kennedy gravesite.

Kennedy family books abound, but here are some of particular interest: *When John and Caroline Lived in the White House,* by Laurie Coulter (tweens); *The John F. Kennedys: A Family Album,* by Mark Show and Richard Reeves (tweens and teens); *Jackie: Her Life in Pictures,* by James Spada (tweens and teens); *President Kennedy: Profile of Power,* by Richard Reeves (teens); and *Conversations with Kennedy,* by Benjamin Bradlee (teens). A movie about the 1962 Cuban Missile Crisis came out in 2001: *Thirteen Days* (teens).

Smart Stuff

For Tweens and Teens . . . When President Kennedy was assassinated, his widow decided on an eternal flame as his memorial. Why do you think Mrs. Kennedy used this symbol? Do you feel it is effective? Why or why not?

Gravesite of Senator Robert F. Kennedy

The assassination of Robert F. Kennedy on the eve of his nomination as the Democratic Party's presidential candidate in June 1968 was a major event in the turmoil of the Vietnam and civil rights eras. Many of his bereaved, youthful followers lost faith in the effi-

Robert F. Kennedy evoked controversy when he was named Attorney General in his brother President Kennedy's cabinet. He turned out to be a thoughtful and restrained counselor and his brother's most trusted adviser. What do you think about a national leader bringing a family member into his or her administration?

cacy of government as the engine to repair social ills. His absence is still mourned by advocates for the poor, hungry, and disenfranchised in America.

Two books teens might enjoy are *Robert Kennedy: His Life,* by Evan Thomas; and *Robert Kennedy: In His Own Words: The Unpublished Recollections of the Kennedy Years.*

Gravesite of Senator Edward M. Kennedy

Closing another chapter in the saga of this famous American family, Senator Edward "Ted" Kennedy was laid to rest next to his two famous brothers, Senator Robert F. Kennedy and President John F. Kennedy, at sunset on a Saturday evening in August 2009. His lifelong advocacy for the "forgotten" members of society earned him the admiration of representatives from both sides of the political aisle.

Tomb of Pierre L'Enfant

The original planner of the District of Columbia, French engineer Pierre L'Enfant had to wait more than 100 years to be recognized for his genius. True to his name, L'Enfant often behaved in a juvenile fashion and managed to alienate everyone he worked with, finally in-

Smart Stuff

For Tweens and Teens . . . Pierre L'Enfant provided the broad tree-lined avenues and open green spaces reminiscent of what European city? Compared to other cities you know, how pedestrian-friendly is D.C.'s downtown area? (C.)

curring the displeasure of the man who hired him, General George Washington. After L'Enfant was fired, it fell to his remarkable assistant, Benjamin Banneker, to bring the work to fruition. L'Enfant died practically penniless, and was buried in a pauper's grave in nearby Prince George's County, Maryland.

In 1908 the city's Board of Commissioners realized the debt owed to this talented man and requested the secretary of war to make a burial site available in Arlington. In 1909 L'Enfant's body (removed from its original gravesite) was reinterred in Arlington National Cemetery after first lying in state in the Capitol Rotunda. His original design for the city is depicted on the top of his gravesite, located in front of Arlington House. The view of the city he designed is breathtaking.

Smart Stuff

For Tweens and Teens . . . What governor vowed to "stand in the schoolhouse door" to prevent integration of his state's public schools? What happened? **(D.)**

Gravesite of Joe Louis

Known affectionately as "the Brown Bomber," Joseph Louis Barrow avenged his 1936 loss to German boxer Max Schmeling to gain the title of heavyweight champion of the world in 1938, a title he retained for 12 years. He brought special pride to African-Americans living in a less tolerant time. With the German fascist creed of Aryan supremacy looming across Europe, all Americans, of many ethnic backgrounds, felt invested in Louis's success.

Two books we suggest for teens are *Champion Joe Louis: A Biography,* by Chris Mead; and *Joe Louis: The Great Black Hope,* by Richard Bak. A movie classic, starring James Earl Jones, is *The Great White Hope* (teens).

Gravesite of Justice Thurgood Marshall

The nation's first black Supreme Court justice, Thurgood Marshall gained renown when he argued on behalf of the National Association for the Advancement of Colored People for desegregation of America's public schools in the landmark case *Brown v. (Topeka, Kansas) Board of Education.* The successful outcome effectively ended the practice of mandating two unequal school systems in the United States—one for blacks and one for whites. In one of history's delightful twists, the African-American lawyer who asked the land's highest court to ensure the educational rights of black children rose to become the first black member of that court.

Some books to consider are *A Picture Book of Thurgood Marshall* (Picture Book Biography), by David A. Adler and Robert Casilla (tykes and tweens); and *Thurgood Marshall: American Revolutionary,* by Juan Williams (teens).

Nurses Memorial

A white stone statue of a nurse in uniform overlooks the Army, Navy, and Air Force nurses buried with their service colleagues in Arlington National Cemetery. Sculpted by Frances Rich, this monument originally honored the nurses who served so valiantly in World War I. In 1971 the monument was rededicated to commemorate "devoted service to country and humanity by Army, Navy, and Air Force Nurses."

Colonel Anita Newcomb McGee, founder of the Army Nurse Corps in 1901, was the only woman with the rank of Assistant Surgeon of the U.S. Army. A veteran of the Spanish-American War, she was instrumental in the establishment of this memorial. Dr. McGee was buried with full military honors in the cemetery in 1940.

Several books on nursing that are of interest here are *Angels of Mercy: The Army Nurses of World War II,* by Betsy Kuhn (tweens); and *G.I. Nightingales: The Army Nurse Corps in World War II,* by Barbara Brooks Tomblin (teens).

Memorial Amphitheater, Mast of USS *Maine*

The Grand Army of the Republic, a Civil War group, spearheaded the idea for a ceremonial spot appropriate to the nation's military cemetery. Woodrow Wilson laid the cornerstone in 1915, and it was dedicated on Memorial Day in 1920. There are crowds here for services on Memorial Day, Veterans' Day, and Easter Sunday. It's quite a colorful spectacle to see the miniature American flags on all the graves on Memorial Day weekend.

The mast of the USS *Maine*, the ship blown up in Havana harbor in 1898, brought to this location in 1912, serves as a tribute to the 229 crewmen who died. This incident at sea precipitated U.S. entry into the Spanish-American War. Located behind the amphitheater and just across Memorial Drive, the mast rests on a battleship-style turret, with the names of the dead inscribed around it. It's a dramatic monument to a bygone era of American imperialism.

Gravesite of Robert Edwin Peary

A tireless explorer of the northern reaches of the planet (he proved Greenland was an island rather than a continent), Robert Edwin Peary contributed to our scientific knowledge of the people he encountered. He adapted Inuit survival skills to his arctic travel. After several unsuccessful attempts, he reached the North Pole on April 6, 1909. A civil engineer in the U.S. Navy, Peary retired from exploration in 1911. In recognition of his achievement, Congress bestowed on him the rank of rear admiral before he retired.

A book that tells of Peary's adventures is *Robert Peary and the Quest for the North Pole*, by Christopher Dwyer (tweens).

It's now disputed whether Peary's assistant, Matthew Henson (an African-American), reached the North Pole ahead of him. Browse through *Matthew A. Henson's Historic Arctic Journey: The Classic Account of One of the World's Greatest Black Explorers*, by Matthew A. Henson, Deirdre C. Starr, Booker T. Washington, and Robert E. Peary; it's an interesting view of this history (teens).

Gravesite of John Joseph Pershing

The only American six-star general gained renown as the leader of the American Expeditionary Force in Europe during World War I. He was also General of the Armies of the United States, a rank he shared only with George Washington.

His memoirs, *My Experiences in the World War*, are a vivid

Smart Stuff

For Tweens and Teens . . . Not exactly a major conflict, the Spanish-American War included Theodore Roosevelt's much-publicized "charge up San Juan Hill." (Actually, his men captured Kettle Hill, but don't be dismayed by the discrepancies—that's history.) As the result of clever publicity, Roosevelt emerged from his military adventure as a war hero, and later became U.S. president. What part do you feel "advertising" plays in our perceptions of public figures?

firsthand account of his experiences (teens). *Until the Last Trumpet Sounds: The Life of General of the Armies John J. Pershing,* by Gene A. Smith, is another view (teens).

Rough Riders Monument

Also known as the Spanish-American War Memorial, the Rough Riders Monument commemorates the Spanish-American War fought in Cuba at the end of the 19th century. President Theodore Roosevelt, brought to prominence through his battlefield adventures at that time, dedicated the monument in 1902. Resigning his post as Secretary of the Navy in 1898, Lieutenant Colonel Roosevelt organized the Rough Riders (a band of enthusiastic recruits) in order to get in on the military action in this brief war.

For young readers (and listeners), the Step-Up Book series offers *Meet Theodore Roosevelt,* by Ormonde De Kay Jr., an appealing overview of the life of our nation's youngest president. Another that would be enjoyable for tykes and tweens is *The Legend of the Teddy Bear,* by Frank Murphy. Tweens might enjoy *Bully for You, Teddy Roosevelt,* by Jean Fritz. Teens can explore *The Boys of '98: Theodore Roosevelt and the Rough Riders,* by Dale L. Walker; and *Carry a Big Stick: The Uncommon Heroism of Theodore Roosevelt,* by George E. Grant.

Gravesite of Albert Sabin

Albert Sabin, a lieutenant colonel in the U.S. Army Medical Corps, served more than the armed forces when he developed the first oral polio vaccine. It's estimated that his work prevented millions of cases of paralytic polio and hundreds of thousands of deaths in the years since the vaccine became available in 1961.

Polio, a forgotten disease for today's youth, comes graphically to life in two books for tweens: *Close to Home: A Story of the Polio Epidemic,* by Lydia Weaver; and *Small Steps: The Year I Got Polio,* by Peg Kehrret and Denise Shanahan.

Gravesite of President William Howard Taft

An enormous person with a résumé to match, William Howard Taft, weighing in at 300 pounds, definitely made a mark on his times. As Governor of the Philippines, Secretary of War, President of the United States, and Chief Justice of the Supreme Court, Taft was the *only* person to have held *both* of the latter two positions. Not bad to be Chief Justice after your retirement from the White House!

Tweens can get some of the flavor of the Taft era by reading *Lost at the White House: A 1909 Easter Story,* by Lisa Griest et al., and *William Howard Taft (Getting to Know the U.S. Presidents),* by Mike Venezia. Teens might enjoy *William Howard Taft, American,* by Robert Lee Dunn.

> All of Taft's personal items had to allow for his large girth. There's a tale that he once got stuck in the White House bathtub. Subsequently, a huge new tub replaced it.

Tomb of the Unknown Dead of the Civil War

The 2,111 unidentified soldiers who died on nearby Virginia battle-fields in the Civil War are memorialized by a huge granite marker over their mass grave. The Civil War left more than half a million soldiers dead, a shocking number, considering the fact that the country's population at the time was about 31.5 million. By contrast, the American death toll from World War II numbered just over 1 million, from a population of between 132 and 150 million.

Soldier's Heart: Being the Story of the Enlistment and Due Service of the Boy Charley Goddard in the First Minnesota Volunteers, by Gary Paulsen, is a coming-of-age tale of a 15-year-old volunteer in the Minnesota militia of the Union army (tweens and teens).

Tomb of the Unknowns

"Here rests in honored glory an American soldier known but to God" is the inscription on the Tomb of the Unknowns, one of Arlington National Cemetery's most-visited sites. Troops from the Third U.S. Infantry Regiment (known as the "Old Guard") stand as sentinels here 24 hours a day. Children are especially fascinated by the drills these troops carry out, facing the tomb, marching, and shifting their M-14 rifles in precision time.

There's *no* soldier buried in the Tomb of the Unknowns from the Vietnam War. DNA tests identified the soldier buried there as Lieutenant Michael Blassie, who was shot down in his A-37 plane in 1962. He was subsequently buried in his hometown at the request of his family.

At the Tomb of the Unknowns

The secret to the sharp sound of the sentinels' clicking heels is taps on the bottoms of their shoes. If their hands look cold in winter, it's because they're required to wet their gloves in order to have a firmer grip on their custom-made guns. To see the ceremony of the changing of the guard, visit on the half hour (April to September, 8 to 7) or on the hour (October to March, 8 to 5). The guard is changed every two hours at night. They have kept watch here since 1930.

Women in Military Service for America Memorial

Finally, a little attention for the distaff side. Completed in 1997, the Women in Military Service for America Memorial commemorates the service of the 1.8 million women who served the nation from the American Revolution through the present. In nearly every American war women have played a military role, frequently as spies but occasionally as soldiers disguised as men, in addition to serving as soldiers in uniform for their country. It took many years for the United States to commission women as officially acknowledged members of our armed forces. But by the turn of the 21st century women had earned commanding positions in all branches of the armed services.

Set into the side of a hill, an **Education Center** with a Hall of Honor exhibits photographs and artifacts that depict the history of U.S. servicewomen. There's also a computer register to trace specific history and individuals, as well as informative films, a bookstore, and a gift shop. A brochure offers a self-guided tour through the memorial.

Even the Marines finally commissioned women. In 1943 Oveta Culp Hobby was sworn in by President Franklin D. Roosevelt as the first female American Marine.

The site itself affords a spectacular view of Washington. Constructed of reinforced concrete and several shades of granite, a semicircular wall, glass tablets of etched quotations, and a Court of Honor, with a fountain in front, the memorial is a dramatic tribute to the individual and collective efforts of women in service to the military. A book of special interest here is *Band of Sisters: American Women at War in Iraq*, by Kirsten Holmstedt (teens).

At the entrance to the cemetery

Education Center open April through September, daily 8 to 7; October to March, daily 8 to 5; closed December 25

Tours can be arranged by calling 703/892–2606

703/533–1155 or 800/222–2294

www.womensmemorial.org

A sign of the times: a 1979 recruitment ad for the U.S. Army read, "Some of our best men are women."

Getting hungry at this point? If you have students of French with you, you might want to try **Café Parisien Express** (4520 Lee Highway, near the intersection of Old Dominion Drive; 703/525–3332) for bistro fare in a delightful café environment. Sandwiches and hot entrées are favorites. Crepes, omelets, and delicious desserts round out the menu. If you call ahead, you'll be encouraged to speak to the waiters in French and learn to order in French as well. Seating in a private room is available for parties up to 20. For chicken, head straight for **El Pollo Rico** (932 N. Kenmore Street; 703/522–3220), a Peruvian eat-in/take-out place with some of the tastiest chicken around. It's open daily 11 to 10. Once you're in this area, you can find other restaurants to try—please let us know what *you* discover.

Smart Stuff

For Tykes . . . When you salute the flag, where do you put your hand? Where does a soldier put his or her hand? Try "standing at attention." What do you do with your feet? (E.)

United States Air Force Memorial

For All Ages . . . Honoring the service of the members of the U.S. Air Force and its predecessors, this cluster of three soaring steel arcs makes a dramatic addition to the skyline. The Memorial, dedicated in 2006, stands on the grounds of Fort Meyer, just south of Arlington National Cemetery. The design evokes the vapor trails of the famous Thunderbirds in their signature "bomb burst" maneuver. Images of four F-16 jets flying in "Missing Man" formation are engraved on a glass wall on the north side of the Memorial. Through the wall you can glimpse a granite inscription wall with the names of Air Force recipients of the Medal of Honor. On the opposite side of the Memorial is another granite wall with inspirational quotes, including the "core values" of the Air Force: "Integrity first, service before self, and excellence in all we do."

> Metro: no access; drive or taxi
> One Air Force Memorial Drive at Columbia Pike, just off
>   Route 395 South
> Open April to September, daily 8 AM to 11 PM; October to
>   March, daily 8 AM to 9 PM
> 703/247–5808
> www.airforcememorial.org

Iwo Jima Memorial

For All Ages . . . Appropriately situated on a promontory at the north end of Arlington National Cemetery overlooking the city, the Marine Corps War Memorial commemorates the battle at Mount Suribachi in 1945, where 6,321 U.S. soldiers died. It's an image etched in our national memory—six American Marines struggling to raise the flag on a rocky hilltop their comrades died trying to secure. Sculpted by Felix W. de Weldon and based on the Pulitzer Prize–winning photograph by Joe Rosenthal, the statue is inscribed with a comment from Admiral Chester Nimitz: "Uncommon valor was a common virtue."

*Iwo Jima
Memorial*

A good time to visit is sunset parade, which includes music by the U.S. Marine Drum and Bugle Corps and precision drill by the Marine Corps Silent Drill Platoon. It's held at 7 PM from the first Tuesday in June through the third Tuesday. There's free shuttle-bus service from Arlington National Cemetery.

Metro: Rosslyn, then a five-minute walk east on Fort Myer
   Drive
Free
202/433–6060 sunset parade info
www.nps.gov/gwmp/usmc.htm

Netherlands Carillon

For All Ages ... Commemorating Holland's liberation from the Nazis on May 5, 1945, the Netherlands Carillon holds a set of 49 bells, each given by a different segment of that country's population. Housed in a 127-foot tower, the carillon was a gift in gratitude for U.S. aid during and after World War II. Park rangers give a brief explanation a half hour before each concert. Sometimes visitors can climb the tower and watch the bell ringers perform—an ap-pealing experience.

Off U.S. Route 50, just outside Arlington National Cemetery
   and near the Iwo Jima Memorial

Call for bell schedule
703/289–2500
www.nps.gov/archive/gwmp/carillon.htm

Smart Stuff

For Teens . . . Journalists frequently make tough choices. Editors, publishers, the story "source," and even the government of the location where the story is taking place may exert pressure to "kill" a story or slant it in a specific direction. Assume you were covering a story about worker abuse (intolerable working conditions, unacceptably low pay, discrimination against particular categories of workers, or any combination of your choosing) in a factory located in a distant country (in Asia or South America, for example) and you found your publisher was part of a conglomerate that owns the plant. Your editor wants you to "kill" the story, and the foreign government is beginning to harass you for your "interference." You have just been told that your passport will be confiscated until you agree to leave the country, and you realize that your next visit to the factory will likely land you in a foreign jail. What would you do? (P.S.: you are *not* Clark Kent.)

Not far away is Freedom Park, at 1101 Wilson Boulevard in Rosslyn. The **Freedom Forum Journalists Memorial**, in memory of journalists who gave their lives in pursuit of their calling, reminds us that a free press, like a free society, often comes with a high price. Replicas of the Goddess of Democracy from Tiananmen Square, a model of a Cuban refugee kayak, and a sculpture of the door from Martin Luther King Jr.'s Birmingham, Alabama, jail cell are all tangible reminders of some of freedom's milestones in the second half of the 20th century.

If at this point you're in search of a place for lunch or a big

Smart Stuff

For Tykes . . . If you could have your very own island, what would be on it? Draw a picture of your make-believe island. What kind of house would you have?

snack, try the **Lynn Street Café** (1735 N. Lynn Street, Rosslyn; 703/525–0384) for great turkey sandwiches. For Vietnamese fare, head for **Pho 75** (1721 Wilson Boulevard; 703/525–7355). Here you can try every imaginable variation of beef-noodle stews. For food from "south of the border" (and we don't mean the Mason-Dixon line), try **Guajillo** (1727 Wilson Boulevard; 703/807–0840). Known especially for yummy goat-cheese enchiladas, it also has quesadillas, tacos, and burritos for younger taste buds. It's open Monday through Wednesday 11 to 9, Thursday 11 to 2 and 5 to 10, Friday 11 to 10, Saturday 5 to 10:30, and Sunday noon to 3 and 4 to 9:30.

Smart Stuff

For Tweens . . . Theodore Roosevelt was known as our first "environmental" president. One of his legacies is our series of national parks. If you had to name a special area to preserve in your home state, what would it be, and why would you choose it? (Would you have to "fight" any "special interests" to get this place protected?)

Theodore Roosevelt Island

For All Ages . . . How appropriate it is that our nation's first "environmental" president should be memorialized on his own island, an oasis of greenery devoid of the trappings of business, government, and even of human habitation. Two and a half miles of (sometimes challenging) hiking trails diverge off into the woods. On a wide plaza, an imposing statue of "T. R.," emphasizing his characteristic vigor, stands guard over this pastoral 88-acre setting. It was primarily from his prior initiatives that the National Park Service, which oversees many of the outdoor settings in Washington, D.C., as well as the White House building and grounds and both the Kennedy Center and Wolf Trap Center for the Performing Arts, was established in 1916. Near the larger-than-life statue, four massive stone tablets carry quotations from his speeches. Roosevelt's eternal "bully pulpit" continues in the national parks he initiated across the country.

Smart Stuff

For Teens . . . In Theodore Roosevelt's day, there were fewer clashes between industry and conservationists. What do you see as our country's biggest environmental disaster? If you were president, what course of action would you advocate?

Restrooms are located only at the southwest corner of the island, near the Theodore Roosevelt Bridge.

Some books of interest to teens are *Theodore Roosevelt: A Life,* by Nathan Miller; and *Theodore Roosevelt: A Strenuous Life,* by Kathleen Dalton. The movie *The Indomitable Teddy Roosevelt* brings Roosevelt to life (teens).

Metro: Rosslyn, but a long walk from there

Between the District and Virginia, on the Potomac River, just north of the Theodore Roosevelt Bridge

Open daily dawn to dusk

National Park Service rangers give nature and history tours of the island during summer months, as well as a variety of other activities, including children's programs

703/289–2500

www.nps.gov/this

DEA Museum

For Tweens and Teens . . . Kids will be intrigued with a visit to this museum in the headquarters of the Drug Enforcement Administration, in spite of the "lessons" to be learned through the exhibits. Both the permanent and changing displays include factual information, current issues, and some quite graphic anti-drug commercials from the 1980s (that kids, of course, should love).

> Metro: Pentagon City
> 700 Army Navy Drive, Arlington, VA
> Tuesday to Friday 10–4
> Free; make reservations for groups of 10 or more
> 202/307–3463
> www.deamuseum.org

The Pentagon

For Teens . . . The only building in the city visible from space, the Pentagon is a fitting symbol of the size of the nation's military. In July 1941, with another world war looming, the War Department required larger quarters and demanded that its planners come up with a suitable building. The familiar edifice took only 16 months and $50 million to build, and is overwhelming in its statistics. The 6.5 million square feet (with 131 stairways, 19 escalators, and 17½ miles of corridors) house the offices of the U.S. Army, Navy, Marine Corps, and Air Force under the umbrella of the (since-named) Department of Defense. The military establishment here is so mammoth, it even has four zip codes of its own.

The tour is quite zippy, because it takes a whole hour to cover more than 1½ miles. As befits this kind of marathon, prepare yourself (and all those accompanying you): eat and drink before you come, wear comfortable shoes, and *remember to use the restroom*. The nearest restaurants are at Pentagon City, via Metro.

Note: since the events of September 11, 2001, only group tours are permitted, selected on a case-by-case basis. Tour partici-

The Pentagon

pants must be 14, and visitors under 16 must be accompanied by an adult.

Both shopping and restaurants are abundant at **Fashion Centre at Pentagon City** (1100 S. Hayes Street, Arlington; 703/415–2400). Here you can find **Nordstrom** and **Macy's,** as well as Discovery Channel, Wallet World, Sunglass Hut, the Hat Zone, six movie theaters, and all kinds of food, from hamburgers to seafood to the **Grill at the Ritz-Carlton.** The center is open Monday through Saturday 10 to 9:30, Sunday 11 to 6.

> Metro: Pentagon
>
> In northern Virginia, across the Potomac River from Washington, D.C.
>
> Military, government, and educational groups must e-mail or fax requests for tours between two weeks and three months in advance. You can also contact your congressional representatives about arranging a tour.
>
> 703/545–6700 information only
>
> www.pentagon.afis.osd.mil

Pentagon Memorial

For Teens . . . At 9:37 AM on September 11, 2001, American Airlines Flight 77 slammed into the Pentagon. On a Thursday morning, September 11, 2008, at the same hour, a two-acre memorial park was dedicated to the victims at that site. Trees, water, gravel, and stone combine to form a place of reflection and repose. A young husband-and-wife design team created a quiet space where visitors can come, without tickets or guides, security checkpoints or metal detectors, seven days a week, 24 hours a day.

At the nearest edge of the site, a black granite plaque summarizes the events of 9/11/01; a few paces farther, another slate of black granite holds the names of the 184 victims and the years they were born—a key to finding each one's memorial bench. After entering a gateway plaza, visitors cross a physical and symbolic threshold: a fire-scorched stone band cut from the original walls of the Pentagon reads: "September 11, 2001, 9:37 AM." A bed of fine gravel paves the area around 184 maple trees and 184 benches. Perched above its own rectangle of circulating water, each bench is aligned with the plane's path, and each is inscribed with the name of a victim of the crash.

A stone bench, interspersed with black granite, runs along a perimeter of the site, noting the birth years of the victims. Behind it rises the concrete "Age Wall," reflecting in height the ages of those lost—from three to seventy-one inches. Projecting an aura of light at all times of day, the Pentagon Memorial is a reminder of the timelessness of memory, love, and loss.

Metro: Pentagon
Site is west of Pentagon's South Parking Area
Open daily, 24 hours
703/545–6700 (Pentagon)
www.whs.mil/memorial

National Weather Service

For Older Tweens and Teens . . . "Everyone complains about the weather, but no one does anything about it," Mark Twain is supposed to have quipped. Well, here's a chance to see how our National Weather Service responds. Touring the facility, kids in the 6th grade and up can see the operations area and learn how experts make their forecasts. Evening visitors might get to watch the launch of a weather balloon.

Metro not available; come by car or taxi
44087 Weather Service Road, Sterling, Virginia
Tours weekdays 10 to 1 and 5 to 7
Call for special events
703/996–2200

Steven F. Udvar-Hazy Center

For All Ages . . . The Steven F. Udvar-Hazy Center in Chantilly, Virginia, is a well-stocked addition to its parent museum, the National Air and Space Museum (see Chapter 3). Together, the two museums comprise the world's largest aviation and space complex.

Full-size aircraft hanging from the ceiling like balsa-wood models occupy only a part of the hangar-size building. On the floor is an impressive array of missiles, rockets, and spacecraft. One highlight is the 69-foot-tall Redstone missile, used to send the first U.S. astronauts into space. In addition to these crowd-pleasers, the museum boasts a serious collection of the "innards" that make aircraft and spacecraft run. Engineers and budding engineers will be fascinated by this unique collection.

The centerpiece of the facility is the refurbished Space Shuttle *Enterprise*—a poignant reminder of the continuing dream of space travel and of the human price we often pay.

Metro: no access; come by car or taxi
14390 Air & Space Museum Parkway, Chantilly, Virginia
Open September to March, daily 10 to 5:30; April to August,
     daily 10 to 6:30; closed December 25
202/633–1000 or 793/260–0107
www.nasm.si.edu/museum/udvarhazy

Where to Stay in Arlington

For a whole different flavor from the downtown Washington, D.C., areas, maybe you'll want to stay in Arlington, where there are often lower prices than in Washington itself.

The Virginian Suites
1500 Arlington Boulevard
703/522–9600 or 800/275–2866
www.virginiansuites.com
Metro: Rosslyn (via free shuttle bus)

Radisson Reagan National Airport
2020 Jefferson Davis Highway (U.S. 1)
703/920–8600 or 800/333–3333
www.radisson.com
Metro: Crystal City

Answers to Smart Stuff Questions

A. Traveler. This horse was the stuff of legends.

B. General Omar Bradley. He was an unpretentious, straightforward leader whose concern for his troops made him a beloved figure in World War II. The present-day Bradley fighting vehicle (tank) is named in his honor.

C. The design of the capital of L'Enfant's adopted country looks much like that of Paris, capital of his native country, France.

D. In 1957 Arkansas Governor Orval Faubus brought state troopers to the door of Little Rock High School, forcing a reluctant President Dwight D. Eisenhower to send federal troops to escort embattled black students to school. News photos of the day show Little Rock citizens, old and young, hurling taunts and jeers as the frightened teenagers walked through the crowd.

E. We place our right hand over our hearts when saluting the American flag. Soldiers place their right hands to the right sides of their foreheads. Standing at attention entails placing your feet together, side by side and touching.

CHAPTER 12

Olde Virginia

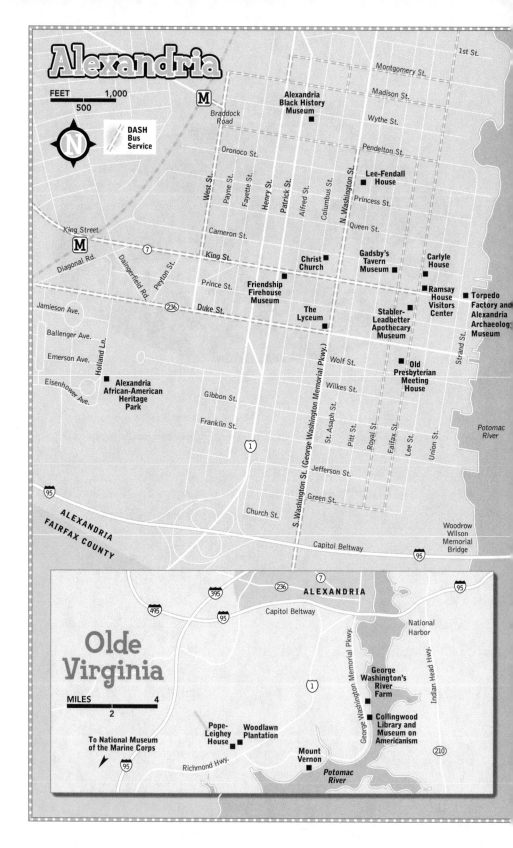

A beautiful time warp on the Potomac River, Alexandria, Virginia, exemplifies the graciousness of colonial America. From the quiet elegance of **Carlyle House** to the lively environment of the restored **Gadsby's Tavern,** from the modern handicrafts at the **Torpedo Factory** to the artifacts at the **Alexandria Archaeology Lab,** from the rustic setting of **Claude Moore Colonial Farm** to the timeless grace of George Washington's **Mount Vernon,** there's no shortage of interesting sites to explore. Calling herself "Washington's older sister," Alexandria (and surroundings) reminds us in our modern society to have respect for age. Many places in this area are closed on Monday, no doubt the effect of the gracious living of a bygone era.

★Old Town Alexandria

For All Ages . . . So why are all those guys marching down the street in *skirts* in the middle of December? It's the annual Scottish Christmas Walk, a yuletide parade held here because of Alexandria's Scottish roots. It was a group of Scottish tobacco merchants who founded the town in 1749. Named for a tobacco merchant (not for a city in Egypt), John Alexander, who purchased the site from its

Quick Guide to

Attraction	Location
★Old Town Alexandria	On and around King Street, Alexandria, VA
★Claude Moore Colonial Farm at Turkey Run	6310 Georgetown Pike, McLean, VA
★Mount Vernon	South end of GW Memorial Parkway
George Washington's River Farm	7932 E. Boulevard Drive, Alexandria, VA
Collingwood Library and Museum on Americanism	8301 E. Boulevard Drive, Alexandria, VA
Woodlawn Plantation	9000 Richmond Highway, Alexandria, VA
Pope-Leighey House	9000 Richmond Highway, Alexandria, VA
National Museum of the Marine Corps	Off Route I–95, Quantico, VA

Olde Virginia Attractions

Age Range	Hours	Details on
All Ages	See individual sites for hours	Page 303
All Ages	April–mid-Dec., Wed.–Sun. 10 AM–4:30 PM	Page 320
All Ages	Open daily. April–Aug., 8 AM–5 PM; Sept.–Oct., 9 AM–5 PM; Nov.–Mar., 9 AM–4 PM	Page 321
All Ages	Mon.–Fri. 9 AM–5 PM	Page 325
Teens	Mon., Wed.–Sat. 10 AM–4 PM; Sun. 1 PM–4 PM	Page 326
Tweens and Teens	March–Dec., Thurs.–Mon. 10 AM–5 PM	Page 327
Tweens and Teens	March–Dec., Thurs.–Mon. 10 AM–5 PM	Page 328
All Ages	Open daily 9–5	Page 329

English owner in 1669, Alexandria was a major colonial port, as well as a trade, social, and political center, in Revolutionary times. During the Civil War Alexandria was occupied by Federal troops and used as a base for Union campaigns in Virginia. In 1801 Congress officially accepted Alexandria as a part of the District of Columbia, but by 1846 Alexandria residents were disillusioned with their disenfranchisement as citizens of the District. They incorporated themselves back into the county of Alexandria. (Current D.C. residents, still disenfranchised, consider this a smart move.) The now-restored historic area of Old Town Alexandria still looks like it's part of an earlier century.

Old Town is about 8 mi south of Washington, along the Potomac River. It's easy to get to, either by Metro or by car. Parking, however, is at a real premium. You need a pass from Ramsay House Visitor Center if you want to park, so stop there first.

Smart Stuff

For Tykes . . . Alexandria began as a colonial town growing up around a port. In the early days of America, many goods had to be imported from other countries. If you lived in Alexandria in colonial times, what would you want to receive by ship?

Metro: King Street, plus a 15-minute walk; you can also take a shuttle bus or a DASH bus down King Street

Ramsay House Visitors Center

In this port city even the buildings sometimes come from elsewhere. This yellow clapboard house came up the river from Dumfries, Virginia, in 1749 (not all by itself, of course!). It was the home of Lord

Helpful Hint

At Ramsey House Visitors Center, be sure to pick up the *Official Visitors Guide of Alexandria*, which has coupons for good deals inside.

Mayor (and Scottish merchant) William Ramsay. Cigars were manufactured here after the Civil War. Today it's a visitor center, offering free maps, brochures, and parking passes for the area, all more useful here than cigars.

Metro: King Street
221 King Street
Free
703/838–4200 or 800/388–9119
www.funside.com

★Torpedo Factory Art Center

For All Ages . . . Talk about recycling! The Torpedo Factory, a World War I munitions plant, is now home to artists and archaeologists. More than 160 professional artists are at work here. Sculptors, painters, photographers, printmakers, potters, weavers, glassblowers, stained-glass designers, and jewelry designers display and sell their original creations. Kids of all ages enjoy watching the artists and asking them questions. Because the building backs on the waterfront, this is also a pretty place to picnic or stroll. The **Food Pavilion** behind the building offers several different selections and a pretty outdoor seating area.

Money-Saving Tip

Purchase a "block ticket" to get discounted entry to some of the major attractions in Old Town, a saving if you plan to visit several of the places included.

Headquartered in the Torpedo Factory is the **Alexandria Archaeology Museum** (703/838–4399; www.alexandriaarchaeology. org), designed to preserve and reconstruct information about the history of Alexandria. You can explore the exhibits and observe volunteers at work cleaning and cataloging artifacts found in the area. Kids are astonished to learn firsthand that these relics of another time were found by digging within what are now the city limits.

Old-fashioned fun

This might lend new meaning and value to that old collection of baseball cards or bottle caps. Volunteers are happy to answer questions, and there are videos to see as well. Tours can be arranged for students in grades 3 through 12. The facility is open Tuesday through Friday 10 to 3, Saturday 10 to 5, Sunday 1 to 5.

Of interest to the older tweens and teens might be: *In Small Things Forgotten: An Archaeology of Early American Life*, by James Deetz.

Metro: King Street

105 N. Union Street, at the waterfront

Open daily 10 to 6; closed January 1, Easter, July 4, Thanksgiving Day, December 25; call first—hours change for special events

Free

703/838–4565 recorded information

www.torpedofactory.org

Carlyle House

For Tweens and Teens . . . This Palladian-style stone mansion was patterned after English and Scottish manor houses and was built between 1751 and 1753 by Scottish merchant John Carlyle. A man of substantial means, he imported the finest furnishings from Europe and hired the most skilled local craftsmen to produce the beautiful woodwork found throughout the house. Most of the original furnishings, unfortunately, have been replaced with similar period pieces, and the original residents have been replaced by mannequins in period dress. You can listen to some recorded conversations and pick up a 22-pound bucket of water, similar to those that slaves were expected to carry. Construction of this 18th-century house is demonstrated in one unrestored room upstairs, with its exposed beams, hand-wrought nails, and unplastered walls.

Smart Stuff

For Tweens . . . If you were building a home in colonial times, what materials would you have needed to import from England? What would you most likely have used from local sources? (A.)

Of all the historic encounters in this house, where George Washington was a frequent visitor, the most notable was likely the 1755 meeting between Major General Edward Braddock, commander in chief of the king's forces in North America, and five colonial governors. He asked them to financially support Britain's war with the French and Indians through a special tax. The five colonial legislatures refused, exercising the colonies' newfound feelings of separation from their mother country. The buck started here.

Behind Carlyle House is a pretty garden with a gazebo. Picnickers are welcome.

Metro: King Street
121 N. Fairfax Street, at Cameron Street
Open Tuesday to Saturday 10 to 4, Sunday noon to 4
Tours every half hour
Call ahead for special programs and tours
Admission fee
703/549–2997
www.nvrpa.org

Gadsby's Tavern Museum

For Tweens and Teens . . . The "in" place during the 18th century, Gadsby's Tavern was the social center for Alexandria. The innkeeper, John Gadsby, who purchased the original tavern from John Wise, joined two buildings (one a tavern and one a hotel) to provide guests with food, lodging, entertainment, the wares of itinerant merchants, and even the services of doctors and dentists. George Washington might not have slept here (his kitchenless house was nearby), but he and Martha certainly ate here often. Other visiting notables included James Madison, John Adams, John Quincy Adams, Thomas Jefferson, and the Marquis de Lafayette. Overnight stays meant paying for a space in a bed or on the floor; your roommate or bedmate was entirely up to chance. Because this was also the scene of numerous political meetings, it's likely that the phrase "politics makes strange bedfellows" was coined here. These days, most travelers choose their *own* bedfellows, regardless of their politics.

Thanks to archaeological excavations and inventories of colonial furnishings, the rooms have been painstakingly restored. The tour includes a sampling of the different kinds of entertainment and meeting rooms, as well as bedrooms. It also visits the underground icehouse. (Talk about water in the basement!)

Gadsby's Tavern Restaurant (703/548–1288) harks back to those thrilling days of yesteryear when entertainment came with your meal and everybody dressed up for dinner. The menu features delicious homemade soups, fresh Virginia ham, roasted turkey and duckling, Sally Lunn bread, English trifle, and buttermilk custard pie, as well as a selection of half-price children's entrées. A good-size helping of modern-day dough is essential here, but strolling musicians (Sunday at brunch and Sunday and Monday at dinner) are free. Don't worry—the *food* is not genuinely antique. The restaurant is open Monday to Saturday 11:30 to 3 and 5:30 to 10, Sunday 11 to 3. Reservations are a good idea.

Metro: King Street

134 N. Royal Street, at Cameron Street

Open April through October, Monday 1 to 5, Tuesday to Saturday 10 to 5, Sunday 1 to 5; November to March Wednesday to Saturday 11 to 4, Sunday 1 to 4; closed Thanksgiving Day and December 25

Guided tours begin a quarter before and a quarter after the hour; the last tour begins 45 minutes before closing

Call ahead about special children's activities

Admission fee
703/838–4242
www.gadsbystavern.org

Lee-Fendall House

For Teens . . . Though this house was built by a civic leader, Philip Richard Fendall, the Lees far outnumbered the Fendalls in residency—37 Lees called this place home between 1785 and 1903. Actually, even Fendall was a distant Lee relative. Since he married, at various times, three different Lee women, he was certainly an in-law. From 1937 to 1969, ironically, it was the residence of someone anathema to Virginia conservatism: labor leader John L. Lewis.

The house, originally Federal white clapboard, was treated to a revival of a different sort during the 1850s. It was renovated in the Greek Classical Revival style and was accented with ornate woodwork and decorations, some of which remain. A treat for miniaturists is the third floor, with its exhibit of antique dollhouses.

On display in the Lee-Fendall House is an original copy of the newspaper eulogy written by Harry Lee

Smart Stuff

For Teens . . . During the eight years of the American Revolution, imports from England were nearly nil. If you were a colonial merchant, what kinds of goods would you be lacking? (B.)

for George Washington. Look for the famous phrase "First in war, first in peace, and first in the hearts of his countrymen." This family did have a way with words. As Alexandria was taken over by the government to give the capital more security during the Civil War, the Union forces appropriated the house for use as a hospital. The beautiful colonial garden includes a 200-year-old magnolia tree and boxwood-lined paths. The Lee-Fendall House was undergoing some renovations at this writing, so be sure to call in advance.

There are numerous appropriate books, but we suggest: *Outrageous Women of Colonial America*, by Mary Rodd Furbee (older tweens and teens); *Prisoners of Hope: A Tale of Colonial Virginia*, by

Mary Johnston (teens); and *Homebuilding and Woodworking in Colonial America*, by C. Keith Wilbur (teens).

Metro: King Street
614 Oronoco Street
Open Wednesday to Saturday 10 to 4, Sunday 1 to 4; closed
    Thanksgiving Day and mid-December until February 1;
    house is sometimes closed on weekends for private events
30- to 45-minute guided tours begin on the hour
Admission fee
703/548–1789
www.leefendallhouse.org

Alexandria Black History Museum

For Tweens and Teens . . . Located in the Parker-Gray Historical District, this 20th-century building was the product of a protest. It was built in 1940 after a sit-in was staged to protest the segregation of local libraries. In two rooms you can study photographs, paintings, books, and other documentation about the black community from 1749 to the present. One gallery tells the history of the

> Only one pair of brothers signed the Declaration of Independence, both Lees. Richard Henry Lee and Francis Lightfoot Lee were, ironically, ancestors of Robert E. Lee, who served as leader of the Confederate forces attempting to separate from the Union.

Parker-Gray District, while the other hosts changing exhibits. The annex, referred to as the **Watson Reading Room,** holds many books and documents on African-American topics. Anyone is welcome to come here to do research. Pick up a printed walking tour of historic sites at the information desk. Of note on this tour are the Franklin and Armfield Slave Market and the house of a free black master carpenter, George Seaton, elected to the city council and the legislature during Reconstruction.

Helpful Hint

Because this site is basically a research center, there's not much here for small children. African-American children of all ages, however, will take great pride in the accomplishments of black Americans highlighted in the displays.

Teens might enjoy reading *American Slavery, American Freedom: The Ordeal of Colonial Virginia*, by Edmund S. Morgan.

Metro: King Street or Braddock Road
902 Wythe Street
Open Tuesday to Saturday 10 to 4; closed major holidays
Call in advance for guided tours
Donation suggested
703/838–4356
www.alexblackhistory.org

Several blocks south and west of the Alexandria Black History Museum, the **Alexandria African-American Heritage Park** sits on Holland Lane between Duke Street and Eisenhower Avenue. Here you can find an 8-acre cemetery, a preserved wetland, and a memorial site. If you have a chance to wander through, you can find numerous memorial sculptures.

Helpful Hint

Call ahead to ask for copies of the Alexandria Black History Resource Center's walking tour of African-American sites.

Christ Church

When Franklin D. Roosevelt brought Winston Churchill to attend services here on the World Day of Prayer, January 1, 1942, he was maintaining a tradition. Twentieth-century presidents attended ser-

*The gates to historic
Christ Church*

vices here, usually on a Sunday close to George Washington's birthday, sitting in his pew, No. 60. The Lee family also had pews here; Robert E.'s was No. 46. In continuous use since 1773, the church has been restored to its original Georgian-style beauty. Some parts are original—the hand-blown glass windows, for example—and the cut-glass chandelier that was one of the most advanced types of light fixtures available at the beginning of the 19th century. In the early 1800s the galleries, organ, bell tower, and church bell were added. Modern heating, which came later, was probably the most appreciated innovation.

The old **Parish Hall** is now a gift shop, and houses an exhibit on the church's history. The graveyard was Alexandria's only burial ground until 1805. It holds the graves of thirty-four Confederate soldiers.

Metro: King Street
118 N. Washington Street, near Columbus and Cameron
    streets
Open Monday to Saturday 9 to 4, Sunday 2 to 4:30, except
    during services; closed holidays and after services
    January 1, Easter, Thanksgiving Day, and December 25
Call ahead for 20-minute guided tours
Donation suggested
703/549–1450
www.historicchristchurch.org

Friendship Firehouse Museum

For All Ages . . . It's always nice to know people in high places. When the Friendship Fire Company was organized in 1774, it had an impressive list of "honorary" volunteers, including high-ranking political figures like George Washington. Before it had a building, the fire company met in taverns, storing its equipment in nearby barns. Ironically, the company's first building was destroyed by fire in the 1850s. The first-floor exhibit room of this restored Italianate building houses firefighting equipment such as leather buckets, speaking trumpets, and an ornate hand-drawn fire engine from the 18th and 19th centuries.

On the second floor, furnished in Victorian style, is the firemen's meeting room, testifying to the fraternal character of its organization in the community. Although it ceased fighting fires in the 1870s, the current Friendship Veterans Fire Engine Association continues as a historic and ceremonial organization.

Metro: King Street
107 S. Alfred Street, between King and Prince streets

Friendship Firehouse Museum

Open Friday and Saturday 10 to 4, Sunday 1 to 4; closed January 1 and December 25
703/838–3891
http://oha.alexandriava.gov/friendship

The Lyceum

For Teens . . . In addition to serving as Robert E. Lee's schoolteacher, Benjamin Hallowell was the prime motivator behind the establishment of a cultural center in the city of Alexandria. In 1839 this Greek Revival building boasted a library, lecture halls, natural-history exhibits, and programs with guest speakers such as Daniel Webster. Despite a slight hiatus during the Civil War, when it was used by both Confederate and Union troops, the Lyceum continues to host lectures, concerts, and educational programs on local and state history. Exhibits include photographs, prints, silver, period furniture, ceramics, and Civil War artifacts.

Adjacent to the Lyceum is a gift shop with reproductions of early pewter, silver, brass, and glassware, as well as prints, posters, needlepoint patterns, toys and games for kids, and regional foods that make great Old Town mementos. You can also stock up on maps and brochures and consult the knowledgeable staff if you have any questions.

Tykes might enjoy *School in Colonial America*, by Mark Thomas (Welcome Books series). For older tweens and teens, take a look at *Alexander the Servant Boy Who Became a Colonial Virginia Frontiersman*, by Charles Stinson.

Metro: King Street
201 S. Washington Street, between Prince and Duke streets
Open Monday to Saturday 11 to 5, Sunday 1 to 5; closed January 1, Thanksgiving Day, and December 25
703/838–4994
http://oha.alexandriava.gov/lyceum

Old Presbyterian Meeting House

The Presbyterian-leaning clergyman Alexander Whitaker converted Pocahontas in 1614 in Jamestown, and ever since, Presbyterians have been worshipping in Virginia. Alexandria, with its Scottish heritage, was an obvious spot for this brick church built in the mid-1770s. George Washington's memorial service was held here in 1799, and in the graveyard lies, among others, Dr. James Craik, Washington's doctor and surgeon general of the Continental Army. The tomb of an unknown Revolutionary War soldier is enclosed in a sarcophagus marked by a wrought-iron rail. An active church until 1889, the Meeting House again opened its doors in 1949 and, fully restored, still uses its old-fashioned gate pews in its original building.

> Metro: King Street
> 321 S. Fairfax Street, between Wolfe and Duke streets
> Open weekdays 9 to 3; stop by the church office to visit the
>   sanctuary
> 703/549–6670
> www.opmh.org

Stabler-Leadbetter Apothecary Museum

For Tweens and Teens . . . The family that sells together sometimes stays in business 141 years. At least that's what happened to the Stabler family, who in 1792 founded the Apothecary Shop, Alexandria's oldest mercantile establishment. Of course it helped to have high-class patrons such as Henry Clay, John C. Calhoun, Robert E. Lee, James Monroe, George Mason, and, of course, the father of our country, George Washington. Martha was a frequent customer, too. Her letter requesting a quart of castor oil still hangs in a glass case in the shop. Looking much as it did in colonial days, the Stabler-Leadbetter Apothecary Museum displays its original collec-

Smart Stuff

For Tweens and Teens . . . Several of our modern-day medicinal and food products come from herbs and plants. Ginger ale, a popular drink and aid for calming upset stomachs, is made from ginger root. What present-day herbal products can you name? **(C.)**

tion of 900 colorful hand-blown medicinal bottles with gold-leaf labels, as well as other antique artifacts, including old-fashioned scales, account books, prescriptions, and medical wares such as equipment for bloodletting.

The adjoining gift shop sells antique books on medicine, antique medicine bottles, and candy (*not* antique). All proceeds support the museum.

> Metro: King Street
> 105 S. Fairfax Street, between Royal and Fairfax streets
> April through October, Tuesday to Saturday 10 to 5, Sunday and Monday 1 to 5; November through March, Wednesday to Saturday 11 to 4, Sunday 1 to 4; closed January 1, Thanksgiving Day, and December 25
> Admission fee
> 703/838–3852
> http://oha.alexandriava.gov/apothecary

If you've been plodding along with us all this time, you *must* be hungry, or at least thirsty, by now. Up and down King Street is a variety of eateries. Two popular spots for homemade ice cream are **Pop's Old Fashioned Ice Cream** (109 King Street; 703/518–5374) and **Scoop Grill and Homemade Ice Cream** (110 King Street; 703/549–4527). The **Farmers' Market** (301 King Street; 703/838–5006) is a good stop for fresh fruits and veggies, as well as for baked goods.

Near Gadsby's Tavern, the cafeteria-style **La Madeleine** (500 King Street; 703/739–2854) serves wonderful baked goods, fresh salads, and homemade soups, as well as delectable entrées from quiche to salmon, all in a cozy setting. It's open Sunday to Thursday 7 AM to 10 PM, Friday and Saturday 6:30 AM to 11:30 PM. A block from the Lyceum, **Bread and Chocolate** (611 King Street; 703/548–0992) serves sandwiches and scrumptious desserts. It's open Monday to Saturday 7 to 7, Sunday 8 to 6. An outpost of the chain **Così** (700 King Street; 703/299–9833) offers fresh-baked pizza from its wood-burning oven and—talk about a treat!—allows kids to make their own s'mores on a tiny burner brought to their table.

Drop by Monday to Thursday 7 to 10, Friday 7 to midnight, Saturday 8 to midnight, and Sunday 8 to 10.

Near Christ Church and the Friendship Firehouse Museum, **Asian Bistro** (809 King Street; 703/836–1515) serves specialties from all over Asia. It's open Monday to Thursday 11:30 to 10, Friday 11:30 to 11, Saturday noon to 11, and Sunday 4 to 10. **King Street Blues** (112 North St. Asaph Street; 703/836–8800), which *isn't* on King Street, is a Southern-style roadhouse diner with music to accompany your meal. Head here for a bargain on chicken, beef stew, or meat loaf accompanied by garlic potatoes. Drop by Monday to Thursday 11:30 to 10, Friday and Saturday 11:30 to 11, Sunday 11 to 10. Near the King Street Metro is the **Hard Times Café** (1404 King Street; 703/837–0050), a good bet for inexpensive entrées accompanied by cornbread, steak fries, and onion rings. For atmosphere, it has jeans-and-T-shirted staff, historic photos, and a jukebox filled with music. It's open daily 11 to 11.

Shopping in Old Town is an adventure in itself. There's no shortage of ways to spend your money. Most of the shops are along King Street and Washington Street. (We start near Ramsay House Visitors Center, but if you follow our list backward, you can start near the King Street Metro.) All that glitters isn't gold—sometimes it's silver. **The Silver Parrot** (113 King Street) has handcrafted and contemporary jewelry from around the world. Take a peek inside and decide whether your kids would like this as much as you would! A popular place for kids is **Why Not?** (200 King Street), with books, toys, and other wares. It takes **Ten Thousand Villages** (915 King Street), not just one, to make this fascinating shop that will appeal to the idealists in your group. Run by a nonprofit organization, it has products from developing countries, returning the profits to the artisans. This is a worthwhile place to spend a buck. For the comic-book collectors, **Aftertime Comics** (1304 King Street) stocks not only hard-to-find collectors' items but also back issues of *MAD* and *Eerie* magazines. **A Likely Story** (1555 King Street) has a play area for younger kids while you search for something to read. These are just a few suggestions. Please keep us posted when you find gems we can share with other readers.

★Claude Moore Colonial Farm at Turkey Run

For All Ages . . . At this reconstruction of a humble family farm from the 1770s, kids can find out what the good old days were *really* like. Although their colonial-era counterparts didn't have to go to school, wait until your youngsters find out what they *did* have to do. Planting and harvesting tobacco, wheat, and vegetables; tending farm animals; chopping wood; and cooking meals were all part of the daily routine. Costumed guides (and school-age volunteers on weekends) demonstrate these chores using period tools. An orchard, fields, hog pen, and single-room farmhouse are accessible via dirt paths that wind around the property. Eighteenth-century market days featuring period music, puppet shows, and craft demonstrations are held the third weekend of the month in May, July, and October. You can munch on delicious food and shop for reproductions of 18th-century clothing, soap, jewelry, pottery, and toys. A visit here makes a wonderful contrast with Mount Vernon. Maybe after seeing this, kids will think it's better to go to school.

How about some play reading? Try *Read-Aloud Plays: Colonial America*, by Marci Appelbaum and Jeff Catanese (tweens). A book teens might enjoy is *Everyday Life in Early America*, by David Hawke.

Smart Stuff

For Tykes . . . Make a toy you would like to have played with if you had lived in colonial times. Toys were extremely simple then, made from sticks, pebbles, cornhusks, cloth, and other natural materials.

Remember to use modern restrooms *before* you come to the farm. The portable toilets aren't exactly outhouses, but they're today's equivalent.

No Metro station; accessible by bus or car
6310 Georgetown Pike, McLean, Virginia

Open April to mid-December, Wednesday to Sunday 10 to
4:30; closed rainy days, July 4, and Thanksgiving.
Schedule group visits in advance; call for a calendar of special
events
703/442–7557
www.1771.org

★Mount Vernon

For All Ages . . . Whereas adults are impressed with this beautiful
waterfront property and its gorgeous views, kids are more interested
in the outbuildings that housed the smokehouse, the kitchen, the
stables, the blacksmith shop, the cobbler shop, the spinning house,
the carriage house, the greenhouse, and all the others on the
grounds of George Washington's home plantation in Virginia. You
can visit the tomb and the gardens as well. Washington believed a
farm should be completely self-sufficient, so all its needs had to be
met on site, even those of the "spirit." Washington's Scottish-born
farm manager persuaded him to include a working distillery on his
property. (The reconstructed still does *not* actually produce any liq-
uid refreshment.) On days when there are no specific demonstrations, youngsters can still peer into these various outbuildings and
see how food was prepared, how shoes were made, how laundry was
done, and how the father of our country got around, since he didn't
have a presidential limousine. The **Mount Vernon Forest Trail** provides a ¼-mile hike, which kids enjoy.

Helpful Hint

There are plenty of special activities that will appeal to
kids, from the "Slave Life at Mount Vernon" tours that
take them into the former slave quarters to the "Hands-
on History" area that lets them handle 18th-century toys
and tools. Be sure to request all the details in advance.
Call 703/780–2000, or write to Mount Vernon Education
Department, Box 110, Mount Vernon, VA 22121.

Activities abound at Mount Vernon. Kids can spin wool, dig for archaeological artifacts, learn slave songs, play with colonial toys, construct wooden buckets, hike nature trails, and even pop into a Revolutionary War tent filled with soldiers' gear and an imposing life-size statue of George Washington. An eye-opening contrast to the gracious main building is a visit to the slaves' quarters. Pick up an Adventure Map to help you decide where to go and what to see while exploring George and Martha Washington's estate. Guides in 18th-century costumes are stationed at various spots on the grounds and in the mansion.

For somebody who had a war to fight and a young country to run, it's amazing that Washington was able to take time to run his plantation and entertain nearly 800 guests per year. It was nice to come home to this lovely mansion, a convenient inheritance from his older brother Lawrence. In addition to the beautiful period furnishings and accessories (many of which are original), Mount Vernon holds some interesting curiosities. One is the key to the Bastille (displayed in a glass case), a gift to Washington in 1790 from his wartime buddy, the Marquis de Lafayette. There's a foot-operated fan chair to keep away the flies when Washington sat down to read (remember, screens hadn't been invented yet). The gracious formal rooms reflect the Washingtons' focus on entertainment, particularly dancing and dining.

The Georgian mansion, with its tall white columns, is not only a study in

The mansion at Mount Vernon

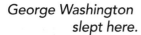

George Washington slept here.

elegance but an example of artifice as well. Its "stone" blocks are really wood coated with sand, edges carefully beveled, and painted white! Since air-conditioning was not available in the 18th century, George and Martha and their guests enjoyed the cool breezes from the Potomac sitting out on their large veranda. Nowadays, whenever Navy ships pass the mansion, they offer a salute in tribute to our first president.

In recent years Mount Vernon has seen some ambitious new additions, including theaters, galleries, and an incredible scale-model mansion. There's an impressive collection of artifacts from Washington's time (some, like the famous false teeth, owned by Washington himself), and remarkable likenesses of George set in significant scenes from his life. The highlight for kids will most likely be the sensory-stimulating movie in the Revolutionary War Theater, where cannon volleys rock the seats, fog descends from the ceiling, and "snow" falls during winter scenes at Valley Forge.

There's a huge list of books about George Washington, but here are a few we suggest looking at: *George Washington's Breakfast*, by Jean Fritz (tykes); *George Washington,* by Lenny Hort (tweens); and *The Unexpected George Washington: His Private Life*, by Harlow Giles Unger (teens).

If you get hungry at Mount Vernon, you're in luck. There's a snack bar with breakfast, lunch, and, of course, snacks. The **Mount Vernon Inn** (703/780–0011), open for lunch daily and dinner every day but Sunday, is a little on the pricey side. Reservations are recom-

Helpful Hint

To avoid spring and summer crowds, arrive at Mount Vernon before 11 AM or after 3 PM.

mended. People dressed in period costume serve up colonial-style fare. Call first, as the restaurant is sometimes closed for private events.

Now for the gift shops (yes, that's plural). The **Mount Vernon Gift Shop** sits beside the entrance gate (no admission ticket needed). It sells jewelry, toys, postcards, reproductions and furniture, and books, some especially for kids, published by Mount Vernon. There are also a Christmas shop and a plant shop selling seeds for colonial-style gardening. The **Lady Washington Shop,** near the upper garden and the slave quarters, carries the same types of merchandise but in a smaller setting. If you happen to arrive by boat, you can shop for souvenirs at the **Wharf Shop,** open March through October. The shops are open daily 9 to 6.

Smart Stuff

For Teens . . . The Washington family, like so many others in the South, relied on numerous slaves to maintain their lifestyles and livelihoods. If you had lived on such a plantation, what changes would you have implemented in order to maintain your farm and home with the employment of (freed) hired hands?

Metro: Huntington, and then Bus 101 (called the "Fairfax Connector"); it's most convenient to come by bus or car

South end of the George Washington Memorial Parkway, overlooking the Potomac River

Open April through August, daily 8 to 5; March and September through October, daily 9 to 5; November to March, daily 9 to 4

Smart Stuff

For Tykes and Tweens . . . The Washington family entertained a great deal, and even George Washington found time to fuss over his menus. If you had lived at Mount Vernon, what kinds of foods would you have had to eat? Look around the dining room for some hints. Keep in mind that a single meal consisted of many courses. **(D.)**

Boat trips on Spirit Cruises depart March to October from
    Pier 4 at 6th and Water streets, SW; fares include admission to Mount Vernon; for details, call 202/554–8013
Tourmobile (202/554–5100; www.tourmobile.com) offers
    tours to Mount Vernon mid-June to Labor Day
Martz Gold Line/Gray Line (301/386–8300; www.graylinedc.
    com) offers year-round tours to Mount Vernon and
    Alexandria
Admission fee
703/780–2000
www.mountvernon.org

George Washington's River Farm

For All Ages . . . One of George Washington's five farms, purchased in 1760 and rented out to tenant farmers who grew tobacco, River Farm is not your average colonial farm. There's an elegant main house with vistas of the Potomac River, as well as a special garden area for children. You can visit a "pizza garden" that grows basil, thyme, oregano, and other herbs essential to this favorite dish. You can explore a bat cave, a fortlike structure covered with plants and vines, and gardens that specifically attract bats, but-

Smart Stuff

For Tykes . . . Farmers have to decide what to plant on their land. What would you plant if you had a farm?

Smart Stuff

For Tweens . . . Do you know what tenant farming is? What are some of the differences between being a tenant farmer and owning a farm? **(E.)**

terflies, birds, and bees. There are even special child-size rocks for sitting on in the stone garden. Visitors—both young and grown-up—can enjoy self-guided tours of the 1757 main house, with its period furnishings, and the elaborate gardens, with their labeled plants. Today George Washington's River Farm is owned by the American Horticultural Society, which purchased it in 1973. The society maintains both display and test gardens on the 27-acre site.

Smart Stuff

For Tweens and Teens . . . George Washington's first job was as a surveyor. What does a surveyor do? See if you can find out whether the tools used in Washington's day are the same kinds used today. **(F.)**

No Metro station; come by bus or car only
7931 E. Boulevard Drive, Alexandria, off George Washington
    Parkway
Open weekdays 9 to 5; closed holidays
703/768–5700 or 800/777–7931
www.ahs.org

Collingwood Library and Museum on Americanism

For Teens . . . Like red, white, and blue? Have we got a place for you to visit! A research facility devoted to Americanism, the Collingwood Library and Museum was once actually part of George Washington's property at River Farm. Now owned by a nonprofit group, this white-columned mansion houses an extensive collection of books, slides, and videos on patriotic subjects. Flags of all 50 states, along with those of the Dis-

Helpful Hint

Collingwood Library and Museum is more of a research facility on patriotism than a full-fledged museum.

trict of Columbia and the five armed services, are on display. Of special interest is a Sioux chief's full-length ceremonial headdress of 87 eagle feathers, along with a collection of American Indian artifacts, basketry, pottery, and beaded belts.

No Metro station; come by bus or car only

8301 E. Boulevard Drive, Alexandria, off George Washington Parkway

Open Monday and Wednesday to Saturday 10 to 4, Sunday 1 to 4; closed holidays

703/765–1652

www.collingwoodlibrary.com

Woodlawn Plantation

For Tweens and Teens . . . The kind of wedding gift *everyone* would want, Woodlawn Plantation was given by George and Martha Washington to their granddaughter Eleanor (Nelly) Park Custis when she married Lawrence Lewis (Washington's nephew and personal secretary) in 1797. At the same time, Washington turned over to the young couple a distillery and a mill, hoping they would thus have a means of employment, he said, because "idleness is disreputable." In the late Georgian mode, this typical Virginia plantation home echoes the style of the groom's boyhood home, Kenmore, in Fredericksburg, Virginia. Still decorated with period antique furnishings, including some pieces brought from Mount Vernon, Woodlawn also has a formal garden, with lovely roses in summer. The drawing room still houses the harp and piano that Nelly and her daughters used in their frequent informal concerts.

Books of interest are: *Colonial Days: Discover the Past with Fun Projects, Games, Activities, and Recipes*, by David C. King (tweens); and *Colonial Kids: An Activity Guide to Life in the New World*, by Laurie Carlson (tweens and young teens).

Metro: Huntington, and then take the "Richmond Highway Express" bus; come by bus or car
9000 Richmond Highway, Alexandria, Virginia
Open March through late December, Thursday to Monday 10 to 4; closed Tuesday and Wednesday
Guided tours begin on the half hour; no tours in March
Admission fee; discounted combination ticket for Woodlawn and Pope-Leighey House
703/780–4000
www.woodlawn1805.org

Pope-Leighey House

For Tweens and Teens . . . A visit to the Pope-Leighey House on the grounds of the Woodlawn Plantation provides a distinct contrast to the graciously detailed colonial architecture of the past. Only a few minutes' walk from the colonial mansion, this is a stark, modernist structure from the 20th century. An example of what its architect, Frank Lloyd Wright, called his "Usonian" architecture (an abbreviation for the "United States of North America"), the house was to be a no-frills, simply designed home, theoretically affordable for the American middle class. Built for Washington-area journalist Loren Pope in 1941, it was sold to the Leigheys five years later. It was then threatened with demolition by highway construction, at which point the Leighey family turned it over to the National Trust for Historic Preservation.

The flowing space and strong horizontal lines, typical of Wright's work, take precedence over the potential attic and basement storage. Wright liked living space, not closets. Maybe he never had to store outgrown clothing or toys. An added attraction to this house is the furniture, designed by the architect himself. Whereas the house is built of cypress, glass, concrete, and brick, the furniture

Smart Stuff

For Tweens and Teens . . . Frank Lloyd Wright was one of the 20th-century's foremost architects. His focus was fitting a structure into its natural surroundings, as though it had grown from its environment. In what ways does this house fit that description? (For a surprise tidbit, see the answers list.) **(G.)**

is more inviting comfort-wise. Unfortunately, the architect is no longer available to design any for you.

> Metro: Huntington, and then take a 9-A bus; come by bus or car
> 9000 Richmond Highway, Alexandria, Virginia
> Open March through December, Thursday to Monday 10 to 4; closed Tuesday, Wednesday, Thanksgiving Day, and December 25
> Admission fee; discounted combination ticket for Woodlawn and Pope-Leighey House
> 703/780–4000
> www.popeleighey1940.org

National Museum of the Marine Corps

For Older Tweens and Teens . . . On 135 acres near Quantico, Virginia, this museum explores the role of the Marine Corps in American history. The building, with its angled, sky-swept tower, is meant to evoke the image of the famous flag-raising at Iwo Jima.

"Enter and Experience What It Means to Be a Marine" is engraved in stone at the museum's entrance. The museum takes you to a replica of a recruiting station, to a bus whose windows are actually video monitors presenting oral histories of young men and women departing for basic training, to a replica of a boot camp, complete with a drill instructor. If hearing "The Marine Corps Hymn" sends chills down your back, this is clearly the place for you.

A **Rifle Range Simulator** offers kids over 8 the opportunity to "fire" an M-16 rifle at a target. **Semper Fidelis Memorial Park** is adjacent to the museum; several thousand bricks along the sidewalks are engraved with the names of specific marines.

The **gift shop** has a model of the Iwo Jima flag raising done in Legos! A playground for young children is located near the parking area—a real one, not made with Legos.

There are two restaurants at the museum: the **Tun Tavern** is a replica of an 18th-century Philadelphia tavern; it opens for lunch only. The **Mess Hall**, cafeteria-style food, is open the same hours as the museum.

Two books of special interest to visitors here are: *Marines: An Illustrated History: The United States Marine Corps from 1775 to the 21st Century*, by Chester G. Hearn (older tweens and teens); and *Semper Fi: Stories of the United States Marines from Boot Camp to Battle*, edited by Clint Willis (teens).

No Metro station; come by bus or car only
18900 Jefferson Davis Highway, outside the Quantico Marine
    Corps base
Daily 9 to 5; closed December 25
800/397–7585or 877/635–1775
www.usmcmuseum.org

Smart Stuff

For Tweens and Teens . . . The Marine Corps has always prided itself on being a special, small service within the military. What is its unique function? **(H.)**

Where to Stay in Olde Virginia

These days, visitors don't have to share beds unless they choose to, but there are some bargains to be found in Alexandria. For more information on Old Town hotels, call the Alexandria Chamber of Commerce (703/549–1000).

Sheraton Suites Old Town Alexandria
801 N. St. Asaph Street
703/836–4700 or 800/325–3535
www.starwoodhotels.com
Metro: King Street

Answers to Smart Stuff Questions

A. You would have needed to import doorknobs and other hardware, perhaps of brass or wrought iron, and some construction tools. If you were prosperous, you might also have ordered fine fabrics and elegant furniture. From local sources, your building materials might have been lumber, stone, or bricks (made from local clay).

B. Youngsters might want to consider that England had far greater manufacturing capacity than the colonies, and yet the colonies were home to abundant natural resources, such as wood and plants like cotton and corn.

C. Some herbal products used today are aloe vera, from aloe plants, for soothing skin irritations and burns; herbal teas from fruits and leaves, such as mint, lemon, or raspberry; dried herbal seasonings, such as rosemary, thyme, and basil; and calendula (from marigolds), found in ointments, for healing cuts and bruises.

D. The displays here change. Some include breakfast foods, such as hoecakes, from cornmeal (like our pancakes), served with butter and honey. The main meal featured smoked ham, fish or shellfish, chicken, duck, game birds, or lamb; fresh vegetables from the garden (such as lettuce, carrots, cucumbers, or beans); a variety of potatoes; homemade bread; and desserts such as jellies (like modern gelatin), cakes, and pies from local fruit (peaches, pears, cherries, apples, currants, and figs). No one was expected to eat everything. The presentation was done like a modern smorgasbord.

E. Tenant farming is growing produce on land that belongs to someone else. Some of what you grow as a tenant farmer can be used as rent payment for the land. Any improvements you make to the property belong to its owner.

F. A surveyor studies and measures the land's topography, maps specific areas and boundaries, and might even evaluate the quality of the land for particular building types. In colonial times surveyors relied on a 32-point compass card, different lengths of chain for measurements, and markings by tree locations. At some point the sextant, the telescope, and the leveling rod were developed as well. These tools can still be used, but today we also have cameras, complex technological tools, and global positioning satellite systems to help surveyors with their work.

G. The house was actually *moved* from its original site in Falls Church, Virginia, when it was threatened with demolition because of highway construction. Mrs. Leighey donated it to the National Trust for Historic Preservation. This modern structure is on the grounds of the Woodlawn Plantation.

H. If the United States is attacking by sea, the Marines always go first. They are the official amphibious landing force of the United States armed services and are thus in great personal danger.

APPENDIX I
For the Fun of It

Not usually thought of as Fun City, U.S.A., Washington, D.C., *can* be a really entertaining place, and we're not just talking about those exciting state dinners in the White House. (Move along—don't wait for your invitation *there*!) Each season brings its own special events, and almost every imaginable sports and cultural activity is available for the choosing. As with hotels, when you're investigating where to go and when, ask for any conceivable discount. Student? AAA? Senior citizen? Military? Birthday? Get creative—who knows *what* might be available—but you have to *ask*.

Seasonal Events

In addition to the permanent monuments and buildings in Washington, D.C., there are other things to see that depend on *when* you come to town. Each month brings special events and festivities. This being the nation's capital, new and interesting celebrations often evolve. Unless otherwise noted, most events offer something for all ages. Be sure to check the local newspapers (especially the *Washington Post*'s "Weekend" section) for the most up-to-date information, and have a great time.

Spring

Even before the cherry blossoms decorate the city in pink and white, Washington's spring rituals begin.

St. Patrick's Day Parade

Bagpipes, floats, and marchers with festive costumes and banners bring in the "green" (no, not money—that's only at the Bureau of Engraving and Printing) in the St. Patrick's Day Parade. It winds down Constitution Avenue, from 7th to 17th streets, NW, traditionally the second Sunday in March. Check local newspaper listings for details.

Woodlawn Plantation Spring Needlework Show

The oldest continuous needlework show in the U.S. showcases exquisite pieces during the month of March at Woodlawn Plantation. Come admire the work of nimble fingers.

>703/780–4000
>www.woodlawn1805.org

Smithsonian Kite Festival

Late in March, usually the last Saturday, while the winds are still impressive, the Smithsonian holds its annual kite festival near the Washington Monument. Adults and kids bring their colorful and creative homemade kites to fly and compete for prizes. Registration is from 10 to noon, and the festival lasts until 4.

>202/633–3030
>www.kitefestival.org

Ringling Brothers and Barnum & Bailey Circus

Always a tremendous draw for both adults and children, "the greatest show on earth" comes to D.C. from late March into early April. You can watch the animals parade from the circus train on the morning before the circus opens.

>703/448–3639
>www.ringling.com

National Cherry Blossom Festival
In this city of monuments to war and government, it's nice that there's a special holiday to celebrate natural beauty. At the center of the festivities are the trees themselves, magnificent in bloom, attracting crowds of visitors all day and even after dark, under the huge floodlights. Capping the celebration is the annual Cherry Blossom Parade, with its floats, concerts, and princesses from all 50 states. Sometimes the blossoms *do* actually bloom during this two-week celebration.

877/442–5666
www.nationalcherryblossomfestival.org

The White House Easter Egg Roll
An event only for youngsters age 8 and younger, who are not likely to be so hard-boiled yet that they mind the crowds and commotion, the annual Easter Monday egg roll is really a treasure hunt. Children search for colorful wooden eggs, many with celebrity autographs, hidden on the grounds of the South Lawn of the White House. Puppet and magic shows, dancers, clowns, military drill teams, egg-decorating exhibits, and an egg-rolling contest are all part of the festivities. Besides the tickets (available starting at 7 AM—and yes, get there very early—at the Visitor Pavilion on the Ellipse), an accompanying grown-up is the only other requirement for admission. Check to see whether any tickets will be distributed in advance. With changing security measures, it's a good idea to check in advance to be sure this event is open to the public.

877/442–5666
www.whitehouse.gov

The White House Spring Garden Tour/Children's Garden
In mid-April visitors can tour the lovely landscaped Rose Garden and Children's Garden. Don't be put off by the lines of people—get *into* the line. Watch for the bronze impressions of the hands and

feet of White House children. Again, with changes in security measures you should check in advance.

202/208–1631
www.nps.gov/whho

D.C. International Film Festival

For two weeks in mid- to late April filmmakers from around the world show their work in movie theaters, embassies, and other screening facilities all over the city. It's an artistic treat. Some films are free, some have admission fees.

202/274–5782
www.filmfestdc.org

Shakespeare's Birthday at the Folger

A birthday by any other name isn't quite the same as this one. On the Sunday closest to April 26, the Bard's real birthday, the Folger Shakespeare Library celebrates in style. Elizabethan music (what else?), theatrical productions, exhibits, food, and children's events make this a festive day indeed.

202/544–4600
www.folger.edu

National Cathedral Flower Mart

Tra-la, it's May. While adults tiptoe through the tulips (and other plants and herbs), kids can enjoy international food booths, rides, and activities, including an antique carousel and puppet shows. This is held the first Friday and Saturday in May.

202/537–6200
www.cathedral.org

Air Show at Andrews Air Force Base

The Department of Defense Joint Services hold their annual Open House at Andrews Air Force Base every May. Ground displays and exciting aerial events lure thousands of spectators every year. Up, up, and away!

301/981–0057
www.jsoh.org

Jazz in the Garden at the National Gallery of Art
Beginning at the end of May, the National Gallery of Art's Sculpture Garden is the site of free Friday concerts featuring an eclectic mix of Washington area jazz artists. The concerts are usually held from 5 to 8 next to the grand reflecting pool and fountain. There's light fare available at the Pavilion Café.

Memorial Day
At 8 PM on the Sunday before Memorial Day the National Symphony (202/619–7222) performs its memorable concert before thousands on the West Lawn of the Capitol. Make sure to bring a blanket.

At the Tomb of the Unknowns in Arlington National Cemetery a high-ranking government official (sometimes the president) lays a wreath in the 11 AM ceremony, which includes military band music, a service, and a speech. The Vietnam Veterans Memorial and the U.S. Navy Memorial also host commemorative ceremonies. Check the newspaper for additional listings and local events.

Summer
What a nice time to have a birthday. In addition to the Fourth of July, Washington celebrates all summer long. Be sure to check local newspaper listings for schedules of the many free musical programs and midday entertainment activities around the city.

Dupont–Kalorama Museum Walk Day
For Teens . . . On the first Saturday in June, when the weather is usually gorgeous, take a stroll through Dupont Circle and Kalorama. Museums and historic houses offer tours, crafts demonstrations, live music, and free refreshments. Shuttle service is provided.

202/387–4062, ext.12
www.dkmuseums.com/walk.html

DanceAfrica DC

During the first week in June, Dance Place (8th Street, NE, near Catholic University) hosts a celebration of African culture featuring music, dance, visual arts, clothing, crafts, and food.

202/269–1600
www.danceplace.org

Alexandria Red Cross Waterfront Festival

The romance of the high seas comes to Alexandria on the second weekend in June. At the Alexandria Red Cross Waterfront Festival, in Old Town's Oronoco Bay Park, you can tour the tall ships and learn about the seaport through historic reenactments. Food from the local restaurants, music, clowns, children's activities, rides, a petting zoo, canoe rentals, and even fireworks enliven this annual event.

703/549–8300 Ext. 500
www.waterfrontfestival.org

Civil War Living History Day

In mid-June "soldiers" dressed in wool uniforms reenact famous battles at the Fort Ward Museum and Historic Site near Old Town, Alexandria. We're impressed with their willingness to sacrifice personal comfort for historical accuracy. One of the original Civil War forts ringing the city, Fort Ward has been partially restored, complete with six mounted guns. Civil War artifacts in the museum here bring this period of history to life.

703/838–4848
www.fortward.org

Maritime Craft Days at the Navy Museum

Yo ho! The Navy Museum's Maritime Craft Days, held for four days in July, are especially fun for kids ages 5 to 12. Some of the free activities include puppet-making, periscopes, and signal flags. Anyone over 16 needs valid ID for these activities.

> 202/433–6897
> www.history.navy.mil

Shakespeare Free for All

For Tweens and Teens . . . The show must go on—and it does, for free. For two to three weeks in June the Shakespeare Theatre brings the Bard to Sidney Harman Hall (6th and F streets, NW).

> 202/547–1122 or 877/487–8849
> www.shakespearedc.org

★*Smithsonian Festival of American Folklife*

Highlighting a specific state each year, this festival incorporates the diverse ethnic traditions that comprise the United States. Children and adults relish the excitement of discovering the native costumes, music, dance, crafts, and food that represent the rich variety in our heritage. The festival runs late June through early July.

> 202/633–1000
> www.festival.si.edu

National Capital Barbecue Battle

This is definitely the place for a hot time. On the third weekend in June, be sure to bring your taste buds to Pennsylvania Avenue between 9th and 14th streets, NW. Thanks to local restaurants, everything here is saucy, spicy, and finger-lickin' good. You could make a fortune here selling wet wipes. There's an admission fee. Check newspaper listings for details.

www.barbecuebattle.com

Independence Day Celebration
The best cakeless birthday party around begins with a 12:30 PM parade along Constitution Avenue and ends with the spectacular fireworks display above the Washington Monument. The afternoon and early evening are filled with the sound of music—free concerts on the Monument grounds (popular music groups), jazz at Freedom Plaza (Pennsylvania Avenue, NW, between 9th and 14th streets), and the National Symphony on the Capitol's West Lawn. Join the crowd to celebrate the birthday of the United States.

800/215–6405
www.july4thparade.com

Greater Washington Soap Box Derby
A capital race without ballots: dozens of 9- to 16-year-olds zoom in their homemade chariots down Constitution Avenue, between New Jersey and Louisiana avenues, NW, on Capitol Hill. This is an exciting summer event for all ages. Check newspaper listings for details. The race usually runs during the second week in July.

Latin American Festival
¡Olé! If you're in town in late July, don't miss this colorful annual event, with live music, international food, arts and crafts, and even a parade. Although it's traditionally centered somewhere near the Washington Monument area, check the *Washington Post* for this year's exact location and time.

Fall
Colorful foliage mixes with colorful events in this delightful season in the nation's capital.

International Children's Festival

For Tykes . . . It's a small world after all at this annual festival for children, offering arts-and-crafts workshops, crafts, music and dance, and numerous performances. Kids can get their faces painted, banter with clowns, watch puppet shows, try out hula hoops, and enjoy this beautiful setting in the Virginia countryside. The festival takes place Labor Day weekend at Wolf Trap Farm Park. There's an admission fee.

> 703/642–0862
> www.internationalchildrensfestival.org

Kennedy Center Open House Arts Festival

The halls are alive with the sounds of music. A daylong festival in September celebrates the performing arts inside and outside this Washington landmark. Local and national artists perform on a multitude of stages, and the National Symphony Orchestra usually provides an "instrument petting zoo," where children get to try out a favorite instrument.

> 202/467–4600 or 800/444–1324
> www.kennedy-center.org

Black Family Reunion

It's like one big happy family on the National Mall when gospel music, dance troupes, international foods, and crafts help celebrate the African-American heritage. The event is held in mid-September.

> 202/737–0120
> www.ncnw.org

Greek Fall Festival

On the third weekend in September the Greek Orthodox Church of Saints Constantine and Helen (4115 16th Street, NW) hosts a festival to delight the eye and tummy.

> 202/829–2910

Renaissance Festival

Don your armor. From late August to mid-October a rural setting in Crownsville, Maryland, becomes a Renaissance-era village, complete with jousters, magicians, wandering minstrels, medieval-style food, performances, and crafts. It's a long ride from D.C., but a whole day's worth of fun. Just remind the kids that only in medieval times did people use their fingers for silverware. There's an admission fee.

> 800/296–7304
> www.rennfest.com

Rock Creek Park Day

A day at the park without hitting the swings. Rock Creek Park celebrates its birthday on the Saturday closest to September 25, and you're invited. Environmental exhibits, arts and crafts, live music, and recreational activities for children highlight this event.

> 202/619–7222

Takoma Park Folk Festival

From the middle to the end of September the folk music scene moves front and center. There are free musical performances, dance lessons, craft artists, and ethnic foods. The Grassy Nook Stage hosts activities for kids: storytelling, interactive games, and music-making.

> 301/270–9090
> www.tpff.org

Takoma Park Street Festival

On the first Sunday in October this arts-friendly community celebrates with scores of craft and vendor booths, three stages with hundreds of musical performances, and scrumptious foods from all over the world.

> 301/270–9090
> www.takomafestival.com

Washington International Horse Show

A horse of a different color, this event is a draw for kids of all ages. International teams compete in jumping events, polo matches, and riding and roping exhibitions. Western-style foods, specialty boutiques, and a family day when kids can watch horse shoeing and learn about how to care for their mounts round out the offerings. There's an admission fee. The show is held in late October at the Verizon Center (6th and F streets, NW).

> 301/987–9400
> www.wihs.org

Woodlawn's Haunted History

A Haunted History program is held here the last weekend in October. It includes tours of Woodlawn's house and ghost stories. Reservations required.

> 703/780–4000
> www.woodlawn1805.org

Veterans' Day Ceremonies

For Teens . . . The Tomb of the Unknowns in Arlington National Cemetery is the setting for this memorial service on November 11. A high-ranking government official (often the president) lays a wreath at the tomb. A service takes place at the Memorial Amphitheater nearby. The Vietnam Veterans Memorial, Mount Vernon, and the U.S. Navy Memorial are some other sites for Veterans' Day observances.

> 202/619–7222

Winter

While everyone else is at home by the fire, this is a really good time to visit Washington, since everywhere you go will be less crowded (and usually heated, if you stay inside). Holiday season, however, does bring crowds.

Annual Scottish Christmas Walk Weekend

The guys in the pleated skirts are at it again, but this time it's a parade with whole clans (not to mention horses and dogs), Highland dancers, kilted bagpipers, storytelling, caroling, craft booths, regional foods, and children's activities. Start the season with this event, held the first weekend in December.

> 703/549–0111
> www.campagnacenter.org

Pageant of Peace/Lighting of National Christmas Tree

The first family's lighting of the national Christmas tree in early December inaugurates the three-week-long Pageant of Peace. Along with the 57 additional decorated trees (for each state, the District of Columbia, and the six U.S. territories), there are live reindeer, festive carols, and musical performances from 6 to 9 PM. Wear mittens, earmuffs, wool socks, a muffler, boots—well, you get the idea. Ho ho ho!

> 202/619–7222
> *www.nps.gov/ncro*

Gather the Family at Woodlawn

These December festivities will carry you back to Old Virginny and the days of gracious living. Musicians and carolers stroll the grounds while visitors enjoy wagon rides and refreshments. See how the gentry decorated for the holidays. First and second Sundays in December, though dates can vary; call to reserve at least a week in advance.

> 703/780–4000
> www.woodlawn1805.org

The D.C. Jewish Community Center's Holiday Festival

The D.C. Jewish Community Center celebrates Chanukah, the "festival of lights," with activities for all ages, including puppet shows,

music, stories, games, and arts programs. Call ahead to check the
schedule.

202/777–3218
www.washingtondcjcc.org

Festival of Music and Lights
A delightful display of more than 300,000 lights decorates the trees
at the Washington Temple and Visitors Center of the Church of
Jesus Christ of Latter-day Saints in Kensington, Maryland. A live
Nativity pageant (6 to 9 PM) outside and a visitor center with 17
Christmas trees inside inspire holiday spirit. Particularly striking are
the trees decorated with ornaments from four different embassies
each year. Drama, dance, and musical programs are featured through
the holiday season.

301/587–0144
www.lds.org/dccalendar

Alexandria's Holiday Festivities
Alexandria celebrates the holiday season with a rich variety of
events, from candlelight tours of Mt. Vernon to the Parade of Lights
in the harbor.

888/468–6449
www.funside.com

Anacostia Community Museum Kwanzaa Celebration
December brings a Kwanzaa celebration at this museum with
African-inspired music, dancing, games, and folktales. A holiday
workshop for families is held the first Saturday in December.

202/633–4820
www.anacostia.si.edu

Martin Luther King Jr. Day
Held at the Lincoln Memorial, the birthday celebration for this famous civil rights leader includes a wreath laying, guest speakers, a

military color guard, choral music, prayer vigils, dance, and theater. King is honored the third Monday in January.

Presidents' Day

Although many Americans consider Presidents' Day (the third Monday in February) as a time for shopping, here in D.C. we take these things so seriously that there are also separate celebrations for the birthdays of Abraham Lincoln (February 12) and George Washington (February 22). The usual speeches, ceremonies, and parades abound. The Gettysburg Address is read at the Lincoln Memorial, and a wreath is laid in Lincoln's memory. As for Washington, Alexandria remembers its native son with a weekend-long celebration.

Chinese New Year Festival

Although tykes might not get a bang out of the firecrackers at this celebration, they will love the colorful dragons, lions, dancers, and music makers in the parade. Passing under the elaborate Friendship Archway at H Street between 5th and 7th streets, NW, the revelers wind up and down the street several times so onlookers can enjoy their performance. New Year is celebrated in February or early March.

Sports

Especially if you've been standing in lines and shuffling in and out of important exhibits all morning, your body is probably ready for some liberation. Here are some suggestions.

Bike Rentals

Spring and fall in Washington are absolutely glorious for bike riding. Even some winter days are mild enough for an invigorating outing. We don't recommend hitting the city streets (you might just do that, literally, with all the traffic), but we do suggest finding out about the wonderful trails you can explore. Check out the *Greater*

Washington Area Bike Map, available in bookstores. You can also contact the Washington Area Bicyclist Association (202/518–0524; www.waba.org) for trail information. The National Park Service (202/619–7222; www.nps.gov) has free maps of some of the trails. The most popular bike paths are along the C&O Canal Towpath, through Rock Creek Park, the Capital Crescent Trail, the Mount Vernon Trail, and the Washington and Old Dominion Bike Trail.

Better Bikes

Bikes, equipment, maps of trails, and even backpacks are delivered to your hotel, with daily or multiple-day rentals available. Roadside assistance is available.

> 202/293–2080
> www.betterbikesinc.com

Big Wheel Bikes

There are four area locations: Georgetown (1034 33rd Street, NW; 202/337–0254); Alexandria, Virginia (2 Prince Street; 703/739–2300); Arlington (3119 Lee Highway; 703/522–1110); and Bethesda, Maryland (6917 Arlington Road; 301/652–0192). Call for rental fees.

> www.bigwheelbikes.com

City Bikes

This shop in Adams Morgan (2501 Champlain Street, NW; 202/265–1564) has sales and rentals. A second location in Chevy Chase, Maryland (8401 Connecticut Avenue; 301/652–1777) is on the Crescent Trail.

> www.citybikes.com

Boating

The beauty of the waterfront in almost all seasons will really float your boat. Come give it a try—everyone will sleep better tonight. Wear rubber-soled shoes, and slather on that sunblock. The Potomac River can be treacherous, so be sure to check conditions with the National Weather Service (301/936–1212).

Atlantic Kayak Company

At the Fort Washington Marina (across the Potomac River from Mt. Vernon) the Atlantic Kayak Company rents both singles and tandems for paddling enthusiasts. Riders must be 5 or older. There are also tours and individual instruction available.

> 301/292–6455
> www.atlantickayak.com

Fletcher's Boat House

Canoes, rowing shells, small sailboats, and rowboats are all awaiting rental at historic Fletcher's Boat House (4940 Canal Road, NW, at Reservoir Road). There's gentle water here, making it great for the younger set. You can also rent bikes for rides along the canal path.

> 202/244–0461
> www.fletcherscove.com

Jack's Boathouse

Under Georgetown's Key Bridge, Jack's Boathouse (3500 K Street, NW) rents canoes and kayaks. It's been in business since 1945.

> 202/337–9642
> www.jacksboathouse.com

Pedal Boats in the Tidal Basin

Everyone except the tiniest of tots can get into the act here. The Tidal Basin Boat House (1501 Maine Avenue, SW, off 15th Street) can be very busy on weekends, so call first.

> 202/479–2426
> www.tidalbasinpedalboats.com

Thompson's Boat Center

For the serious as well as amateur paddlers, there are canoes, rowboats, shells, double shells, and sunfish. Rent them all, along with bicycles, at Rock Creek Parkway and Virginia Avenue, NW.

202/333–9543
www.thompsonboatcenter.com

Fishing

You should have seen the one that got away! Fishing licenses for nonresidents cost $10; anglers under 16 and over 65 don't need one. Fletcher's Boat House sells licenses, as well as bait and tackle.

Chain Bridge

Anywhere along the Potomac near Chain Bridge you may drop a line.

Fletcher's Cove

This popular place to cast off is in Georgetown, about a mile north of Key Bridge.

Hains Point

Near East Potomac Park, the wall along the Washington Channel here is a good place to perch.

Golf

There are certainly enough choices for duffers in the Washington area to suit you to a tee.

East Potomac Park

On Hains Point at Ohio Drive, SW, this highly rated practice facility has two 9-hole courses and one 18-hole course, a driving range, a pro shop, and a snack bar. For the younger set, there's Circus Mini Golf Putt-4-Fun. Greens fees for 18 holes range from $15 to $30.

202/554–7660
www.golfdc.com

Langston

This 18-hole course and driving range are across from RFK Stadium at 2600 Benning Road, NE. At the pro shop you can rent clubs, pull carts, and riding carts. The snack bar is popular with locals.

> 202/397–8638
> www.golfdc.com

Rock Creek Park

This 18-hole course is at 16th and Rittenhouse streets, NW. There's a pro shop and a snack bar with an outdoor grill.

> 202/882–7332
> www.golfdc.com

Hiking

A perfect response if someone tells you to go take a hike would be to explore some of the beautiful trails in the D.C. area. Bring your water bottle, insect repellent, and sunscreen. Some useful Web sites are: *www.trails.com/activity* and dc.about.com/od/hiking.

Billy Goat Trail

On the Maryland side of Great Falls Park, 11710 MacArthur Boulevard, Potomac, this 4-mi climb awaits you. Remember the *name* of the trail?

> 301/767–3714
> www.nps.gov/choh, go to "plan your visit" to get a map

C&O Canal Towpath

A favorite with locals, this 184-mile trail offers you several choices for hikes from Georgetown, depending on your stamina: to Glen Echo Park is 7 miles; to Old Angler's Inn is 12.5 miles; to Great Falls is 14 miles; and to Violette's Lock is 22 miles.

> www.nps.gov/choh

Great Falls Park
This beautiful Virginia park features 16 miles of footpaths.

703/285–2965
www.nps.gov/grfa

Rock Creek Park
Here you can have access to a whole network of hiking trails. Guided tours with U.S. park rangers are available.

202/619–7222
www.nps.gov/rocr

Theodore Roosevelt Island
Walk across the footbridge from the parking area on the Virginia side of the Potomac, and enjoy the 2½ miles of shady paths through woods, marshland, and swamp.

703/289–2500
www.nps.gov/this

Horseback Riding
Tired of gasoline prices? Ride a horse!

Rock Creek Park Horse Center
Guided rides on the equestrian trails in Rock Creek Park are offered at this center, located at Military and Glover Roads, NW. Reserve at least one week in advance. The younger set will enjoy pony rides on a special trail.

202/362–0117
www.rockcreekhorsecenter.com

Ice-Skating
In the winter in Washington ice is nice. If we're having one of our wintrier seasons, you can skate free on the **Reflecting Pool** (between the Lincoln Memorial and Washington Monument), on the pond in **Constitution Gardens** (near the Vietnam Veterans

Memorial), or on the **C&O Canal.** For conditions, call the National Park Service.

202/619–7222

Cabin John Ice Rink

In Bethesda, Maryland, at 10610 Westlake Drive, there's an indoor rink that's open year-round. There are rental skates, a snack bar, and a pro shop. Suggestion: this is a good way to keep those kids busy in the *evening.*

301/365–2246
www.cabinjohnice.com

National Sculpture Garden Ice Rink

Get rental skates and snacks at this rink across from the National Archives at 7th Street and Constitution Avenue, NW.

202/289–3360
www.nga.gov/ginfo/skating.shtm

Nature Centers

While not actually a "sport," visiting nature centers is a popular activity for kids and families. Some parks to explore in Virginia include Green Spring Gardens (703/642–5173), Huntley Meadows Park (703/768–2525), and Jerome "Buddie" Ford Nature Center (703/838–4829) in Alexandria; Gulf Branch Nature Center (703/228–3403) and Long Branch Nature Center (703/228–6535) in Arlington; and Riverbend Park (703/759–9018) in Great Falls.

In Maryland, try Brookside Nature Center and Gardens in M-NCPPC Wheaton Regional Park (301/946–9071; www.brooksidegardens.org), Locust Grove Nature Center in Cabin John Regional Park (301/299–1990; locustgrovenature.org).

Swimming

Swimming is a great way for kids to unwind in the evening, but if you're here when the weather during the day is really hot, read on. If you try to swim in the C&O Canal or the Potomac River, you'll be in hot water—they are *not* safe for swimming.

D.C. Department of Parks and Recreation Aquatic Program

To locate the nearest public outdoor or indoor pool, call the D.C. Department of Recreation. Ask for information about the neighborhood where the pool is located and what fees are charged.

202/282–0720
www.dpr.dc.gov

Montgomery Aquatic Center

In North Bethesda, Maryland, you can find this spiffy new indoor facility at 5900 Executive Boulevard.

301/468–4211
www.montgomerycountymd.gov/rec

Tennis

Tennis enthusiasts will *love* the selection of playing sites available in the nation's capital. To locate the courts nearest you and for details and court fees, call the D.C. Department of Recreation (202/698–2250) or Rock Creek Tennis (202/722–5949).

www.dpr.dc.gov

East Potomac Park

Two dozen courts—indoor, outdoor, lighted, and clay—can be found at 1090 Ohio Drive, SW. Reservations are needed up to a week in advance.

202/554–5962
www.eastpotomactennis.com

Spectator Sports

If you'd rather watch *other* people sweat, there are plenty of spectator sports to choose from. You can watch polo, rugby, cricket, and soccer and root for local teams as well as teams from around the world. Call the National Park Service (202/619–7222) for the schedule at West Potomac Park. Now, if you don't mind paying to watch other people work, here are the Washington area highlights.

American University

For sports events uptown at AU, call 202/885–8499.

> aueagles.com

FedEx Field

Here's an attraction you don't even have to get to. Home to the **Washington Redskins,** FedEx Field (Redskins Road and Stadium Drive, Landover, Maryland), only sells season tickets, and they're always sold out. If you're football fans, keep on good terms with your Washington-area friends and relatives. Even if they don't have tickets, you can be sure they know someone who does. As for everybody else, turn on your local TV set, grab a hot dog, and join the excitement. Tweens can read *The Washington Redskins* (Team Spirit Series), by Mark Stewart.

> 301/276–6000
> www.redskins.com/ or www.fedex.com/us/sports

George Mason University Patriot Center

The big events at this 10,000-seat college arena in northern Virginia bring spectators to their feet to cheer.

> 703/993–3000
> www.patriotcenter.com

Georgetown University

If you want to root for the popular Hoyas, you'll have plenty of opportunities.

202/687–2449

www.guhoyas.com

George Washington University

If you're downtown and want to see collegiate basketball, join the gang at GW.

202/994–6050

www.gwsports.com

Verizon Center

At this state-of-the-art facility (601 F Street, NW), there's plenty to do besides watch a game. You can enjoy the high-tech National Sports Gallery and the American Sportscasters Association Hall of Fame, watch the film *Destination DC,* shop at the Discovery Channel Store, and dine in several restaurants. Also, of course, you come here to see the Washington Wizards, the Washington Mystics, and the Georgetown Hoyas play basketball, and the Washington Capitals play hockey.

202/628–3200 (automated) or 202/661–5000

www.verizoncenter.com

Camden Yards

The Baltimore Orioles, now our *second* favorite baseball team, play at **Oriole Park at Camden Yards,** about an hour from D.C. Call Ticketmaster at 202/397–7328 or 410/547–7328, or get tickets online at www.ticketmaster.com. For tickets or baseball souvenirs, visit the **Orioles Baseball Store** (202/296–2173, at 925 17th Street, NW, in D.C. For bus information, check with Metrobus (202/637–7000). Another option is the MARC Train (800/325–7245) that goes from Union Station to Camden Yards.

410/685–9800 or 888/848–2473

www.orioles.mlb.com

The championship Baltimore Ravens football team plays at **M&T Bank Stadium,** also at Camden Yards. With two football teams and two baseball teams, the metropolitan D.C. area has exciting spring and fall sports seasons.

> 410/261–7283
> www.baltimoreravens.com

Robert F. Kennedy Stadium

The fans are going wild! Playing here is the city's major-league soccer team, D.C. United, a powerhouse group that draws enthusiastic fans. The days of the swaying rafters have returned. This is an exciting place to cheer the home team. For tickets, call Ticketmaster (202/397–7328 or 800/551–7328).

> 202/547–9077
> www.washdcsports.com

Nationals Stadium

The city is "batty" for its home team, the Nationals, or "Nats" (not gnats). They began their first season in their new "digs" on opening day, 2008. Tweens might enjoy reading *The Washington Nationals* (Team Spirit Series), by Mark Stewart. Watch out for flying balls and giddy fans.

> 202/675–6287
> www.washington.nationals.mlb.com

University of Maryland

For tickets to see the Terrapins play in College Park, Maryland, call 301/314–7070.

> umterps.com

Entertainment & the Arts

Although politics can be quite entertaining, the city has a sophisticated cultural scene as well. In addition to purchasing tickets directly from a specific venue, you can also get them through several outlets:

At 407 7th Street, NW, **TICKETplace** (202/842–5387; www.ticketplace.org) is Washington's only discount day-of-show source.

Ticketmaster (301/808–2405 or 800/527–6384; www.ticketmaster.com), at the Marvin Center at George Washington University (21st and H streets, NW), charges a fee for ticket purchases.

Tickets.com (800/955–5566; www.tickets.com) is a nationwide phone charge service, also charging a fee for ticketing.

American Film Institute

For Tweens and Teens . . . This is the place for celluloid aficionados to go for classic and art films, as well as the popular variety, domestic and foreign. The AFI Silver Theater and Cultural Center, a beautifully renovated Art Deco theater in Silver Spring, Maryland, also hosts festivals, special events, and educational programs.

Metro: Silver Spring
8633 Colesville Road, at Georgia Avenue
301/495–6720
www.afi.com

Arena Stage

For Tweens and Teens . . . Washington's oldest professional resident theater, the Arena presents top-notch dramatic productions. Shows from this outstanding theater, starring luminaries like James Earl Jones, Robert Prosky, Ned Beatty, and Jane Alexander, have moved on to achieve commercial success on Broadway. Theater temporarily moved to Crystal City.

Metro: Crystal City
1800 S. Bell St. Arlington, VA
202/488–3300
www.arenastage.org

The Bethesda Theatre

The old-fashioned 1938 Art Deco movie palace is now an off-Broadway venue for both musicals and drama. A great bet for theater in the 'burbs. The Green Room on-site serves salads, soups, wraps, and drinks before and after the show. Your tummy will give rave reviews.

301/657–7827
www.bethesdatheatre.com

Carter Barron Amphitheatre

A warm-weather cultural mecca, the Carter Barron is the site for performances sponsored by a variety of musical groups and the National Park Service, running throughout the summer. Some concerts are free, whereas others require tickets. Check the *Washington Post* or the Carter Barron Web site for schedules and details.

Helpful Hint

As for comedy *outside* Congress, check local listings for the most up-to-date information and appropriateness of content for the audience you have in mind. Some of the most popular include **Bethesda Comedy Club** (301/358–5237; *www.bethesdacomedy.com*); **Capitol Steps** (703/683–8330; www.capsteps.com); **Comedy Spot** (703/294–5233; www.comedyindc.com); **Gross National Product** (202/783–7212; www.gnpcomedy.com); and **Evening at the Improv** (202/296–7008; www.dcimprov.com).

No Metro station; take S2 or S4 buses that travel 16th Street
16th Street at Colorado Avenue, NW
202/426–0486
www.nps.gov/rocr

DAR Constitution Hall

An elegant building with an auditorium with seating for more than 3,500, Constitution Hall has hosted a variety of musical performances, from the Boston Symphony to Ray Charles.

Metro: Farragut West or Farragut North
18th and D streets, NW
202/628–1776
www.dar.org

D.C. Armory

This venerable landmark frequently houses the Ringling Brothers and Barnum & Bailey Circus when it comes to town, as well as the National Christmas Show and other special programs like trade shows and antiques shows. The Armory is also the headquarters for the National Guard.

Metro: Stadium-Armory
2001 East Capitol Street, SE
202/547–9077
www.dcsec.com

Folger Shakespeare Theatre

For Teens . . . The Elizabethan-style theater at the Folger Shakespeare Library is the setting for plays, lectures, readings, and musical performances. The Folger Consort, performing Renaissance, medieval, and baroque music, has been wowing audiences for more than 20 years during its season that runs from October through May. The annual PEN/Faulkner fiction readings by major authors also take place here. Yea, verily.

Metro: Capitol South
201 E. Capitol Street, SE
202/544–7077
www.folger.edu

Ford's Theatre

For Tweens and Teens . . . "Other than *that*, Mrs. Lincoln, how did you enjoy the show?" goes the old joke. Without the same risk to life and limb, you, too, can enjoy musical and dramatic performances, some even bound for Broadway, when you visit Ford's Theatre. Thanks to a recent restoration, the theater seats are actually comfortable now. The Ford's Theatre production of Charles Dickens's *A Christmas Carol* is a highlight of the D.C. Christmas season.

> Metro: Metro Center
> 511 10th Street, NW
> 202/347–4833
> www.fordstheatre.org

GALA Hispanic Theater

A celebration in itself, the GALA Theater, in the beautifully reconstructed Tivoli Theater, presents plays in Spanish and English, highlighting the heritage of many D.C. residents. In addition to community-based theater, the troupe hosts programs of music, poetry, dance, and contemporary and classic plays.

> Metro: Columbia Heights
> 3333 14th Street, NW
> 202/234–7174
> www.galatheatre.org

Gallaudet Theater

Spotlight this one if any members of your group are hearing impaired, as performances are all in American Sign Language. The drama department at Gallaudet stages three productions a year. Voice interpretation devices are available for the hearing.

> No Metro station
> 800 Florida Avenue, NE
> 202/651–5502V/TTY or 202/651–5501
> www.gallaudet.edu

George Mason University Patriot Center

For Tweens and Teens . . . Big-name country performances and major rock concerts are staples of this huge 10,000-seat arena.

> No Metro station
> 4400 University Drive, Fairfax, Virginia
> 703/993–3000
> www.patriotcenter.com

Adjacent to the Patriot Center is the new **George Mason University Center for the Arts** (703/993–8888), presenting performances of jazz and classical music, as well as dramas.

Glen Echo Adventure Theater

For Tikes and Tweens . . . Housed in one of the historic buildings at Glen Echo Park, Adventure Theater provides a kid-friendly experience where everyone can nestle on carpeted steps to watch live productions on weekend afternoons. The actors are often available afterward to sign autographs and answer questions.

No Metro station
7300 MacArthur Boulevard, Glen Echo, Maryland
301/320–5331
www.adventuretheatre.org

Greenberg Theatre

For Tweens and Teens . . . American University is home to the Harold and Sylvia Greenberg Theatre. Check local listings for dramatic, dance, and musical performances.

Metro: Tenleytown
4200 Wisconsin Avenue, NW
202/885–2787
www.american.edu/cas/greenberg

Hartke Theatre

The consistently high-quality dramatic productions at Catholic University's Hartke Theatre have featured Academy Award–winning stars as well as talented undergraduate actors. Performances here are a delight.

Metro: Brookland-CUA
620 Michigan Avenue at 4th Street, NE
202/319–5358
drama.cua.edu

Katzen Arts Center at American University

The beautiful Katzen Arts Center accommodates the visual and performing arts programs at American University in one 130,000-square-foot space.

> Metro: Tenleytown
> 4400 Massachusetts Avenue, NW, between Ward and Wesley circles
> Open Tuesday through Sunday 11 to 4
> 202/885–1300 museum, 202/885–3634 box office
> www.american.edu/katzen

Kennedy Center

This modern palace devoted to the performing arts offers productions on five stages, as well as smaller venues within the building. Although a number of family-friendly events are scheduled around holiday seasons (Christmas, Easter, and Labor Day, for example), the Kennedy Center hosts regular performances of opera, classical music, musicals, dance, and drama, many of them appealing to young people. The Theater Lab is famous for staging children's theater by day and a long-running comedy-mystery called *Shear Madness* in the evening. At 6 PM daily the Millennium Stage offers *free* programs especially for families. The newly renovated Family Theater showcases plays for youngsters of various ages. The popular Teddy Bear concerts for the youngest audiences, who are encouraged to bring their favorite stuffed animals and sing along, are sponsored by the National Symphony Orchestra.

Helpful Hint

Although it's sometimes possible to get same-day tickets to performances at the Kennedy Center, it's best to check well in advance if you want tickets to a performance for a specific date. Inquire about specially priced tickets for students, seniors over 65, and members of the military, at 202/467–4600.

> Metro: Foggy Bottom–GWU (free shuttle to station leaves
>   every 15 minutes)
> 2700 F Street, NW
> 202/467–4600
> www.kennedy-center.org

Library of Congress

For Teens . . . Concerts given from September to May in the Library of Congress's Coolidge Auditorium are often free, although some require tickets. You can hear everything from classical music to gospel to rock and roll.

> Metro: Capitol South
> 1st Street and Independence Avenue, SE, across from the
>   Capitol
> 202/707–5000
> www.loc.gov/rr/perform/concert

Lincoln Theater

Situated along the U Street Corridor, which years ago was known as "Black Broadway," the Lincoln has been restored to its former elegance. Audiences again enjoy jazz, rhythm and blues, gospel, and comedy performances.

> Metro: U Street–Cardozo
> 1215 U Street, NW
> 202/328–6000
> www.thelincolntheatre.org

Lisner Auditorium

On the campus of George Washington University, Lisner has everything from rock to opera, plays to ballets. This venue is not for college students only.

> Metro: Foggy Bottom–GWU
> 21st and H streets, NW
> 202/994–6800
> www.lisner.org

Merriweather Post Pavilion

An outdoor summer venue designed by the world-renowned architect Frank Gehry, Merriweather Post (off Route 29, Columbia Pike, Columbia, Maryland) has both pavilion and lawn seating for acts as varied as Joan Rivers, James Taylor, Liza Minnelli, Elton John, and the most currently popular rock bands. Check local listings, and call Ticketmaster (301/808–2405 or 800/551–7328) for tickets. Travel here by car.

No Metro station
Off Route 29, Columbia Pike, Columbia, Maryland
410/715–5550
www.merriweathermusic.com

National Theatre

Giving new meaning to "off-off-Broadway," productions either headed to or touring from the Great White Way are often booked here. This venerable landmark, which has been beautifully restored, offers backstage tours. From October through April the National presents free shows for kids on Saturday mornings.

Metro: Federal Triangle or Metro Center
1321 Pennsylvania Avenue, NW
202/628–6161
www.nationaltheatre.org

Nissan Pavilion

At this outdoor theater 10,000 can fill the covered pavilion, while another 15,000 can spread out on the lawn. Perhaps the Nissan could elect its own representative to Congress with these numbers. Summer highlights here have included such performers as Phish, the Cranberries, the Dave Matthews Band, Rush, REM, and Jimmy Buffett. The giant video screens assure you of a view. You'll need a car to get here.

No Metro station
7800 Cellar Door Drive, Bristow, Virginia
703/754–6400 or 703/754–2156
www.nissanpavilion.com

The Puppet Company Playhouse

At Glen Echo, the Puppet Company Playhouse features professional puppeteers entertaining kids of all ages. After the performances (Wednesday to Friday mornings and weekend mornings and afternoons), the puppeteers frequently demonstrate how the puppets work to their young audience members.

> No Metro station
> 7300 MacArthur Boulevard, Glen Echo, Maryland
> 301/634–5380
> www.thepuppetco.org

Round House Theatre

A popular resident theater company with two locations (4545 East-West Highway, Bethesda, Maryland; and 8641 Colesville Road, Silver Spring, Maryland) presents musical and dramatic productions and can often be a kid-friendly way to see some well-done productions.

> 240/644–1100
> www.roundhousetheatre.org

The Shakespeare Theatre

For Tweens and Teens . . . In a beautifully renovated old building in the heart of downtown, the Bard lives on. Stars such as Kelly McGillis, Richard Thomas, and Stacy Keach have lent their talents to this high-caliber outfit. In addition to its Shakespeare repertoire, this theater also offers works by other well-known playwrights like George Bernard Shaw, Oscar Wilde, and Tennessee Williams. This is a wonderful opportunity for kids to see first-class theater. Defi-

Helpful Hint

Tickets to the Shakespeare Theatre sometimes sell out months in advance, so call way ahead to make your arrangements.

nitely a midsummer night's dream (or midwinter, or mid-fall, or mid-spring . . .). A goodly shew.

Metro: Archives–Navy Memorial
450 7th Street, NW
202/547–1122 or 877/487–8849
www.shakespearetheatre.org

The Strathmore

For Tweens and Teens . . . A modern building in a parklike setting, the Strathmore hosts a variety of musical performers playing everything from jazz and blues to Latin and African music. Many performances are aimed at children and families.

Metro: Grosvenor-Strathmore
10701 Rockville Pike, North Bethesda, Maryland
301/581–5100
www.strathmore.org

Studio Theater

For Teens . . . A completely renovated two-stage theater, the Studio offers contemporary drama on its Mainstage. Its Second Stage produces the works of up-and-coming playwrights. The Studio Theater is the recipient of numerous awards for its outstanding dramas.

Metro: Dupont Circle
1501 14th Street, NW
202/332–3300
www.studiotheatre.org

Warner Theatre

A glamorous older cousin of the Kennedy Center, the Warner opened in 1924 as a combination movie and vaudeville palace. Now restored to its original appearance, complete with crystal

Helpful hint

Tickets for the Warner often sell out, so it's best to ask for the schedule and order tickets way in advance.

chandeliers and velvet draperies, it hosts Broadway shows, rock concerts, and gospel shows, as well as the annual performance of the Washington Ballet's *Nutcracker*. This is a real evening on the town.

> Metro: Metro Center or Federal Triangle
> 13th Street and Pennsylvania Avenue, NW
> 202/783–4000
> www.warnertheatre.com

West Garden Court of the National Gallery of Art

From October to June, the National Gallery hosts free concerts in this beautiful space on Sunday evenings. Many different groups can be seen here, including the National Gallery Orchestra.

> Metro: Archives or Judiciary Square
> North side of the Mall, between 3rd and 7th streets, NW
> 202/737–4215
> www.nga.gov

Wolf Trap

Metropolitan Washington's most popular outdoor theater, offering entertainment almost every summer night, Wolf Trap hosts pop, folk, rock and roll, jazz, rhythm and blues, classical, opera, and country music performances, as well as all kinds of dance troupes and Broadway shows. As an alternative to the seats in the pavilion, there are less expensive lawn tickets available (a good place to bring a blanket and dine under the stars). The Children's Theatre in the Woods, running June through August, has puppet shows, clown acts, and plays.

> Shuttle service available from the West Falls Church Metro
>   station
> 1551 Trap Road, Vienna, Virginia

703/255–1900 or 877/965–8727
www.wolftrap.org

Woolly Mammoth Theater

For Teens... Aspiring playwrights should definitely discover Woolly Mammoth, an alternative theater that welcomes manuscripts from newcomers. Regularly reviewed by the *New York Times,* Woolly Mammoth strives to involve its audience in important issues. Call to check the appropriateness of specific performances for your group.

Metro: Archive–Navy Memorial or Gallery Place–Chinatown
641 D Street, NW
202/393–3939
www.woollymammoth.net

APPENDIX II
Tours: Washington, D.C., Inside & Out

Any way you get around, Washington, D.C., can be inviting, and there are lots of organizations ready to welcome you. If you're totally overwhelmed by all the choice sites we've been describing, you just might want to take a tour. Tantalizing tours range from bikes to boats, from trolleys to ghost walks.

Bike

For outdoor types who must exercise on tour, this is a good workout.

Bike the Sites

For guided bike tours as well as bike rentals for tours on your own, contact Bike the Sites. There are two locations: at the rear of the Old Post Office Pavilion (12th Street between Constitution and Pennsylvania avenues, NW), and in Alexandria, Virginia (1 Wales Alley). The company offers lots of different choices at different times of the year. There's even a summer "Sites at Night Tour"— a picturesque ride beginning at sunset. It's a fun way to see the city! The fee covers your helmet, water, and snacks. Adults must accompany kids under age 14. Trailers, strollers, and motorized wheel-chairs are available.

> 202/842–2453 (BIKE) or 703/548–7655
> www.bikethesites.com

Boat

Since it sits beside the Potomac River, D.C. offers many boat tours.

Capitol River Cruises

This 50-minute narrated tour leaves Washington Harbour in Georgetown every hour on the hour (April through October). Travel past the city's major memorials and monuments on this 65-foot steel riverboat. There's a snack bar on board. Call ahead for schedule and reservations.

> 301/460–7447 or 800/405–5511
> www.capitolrivercruises.com

C&O Canal Boat Rides

Kids are fascinated by these mule-drawn barges. Guides in period costume sing songs and tell stories through the 90-minute voyage along the C&O Canal (April through October). Reserve in advance.

> 202/653–5190 in Georgetown, 301/767–3714 in Great Falls,
>   Maryland
> www.nps.gov/choh

DC Ducks

Can't decide whether to walk or swim? Take the 90-minute guided tours aboard these amphibious open-air army vehicles all decked out in red, white, and blue (March through October). On land you'll bump along past some of D.C.'s major sites, and then—splash!—you'll cruise the Potomac for half an hour. Tours begin at Union Station.

> 202/832–9800
> www.historictours.com/washington/dcducks

National River Tours

With your older tweens and teens, try a 45-foot covered catamaran. Boats scoot from Georgetown's Washington Harbour, at the foot of 31st Street, NW, over to the Pentagon lagoon and back. The 45-minute narrated tour packs in plenty of humor and good fun. Maximum 42 passengers.

202/369–7077
www.nationalrivertours.com

Potomac Riverboat Company

Four different ships can take you sightseeing along the river, including one that drops you off to visit Mount Vernon (April to October). Board at Washington Harbour in Georgetown or at the Torpedo Factory in Old Town, Alexandria. There's a concession stand.

703/684–0580 or 877/511–2628
www.potomacriverboatco.com

Spirit Cruises

This narrated cruise along the Potomac departs from Pier 4, 6th and Water streets, SW (March to October). Some cruises visit George Washington's gracious home, Mount Vernon. The boat departs Tuesday to Sunday, boarding at 8 AM and returning at 3 PM. There's a concession stand on board. Admission to Mount Vernon is included.

866/446–9283
www.spiritcitycruises.com

Buses & Other Vehicles

If you'd like to see a lot of the city in a little bit of time, jump on one of the many tour vehicles cruising the streets daily.

Anecdotal History Tours

Private motorized or walking tours by author and historian Anthony Pitch illuminate specific neighborhoods, including Georgetown, the Mall, or certain subjects, such as political Washington.

301/294–9514
www.dcsightseeing.com

Capital Segway Tours

When you're riding a Segway, you always have the best seat on board. Of course, you actually ride standing up. Oh, well. You must be age 16 or older. Capital Segway is in Franklin Square Park, two blocks from the White House.

202/682–1980
www.capitalsegway.com

Capitol Entertainment Services

This company offers guided bus tours that focus on the city's African-American history. One popular tour is of the Shaw neighborhood, once filled with so many theaters that it was called the "Black Broadway."

202/636–9203
www.washington-dc-tours.com

City Segway Tours

These 3-hour tours (10 AM, 2 PM, 6 PM) meet across from the Gallery Place Metro station (624 9th Street, NW, between F and G streets). You begin with a short training session before taking off to see the sites. You must be age 16 or older.

877/734–8687
www.citysegwaytours.com

Guide Service of Washington

The Guide Service of Washington has licensed guides leading a variety of group tours as well as private tours; some guides speak different languages. The company can meet you at one of the airports and serve as a guide only (no vehicle provided).

> 202/628–2842
> www.dctourguides.com

Martz Gold Line/Gray Line

This bus company offers a wide variety of tours. Choose between tours to Mount Vernon/Alexandria; Capitol Hill, Embassy Row, and Arlington National Cemetery; and a nighttime view of the monuments. Seasonally, tours are also available to Monticello and Gettysburg.

> 301/386–8300 or 800/862–1400
> www.graylinedc.com

Old Town Trolley Tours

Board this replica of a Victorian streetcar for a narrated tour of major attractions in and around Washington, including Embassy Row, Georgetown, the Mall, the Smithsonian museums, the White House, Union Station, and Arlington National Cemetery. Hop on and off as many times as you like. There are evening tours, but reservations are required.

> 800/868–7482
> www.oldtowntrolley.com

Scandal Tours

Can you do justice to the scandals of Washington in only 75 minutes? Well, you can try. Employing actors from the comedy troupe Gross National Product to impersonate some major perpetrators, this mobile comedy show steers you from one infamous site to the next (April through Labor Day). Tours begin Saturday at 1. Pick-up at 1100 Pennsylvania Ave., NW, near the Old Post Office Pavilion. Reservations are required.

> 202/783–7212
> www.gnpcomedy.com

Spies of Washington Tours

Sounds intriguing! The political center of this country has attracted spies and counterspies for the past 200 years. Both automobile and walking tours are presented by a retired U.S. Air Force intelligence officer.

703/569–1875
www.spiesofwashingtontour.com

Tourmobile

All over Washington you can see vehicles as they make their way to 25 stops at historical sites between the Capitol and Arlington National Cemetery. Tourmobile also has trips to Mount Vernon and the Frederick Douglass National Historic Site, and some seasonal twilight tours. Tickets are available online, at information booths around the city, or directly from drivers.

202/554–5100 or 888/868–7707
www.tourmobile.com

Recorded Tours

Will you be driving your own car in Washington, D.C.? Bring along a virtual guide (besides the necessary bottle of aspirin!) in the form of a three-hour-long cassette tape or CD tour through the city, Mount Vernon, and Old Town Alexandria.

www.autotapetours.com

Self-Guided Tours

The advantage of a self-guided tour is that your guide never leaves you. The disadvantage is that he is as ill informed as you are, so take along the appropriate materials to help him out. Enjoy the company.

Arlington National Cemetery Tour

Cars are not permitted in the cemetery, so you'll notice that everyone is either walking or riding the Tourmobile. Pick up a map at the visitor center and spend a few minutes selecting the sites you most want to visit so you can plan your self-guided tour. This is a huge place, so you probably won't want to just wander.

703/979–0690
www.tourmobile.com

Cultural Tourism D.C.

Cultural Tourism D.C. is a nonprofit organization that helps you explore the city's interesting architecture, historic neighborhoods, parks and gardens, museums and galleries, and places of worship. At the D.C. Visitors Center you can pick up maps and cards that describe the major sites in various neighborhoods. There is a weekly e-mail calendar filled with local events.

To visit African-American historical sites, call Cultural Tourism D.C. for a brochure with details of sites, locations, and photos. Included are the Frederick Douglass National Historic Site, the Martin Luther King Memorial in the Rotunda of the U.S. Capitol, and other points of interest.

202/661–7581
www.culturaltourismdc.org

Mount Vernon

However you get to Mount Vernon, you'll need a map to follow while you visit. Pick one up when you arrive. Tours are self-guided, but along the way, both inside and out, you'll meet docents in 18th-century garb. These are the folks who can enrich your touring by answering your questions.

800/429–1520
www.mountvernon.org

Old Town Alexandria Self-Guided Walking Tours

At Ramsay House Visitors Center, pick up the brochures and maps for some interesting tours.

703/838–5005 or 800/388–9119
www.visitalexandria.com

Walking

Perhaps the most dependable source of transportation at your disposal, walking is a wonderful way to explore the area. Stick to the sidewalks *in* the city—and avoid the Beltway!

Alexandria Colonial Tours

Tours are for prearranged groups only, and feature children's programs. There's even a "Ghost and Graveyard" tour.

> 703/519–1749
> www.alexcolonialtours.com

Alexandria's Footsteps to the Past

These history tours and ghost tours are only for the brave.

> 703/683–3451
> www.visitalexandria.com

Ford's Theatre "History on Foot" Walking Tours

With costumed actors portraying characters from Civil War Washington, Ford's offers two tours, each lasting 90 minutes and covering about 1½ miles. One focuses on Mary Lincoln's confidante, the free African-American Woman Elizabeth Keckley, and her role in helping former slaves acclimate to new lives in the capital city. The second features Detective James McDevitt, working on the investigation of the "Lincoln Assassination Conspiracy." Tours run Wednesday, Friday, and Saturday; call for specific dates and times.

> 202/397–7328 (SEAT) or 202/638–2367
> www.fords.org

The Old Town Experience

This Alexandria tour, lasting an hour and a half, can be done on foot or by bus.

> 703/836–0694

TourDC

This outfit leads 90-minute walking tours through Georgetown and Dupont Circle on Saturday in spring and fall.

301/588–8999
www.tourdc.com

A Tour de Force

A Tour de Force customizes guided tours of Washington for groups. Both walking tours and bus tours are available.

703/525–2948
www.atourdeforce.com

Washington Photo Safari

It's a snap! A professional photographer leads walking tours to various sites with special photo ops and photo skills advice. Call to check what's appropriate for your group.

202/537–0937 or 877/512–5969
www.washingtonphotosafari.com

Media Tours

Kids often find media of special interest. It's always exciting to see some familiar voices and faces and to discover that their work is facilitated by real, life-size people doing their jobs here in Washington, D.C.

National Public Radio

For ages 12 and up, this hour-long tour at 11 AM on Thursday focuses on the studios and equipment. (It's rare to see an interview taking place.) Call 202/513–3232 at least four weeks in advance for groups.

635 Massachusetts Avenue, NW
www.npr.org

Voice of America

This is the world's largest radio station, broadcasting on 26 channels in 42 languages around the world. Make reservations in advance. No children under eighth grade. Guided tours depart from a new visitor center. Tours are limited to 25 people, and include a simulated VOA broadcast and a visit to the new newsroom.

> 202/203–4990
> www.voatour.gov

The Washington Post

Call one month in advance to schedule guided tours of the newspaper's offices for kids 11 and up.

> 202/334–6000
> www.washingtonpost.com

Local Radio and Television Stations

WTOP (202/895–5040) has half-hour tours for groups ages 7 and up. The tours include the studios and broadcasting equipment and (if scheduled in advance) a meeting with a reporter. WETA (703/998–2600), the local public radio station, has tours for ages 11 and up. Call in advance to schedule.

Television station WHUT (202/806–3200) offers 45-minute tours that include television production equipment and the studios.

APPENDIX III
Now What?

We've been collecting ideas from parents, teachers, and kids who have visited Washington, D.C. As the answer to the inevitable question after your visit—"Now what?"—here are some follow-up suggestions to build on your travel experiences. These do not preclude sharing your photographs, however, so get moving!

The Capital Scavenger Hunt

Patience is a virtue. If you stuck with the scavenger hunt, you're in luck. The **answers** appear at the end of this appendix, and someone in your group will need to be in charge of the prizes for the most correctly answered questions. We suggest a Washington sweatshirt or T-shirt or baseball cap or snow-scene paperweight (the kind with lots of little white sprinkles coming down over a famous Washington site) or a mug or a pen (containing shredded money, from the Bureau of Engraving and Printing). You name it. And don't forget to send us *your* ideas: parentsper@gmail.com.

Sharing Your Washington Experiences

You will want to reunite with those who shared your delayed plane flights, your missed connections, your weather joys or miseries, and your waits in the long lines for tours. So, share e-mail, Facebook, etc., contact information, and maybe even schedule a **reunion.**

We hope at least some of you kept **journals,** per our suggestion early in the book. This is the time to get together and compare notes. Who wrote what about where and whom? How differently did people experience the same events? Taking turns reading sections aloud is sometimes hilarious or poignant. Enjoy those shared memories.

And those **photographs.** Some groups have told us about **"parties,"** where all members display and share their photos, either online or at an actual party.

Kids can help each other organize what they've got and round out their own collections. Sometimes it's hard to identify everything you've seen all by yourself, so putting heads together should help. At this event, participants can work on the labeling, to protect those memories for good. Some folks will take **videos**—everyone loves to watch videos of themselves and their friends.

One teacher actually posts the photos from each year's trip all over his classroom so parents and students can enjoy looking at them all through the next year. They're quite an enticement for the next group of kids who hope to participate in this kind of trip, and wonderful fun for those who are looking back at what they've done.

No trip is complete without its **awards.** These, of course, are *funny* awards. Everyone can make suggestions for the categories and the recipients. If you talk about possibilities *before* the trip, lots of other ideas will materialize along the way. The *Turtle Award* will, of course, go to the one who has been consistently late for everything. The *Major Gifts Award* goes to the one who, by misplacing his jacket, shoe, backpack, ticket stubs, and so forth, has unwittingly contributed the most to the city of Washington. And the *Good Housekeeping Award* is for the ones whose hotel room needed a backhoe just to clear away the rubble. Everyone can use creativity to come up with the categories. Then have a secret ballot vote to choose the "winners." We're watching our e-mails for whatever else *you* can think up.

Individual & Group Project Ideas

So you thought you were finished learning about Washington, D.C.? Wrong. Here are some suggestions to keep those brain cells thriving.

Tykes

If you could be the president for a day, what would you want to accomplish?

Design an original flag for your room (or classroom). You can make it out of materials from a scrap bag and some glue.

Tykes and Tweens

Make an original "native" mask like those you saw in the museums. Read about some of the uses of masks. How do styles vary from country to country?

Younger children might enjoy creating original stamp designs. Focus on a specific theme, such as a holiday, special event, or famous person. Maybe even commemorate your visit to Washington.

Gather some photos or artwork about your favorite spot in Washington. What makes that place significant for you?

Tweens

The Washington Monument is a building that has no mortar to hold together its stones. See whether you can duplicate it (in miniature) using uniform wood blocks, sugar cubes, or other materials.

Tweens and Teens

If you had to reestablish a capital city for the United States today, where would you locate it, and why? Draw its new location on a map of the United States. (Teams of students could work on this issue and then present their plans to the class.)

For an imaginary country, you and some classmates can write an original constitution. What rights would you want to give to the citizens? What would be the obligations of the government?

Design a museum for an imaginary city. What purpose would your museum serve for the city's population and its visitors?

Washington has a large percentage of its land devoted to public spaces. What is the importance of public spaces in a city? What kinds of public spaces would you advocate in an ideal city?

Teens

Of the government activities you witnessed on your trip to Washington, D.C., what was most impressive? Most disappointing?

There's a controversy over the rights and responsibilities of District of Columbia residents, since they have no voting representation in Congress and no state to provide a base for the city's financial support. What rights and responsibilities would you give to the capital's citizens? Should D.C. be granted "statehood" status? Why or why not?

Look at the public buildings that are the work of architects from the 19th and 20th centuries. What public buildings are most impressive to you? Why?

After visiting the Kennedy Center and other performing arts facilities, as well as some of Washington's art galleries, what recommendation would you make about national support for the arts? What part of our national budget would you want to allocate to support art spaces and artists? Who should decide which projects and people get federal funds?

Research the work of James McNeill Whistler, contrasting his different styles, from the ornate oriental "Peacock Room" in the Freer to his *Arrangement in Black and Gray: The Artist's Mother* in the Louvre (Paris). Where can you find the largest collection of Whistler's work? (Surprise! It's in the Freer Gallery, right here in Washington, D.C.)

Research African music. Trace its use as roots for American music: jazz, blues, rhythm and blues, rock.

Adults pay local, state, and federal taxes. Find out where your area's tax dollars go. If you were in charge of the federal budget, what categories would you want funded? (Think about interstate highways, defense, school lunches for impoverished children, medical research, NASA, etc.) Make a chart to show what percentage of the national budget should go to each category you choose.

Write a letter to an elected official (from your city, county, state, or national government), discussing a problem you would like to see addressed and your suggestions for correcting it. You can find names and addresses online at www.congress.org. Click on "selected legislation" and "write elected officials" (you will need to enter a zip code). For local information, contact the League of Women Voters at www.lwv.org.

Every four years our country goes through a national presidential election, and often there is great controversy about the process. What changes would *you* like to see for the next presidential election? You might want to consider the following questions:

- Should there be a uniform time when all polls across the United States close?

- Should radio and TV commentators not be allowed to predict individual states' outcomes using exit polls?

- Should "live" media in zones where the polls are already closed be accessible in areas where the polls are still open?

- Should states go to a mail-in or an e-mail voting system?

- How can jurisdictions guard against voter fraud?

All Ages

Write a letter to your local newspaper or e-mail us (*parentsper@gmail. com*) telling your impressions of Washington, D.C., from your trip.

Of all the magnificent artwork in the Basilica of the National Shrine of the Immaculate Conception, perhaps the most impressive is the use of mosaic tiles. Try your hand at this medium, using a piece of cardboard for your pencil design, with rubber cement as a base coat. Use cut-up fabric or paper, broken eggshells, or bits of ribbon or colored foil for your creative project.

A Few More Ideas to Think About

After seeing Washington, D.C., build a model of a capital city of a fictitious country. What kinds of monuments and public buildings would you want it to contain?

After seeing artifacts in the Smithsonian museums, construct a time capsule (in a shoebox or similar container). What objects would you include to give future generations an idea of what life in the early 21st century was like?

Scavenger Hunt Answers

1. The ornately carved Columbus Doors, at the main entrance to the Capitol, stand 17 feet high and weigh 20,000 pounds.
2. The lady is Justice, at the U.S. Supreme Court, where we hope she is hard at work.
3. These bronze cranes struggle to break free of their barbed-wire bonds as the central figures of the National Japanese American Memorial.
4. A. Philip Randolph was the founder of the Sleeping Car Porters Union, and his statue stands appropriately in Union Station.
5. Look for these above some of the doorways in Union Station.
6. The Hirshhorn, of course.
7. The *Voyager,* the first aircraft to fly nonstop around the world without being refueled, and made primarily of plastic, is suspended from the ceiling of the National Air and Space Museum.
8. These two boats were handmade by modern Native Americans to ancient specifications. They are on the ground floor of the National Museum of the American Indian.
9. Mercury, the Messenger of the Gods, stands poised over a beautiful fountain in the rotunda of the West Building of the National Gallery of Art.
10. A statue of Alexander Hamilton, first secretary of the Treasury, stands on the south plaza of the Treasury Building, at 15th Street and Pennsylvania Avenue, NW.

11. The Albert Einstein Memorial, outside the southwest corner of the National Academy of Sciences Building at 2101 Constitution Avenue, NW, is a 12-foot bronze sculpture of this famous physicist. The universe is depicted at his feet. You can sit in his lap and pose for a photo (but it still won't make you a genius).

12. At the bottom of the enormous stairway is a plaque adding the names of Alaska and Hawaii, the 49th and 50th states.

13. This wall of gold stars is a centerpiece in the World War II Memorial. Each star represents 100 casualties of the more than 400,000 soldiers lost.

14. Corn and tobacco, the cash crops of Virginia in Thomas Jefferson's day, peek from beneath his coat as he stands in the Jefferson Memorial.

15. A $100,000 bill is on display in the Bureau of Engraving and Printing. It's for official use only, so don't get too excited.

16. On Massachusetts Avenue, NW, near the Embassy of India, of course, is a larger-than-life sculpture of Gandhi, India's most revered national leader.

17. Rung for the opening of Congress and on national holidays (and practiced from 6:30 to 9:30 PM on Thursday) in the clock tower of the Old Post Office Pavilion, the 10 Congress Bells are replicas of those at Westminster Abbey.

18. This quotation from William Shakespeare's *The Tempest* is inscribed on the pedestal under the female figure outside the Pennsylvania Avenue entrance of the National Archives.

19. The shoe was a tool for Soviet spies during the Cold War. Look for it in the International Spy Museum.

20. Historic Ford's Theatre, where President Abraham Lincoln was shot, has had no visitors in the Presidential Box since that fatal day in 1865.

21. There are four of these statues at the National Law Enforcement Officers Memorial.

22. A piece of moon rock is embedded in a stained-glass window commemorating the flight of Apollo 11 in the Washington National Cathedral.

23. *The Turtle,* America's first submarine, was invented in 1776. You can see it at the Navy Museum.

24. *PT 109* was the patrol boat that carried young Navy Lieutenant John F. Kennedy to safety after his ship was destroyed in World War II. It's featured in a Navy Museum exhibit.

25. "The Growlery" was Frederick Douglass's name for a small, one-room building behind his home that was off-limits to his household while he was working.

26. The mast of the USS *Maine* rests in Arlington National Cemetery, across Memorial Drive from the Memorial Amphitheater. The battle cry "Remember the *Maine!*" commemorated the sinking of the American ship the *Maine* in Havana harbor in 1898, helping to provoke the Spanish-American War.

27. The tall spires of the U.S. Air Force Memorial are reminiscent of the contrails of jets streaming skyward.

28. A fitting tribute to President Theodore Roosevelt, his statue stands tall on the island named for him: Theodore Roosevelt Island.

29. The Confederate monument *Appomattox* stands at the intersection of Washington and Prince streets in Old Town, Alexandria, Virginia. Erected in 1889, the statue commemorates Alexandria's Confederate dead.

Index

A

Accessibility, xxv
Adams Morgan, 157–178
  map, 158
  quick guide, 160–161
Aditi ✕, 146
African American Civil War Memorial, 210–211
Aftertime Comics (shop), 319
Air Show at Andrews Air Force Base, 336–337
Airports and airplane travel, 17–18
  map of locations, 2
Albert Einstein Planetarium, 67
Alexandria, 303, 306–319
  map, 302
Alexandria African-American Heritage Park, 313
Alexandria Archaeology Museum, 303, 307–308
Alexandria Black History Museum, 312–313
Alexandria Red Cross Waterfront Festival, 338

Alexandria's Holiday Festivities, 345
American City Diner ✕, 226
American Film Institute, 357
American University, 226–227, 354
Anacostia Community Museum, 262–264
Anacostia Community Museum Kwanzaa Celebration, 345
Anderson House, 158–159, 162
Annual Scottish Christmas Walk Weekend, 344
Appalachian Spring (shop), 147
Arbor House Gift Shop, 257
Arena Stage, 357
Arlington, 299–300
  map, 271
Arlington House, 276–278
Arlington National Cemetery, 272–273, 276–290
Art Museum of the Americas, 101
Arthur M. Sackler Gallery, 59, 62
Arts, 356–368
Arts and Industries Building, 63–64

Asian Bistro ✕, 319
Atrium Café ✕, 77

B

Baltimore-Washington International Thurgood Marshall Airport, 17
Banana Leaves ✕, 177
Barnes & Noble (shop), 147
Bartholdi Park, 39–40
Basilica of the National Shrine of the Immaculate Conception, 249, 252–254
Battery-Kemble Park, 235–236
Bennett Dining Room ✕, 36
Ben's Chili Bowl ✕, 212
Bertucci's ✕, 92–93, 171
Bethesda Circulator (bus), 241–242
Bethesda Comedy Club, 358
Bethesda Theatre, 357–358
Bethune, Mary McLeod, statue of, 258–259
Bicycling, 346–347, 369–370
Bishop's Garden (Washington National Cathedral), 224
Bistro D'Oc ✕, 200
Black Family Reunion, 341
Boating, 347–349, 370–371
Booeymonger ✕, 141
Books about D.C., xxvi–xxviii, 8–9
Bradley, Omar, gravesite of, 278
Bradley's Ice Cream Shoppe ✕, 241
Brass Knob (shop), 176
Bread and Chocolate ✕, 318
BreadLine ✕, 85
British Embassy, 148–149
Brooks Brothers (shop), 169
Bua ✕, 171

Burberry's (shop), 169
Bureau of Engraving and Printing, 126–127
Bus travel and tours, 16, 19, 141, 241–242, 371–374

C

C & O Canal, 137, 140–141
Cactus Cantina ✕, 225
Café at the Corcoran, 99
Café Deluxe ✕, 225–226
Café Luna ✕, 171
Café Milano ✕, 147
Café Parisien Express ✕, 290
Camden Yards, 355–356
Canadian Embassy, 150
Cannon House Office Building, 35
Capital City Brewing Company ✕, 187
Capitol, 27, 29–31, 34–39, 55
Capitol Hill, 27–53
  map, 28
  quick guide, 32–33
Capitol Hill Books (shop), 260
Capitol Hill Suites ☶, 52, 268
Capitol Steps (comedy), 358
Car travel, 15–16, 19
Carlyle House, 303, 308–309
Carlyle Suites Hotel ☶, 178
Carousels, 235
Carter Barron Amphitheatre, 358
Cascade Café ✕, 74
Catholic University, 249, 252
Cemeteries
  Arlington National Cemetery, 272–273, 276–290
  Congressional Cemetery, 259–260
  Female Union Band Society Graveyard, 145–146

Mount Zion Graveyard, 145–146

Challenger Memorial, 278–279

Charters Café ✕, 193

Chesapeake and Ohio Canal National Historical Park, 137, 140–141

Chevy Chase Supermarket, 239

Children's Chapel (Washington National Cathedral), 224

Chinatown, 180–213
map, 180
quick guide, 182–185

Chinatown Friendship Archway, 181, 204–205

Chinese New Year Festival, 346

Chipotle Mexican Grill ✕, 163–164

Christ Church 313–314

Churchill, Winston, statue of, 148–149

Civil War Living History Day, 338

Clara Barton National Historic Site, 237–238

Claude Moore Colonial Farm at Turkey Run, 303, 320–321

Clothes Encounters of A Second Kind (shop), 260

Clothing for the trip, 14–15

Clyde's ✕, 146

Collingwood Library and Museum on Americanism, 326–327

Colonel Brooks Tavern ✕, 249, 252

Columbia statue, 93

Comedy Spot, 358

Comedy venues, 358

Comfort One Shoes (shop), 147

Commander Salamander (shop), 147

Commerce Department, 84–85

Concert Hall (Kennedy Center for the Performing Arts), 104

Confederate Memorial, 279

Congress, 27, 34–39

Congress Bells, 190

Congressional Cemetery, 259–260

Constitution Café ✕, 79

Constitution Gardens and Reflecting Pool, 116–117

Corcoran Gallery of Art, 84, 97–99

Così ✕, 318–319

Crowne Plaza 🏨, 245

D

D.C. Armory, 359

D.C. International Film Festival, 336

D.C. Jewish Community Center's Holiday Festival, 344–345

D.C. Visitor Information Center, 189

DanceAfrica DC, 338

DAR Constitution Hall, 358–359

DAR (Daughters of the American Revolution) Museum, 99–100

Days Inn Connecticut Avenue 🏨, 244

DEA Museum, 296

Decatur House, 95

Deli City ✕, 257

Dennis & Phillip Ratner Museum, 240–242

Department of Commerce, 84–85

Department of State, 84, 102–103

Department of the Interior, 101–102

Designer Ars and Crafts USA, Inc. (shop), 169

Dining
  Capitol Hill, 36–37, 41, 44
  Chinatown/Gallery Place,
    186–187, 193, 194,
    199–200, 202, 203, 204,
    205, 208, 212
  Dupont Circle/Adams Morgan,
    163–164, 171, 177
  Georgetown/Embassy Row,
    141, 146–147, 153–154
  National Mall area, 64, 65–66,
    69, 74, 76, 77, 79
  Northeast/Southeast, 249, 252,
    257, 262
  Northern Virginia, 290, 294,
    297
  Olde Virginia, 303, 307,
    310–311, 318–319, 324,
    330
  Tidal Basin, 127, 130
  Uptown/Suburban Maryland,
    216, 218, 225–226, 235,
    236, 239, 240–241
  White House/Foggy Bottom,
    85, 92, 99, 104
Dinosaur Hall (National Museum
  of Natural History), 76–78
Dirksen Senate Office Building,
  35
Dirksen Senate Office Building
  South Buffet Room ✕, 37
Disabilities and accessibility, xxv
Discount cards, 10
Discovery Center (National
  Museum of Natural History),
  77
Discovery Creek Children's Mu-
  seum, 236–237
Discovery Room (National Mu-
  seum of Natural History), 76
Discovery Theater, 63

District of Columbia War Memo-
  rial, 119–120
Doubletree Guest Suites 🏨, 106
Douglas, Justice William O.,
  gravesite of, 279–280
DSW Designer Shoe Warehouse
  (shop), 241
Dumbarton House, 145
Dumbarton Oaks Garden and
  Museum, 144–146
Dumbarton Oaks Park, 144
Dunkin' Donuts ✕, 262
Dupont Circle, 157–178
  map, 158
  quick guide, 160–161
Dupont Hotel, The, 🏨, 178
Dupont-Kalorama Museum Walk
  Day, 337

E
Eastern Market, 260
Education Center (Women in
  Military Service for America
  Memorial), 289–290
Einstein Brothers Bagels ✕, 239
Eisenhower Executive Office
  Building, 96
Eisenhower Theater (Kennedy
  Center for the Performing
  Arts), 104
El Pollo Rico ✕, 290
Ellipse, The, 92
Ellipse Visitor Pavilion, 92
Emancipation Statue, 249
Embassy of Australia, 150
Embassy of Brazil, 150
Embassy of Chile, 150
Embassy of Greece, 150
Embassy of Grenada, 150–151
Embassy of Ireland, 150
Embassy of Israel, 151

Embassy of Japan, 150
Embassy of Jordan, 151
Embassy of South Africa, 150
Embassy of Sweden, 150
Embassy of the Philippines, 150
Embassy of Togo, 1450
Embassy of Turkey, 150
Embassy Row, 136–155
   map, 137
   quick guide, 138–139
Embassy Suites at the Chevy
   Chase Pavilion ⛺, 244
Emergencies, xxvi
Enid A. Haupt Garden, 59, 62
Entertainment, 356–368
Equestrian monument, 86
Evening at the Improv (comedy),
   358
Evers, Medgar, gravesite of, 280
Expense planning, 9–12
Explorers Hall, National Geo-
   graphic Society, 172–173

F

Fairy Godmother (shop), 260
Family Theater (Kennedy Center
   for the Performing Arts), 104
Farmer's Market ✗, 318
Farragut Square, 94
Fashion Centre at Pentagon City
   (shops), 297
FBI Building, 181
FDR Memorial, 121–123
FedEx Field, 354
Female Union Band Society
   Graveyard, 145–146
Festival of Music and Lights, 345
Festivals and seasonal events, 43,
   333–346
Finnish Embassy, 148
Fire and Ice (shop), 147

Fire Hook Café ✗, 208
Fishing, 349
Flights of Fancy (shop), 52
Foggy Bottom, 84–108
   map, 86
   quick guide, 88–87
Folger Shakespeare Library, 42–43
Folger Shakespeare Theatre, 359
Fondo Del Sol Visual Arts Center,
   167–168
Food Pavilion (Torpedo Factory
   Art Center) ✗, 307
Foot Locker (shop), 52
Ford's Theatre, 181, 198–201,
   359–360
Ford's Theatre Museum, 198
Fossil Café ✗, 77
Franciscan Monastery, 254
Franklin, Benjamin, statue of, 196
Franklin Delano Roosevelt Memo-
   rial, 121–123
Frederick Douglass National His-
   toric Site, 264–265
Freedmen's Hall Gallery of Art,
   211
Freedom Forum Journalists Me-
   morial, 293
Freedom Plaza, 188–189
Freedom's Memorial, 258
Freer Gallery or Art, 58–59
French Embassy, 150 148
Friendship Firehouse Museum,
   315–316
Full Circle ✗, 65–66
Full Kee ✗, 205

G

Gadsby's Tavern Museum, 303,
   309–311
Gadsby's Tavern Restaurant ✗,
   303, 310–311

GALA Hispanic Theater, 360
Gallaudet Theater, 360
Gallaudet University, 255–256
Gallaudet University Kellogg
    Conference Center ⌂,
    268–269
Gallery Place, 180–213
    map, 180
    quick guide, 182–185
Gallery 10, Ltd. (shop), 169
Gather the Family at Woodlawn,
    344
George Mason University Center
    for the Arts, 361
George Mason University Patriot
    Center, 354, 360
George Washington Carver Nature
    Trail, 263
George Washington University,
    103, 355
George Washington University
    Inn, The ⌂, 106
George Washington's River Farm,
    325–326
Georgetown, 136–155
    map, 137
    quick guide, 138–139
Georgetown Inn ⌂, 154
Georgetown Suites ⌂, 154
Georgetown Tees (shop), 147
Georgetown University, 142–143,
    355
Geppetto's ✗, 240–241
Gift shop (National Museum of
    the Marine Corps), 330
Ginza (shop), 169
Glen Echo Adventure Theater,
    361
Glen Echo Gallery, 235
Glen Echo Park, 234–236
Glen Echo Pizza and Subs ✗, 236

Gloria in Excelsis Central Tower
    (Washington National Cathe-
    dral), 224
Glover Archbold Park, 143
Golf, 349–350
Gompers, Samuel, memorial to,
    209
Grand Foyer (Kennedy Center for
    the Performing Arts), 104
Grand Hyatt Washington ⌂, 213
Grant, Ulysses S., statue of, 32
Great Falls Historic Tavern and
    Museum, 140–141
Great Hall (Library of Congress),
    40
Greater Washington Soap Box
    Derby, 340
Greek Fall Festival, 341
Greenberg Theatre, 361
Grill at the Ritz-Carlton ✗, 297
Gross National Product (comedy),
    358
Guajillo ✗, 294

H

H&M (shop), 147
Haad Thai ✗, 187
Hains Point, 126
Hall of Americas (Organization of
    American States Building),
    101
Hall of Heroes and Flags (Organi-
    zation of American States
    Building), 101
Hall of Nations (Kennedy Center
    for the Performing Arts), 104
Hall of States (Kennedy Center for
    the Performing Arts), 104
Hamburger Hamlet ✗, 241
Hampton Inn and Suites ✗, 269
Hard Rock Café ✗, 199–200

Hard Times Café ✗, 319
Hart Senate Office Building, 35
Hartke Theatre, 361
Hattery, The, (shop), 147
Health issues, xxvi
Henry, Joseph, statue of, 56
Herb Cottage (Washington National Cathedral), 224
Hiking, 350–351
Hillwood Museum and Gardens, 227–228
Hilton Washington Embassy Row ⛫, 154–155
Hirshhorn Museum and Sculpture Garden, 64–66
Holiday Inn Georgetown ⛫, 154
Holiday Inn Washington-Capitol ⛫, 81
Horseback riding, 351
Hotel Harrington ⛫, 80, 213
Hotels, 12–13
    Capitol Hill area, 52–53
    Chinatown/Gallery Place, 187–188, 212–213
    Dupont Circle/Adams Morgan, 177–178
    Georgetown and Embassy Row, 154
    National Mall area, 80–81
    Northeast/Southeast, 268–269
    Northern Virginia, 299–300
    Olde Virginia, 330–331
    Tidal Basin, 133
    Uptown/Suburban Maryland, 244–245
    White House/Foggy Bottom, 106
House of Representatives, 27, 34–39
House of Representatives Office Building, 27, 37

Howard University, 211
Hyatt Regency Bethesda ⛫, 245
Hyatt Regency Washington on Capitol Hill ⛫, 53

I

Ice-skating, 75, 351–352
Icons, xii
Idle Time Books (shop), 176–177
Independence Day Celebration, 340
Indian Craft Shop, 102
Indonesian Embassy, 148
Information Center (Arlington National Cemetery), 273, 276
Insect Zoo (National Museum of Natural History), 76–77
International Children's Festival, 341
International Spy Museum, 181, 203–2043
International Student/Teacher Identity Cards, 10
Islamic Center, 151–153
Itineraries, 4–6
Iwo Jima Memorial, 291–292

J

Jackson, Andrew, statue of, 93
James Madison Building, 40, 41
Janet Annenberg Hooker Hall of Geology, Gems, and Minerals (National Museum of Natural History), 77
Jazz in the Garden at the National Gallery of Art, 337
Jefferson Memorial, 124–126
John Adams Building, 41
Jones, John Paul, statue of, 131
Juarez, Benito, statue of, 103

K

K.C. Café ✕, 104
Kahlil Gibran Memorial Garden, 149
Katzen Arts Center at American University, 362
Kenilworth Park and Aquatic Gardens, 249, 266–268
Kennedy, Senator Edward M., gravesite of, 282
Kennedy, President John F., gravesite of, 280–281
Kennedy, Senator Robert F., gravesite of, 281–282
Kennedy Center for the Performing Arts, 84, 104–105, 362–363
Kennedy Center Open House Arts Festival, 341
King Street Blues ✕, 319
Korean War Veterans Memorial, 121
Kramerbooks and Afterwards (shop), 169
Kreeger Museum, 233–234

L

La Madeleine ✕, 318
Lady Washington Shop, 324
Lafayette, Marquis de, statue of, 93
Lafayette Square, 93–94
Langley Theater, 67
Latin American Festival, 340
Le Cadeau (shop), 147
Lee-Fendall House, 311–312
L'Enfant, Pierre, tomb of, 282–283
L'Enfant Plaza, 64
L'Enfant Plaza Hotel ⌂, 81

Liason Capitol Hill Hotel ⌂, 52–53
Library of Congress, 27, 40–41, 363
Likely Story, A (shop), 319
Li'l Thingamajigs (shop), 147
Lillian and Albert Small Jewish Museum, 208–209
Lincoln House Restaurant and Deli ✕, 199
Lincoln Memorial, 55, 117–119
Lincoln Park, 249, 258–260
Lincoln Theater, 212, 363
Lindy's Bon Apetit ✕, 92
Lisner Auditorium, 363
Listrani's ✕, 236
Lodging ⇨See Hotels
Longfellow, Henry Wadsworth, statue of, 171–172
Longworth Building Food Court ✕, 37
Longworth House Office Building, 35
Lou Lou (shop), 169
Louis, Joe, gravesite of, 283
Lyceum, The, 316
Lynn Street Café ✕, 294

M

M & T Bank Stadium, 356
Macy's (shop), 297
Made in America (shop), 52
Main Reading Room (Library of Congress), 40
Mane Restaurant ✕, 218
Mansion on O Street, 174
Maps
    airport locations, 2
    Alexandria, 302
    Arlington, 271
    Capitol Hill, 28

Chinatown/Gallery Place, 180
Dupont Circle/Adams Morgan, 158
Georgetown/Embassy Row, 137
National Mall, 57
Northeast/Southeast, 248
Northern Virginia, 271
Olde Virginia, 302
Tidal Basin, 111
Uptown/Suburban Maryland, 216, 217
Washington, D.C. region, xiv–xv
White House/Foggy Bottom, 86
Marian Koshland Science Museum, 205–206
Maritime Craft Days at the Navy Museum, 339
Marriott Wardman Park Hotel ⛳, 244
Marshall, Justice Thurgood, gravesite of, 283–284
Matchbox ✕, 202
Martin Luther King Jr. Day, 345–346
Mary McLeod Bethune Council House, 209–210
Mary McLeod Bethune Memorial, 258–259
McDonald's ✕, 262
Meadowbrook Recreation Center, 229–230
Media resources, 7–8
Media tours, 377–378
Memorial Amphitheater, Mast of USS Maine, 284–285
Memorial Day, 337
Merriweather Post Pavilion, 364
Meskerem ✕, 177
Mess Hall ✕, 328

Metrobus, 19
Metrorail, 19–20
Mezzanine Café ✕, 186–187
Miss Saigon ✕, 141
Money matters, 9–12
Mount Vernon, 303, 321–325
Mount Vernon Forest Trail, 321
Mount Vernon Gift Shop, 324
Mount Vernon Inn ✕, 323–324
Mount Zion Graveyard, 145–146
Movies, books and games, xxvi–xxviii, 8–9
Mrs. Fields Cookies (shop), 147
Museum Café ✕, 130
Museums and galleries. ⇨*Also* specific museums and galleries
  Capitol Hill area, 50–51
  Chinatown/Gallery Place, 181, 186–187, 191–194, 195, 196–199, 201–204, 205–206, 207–209, 211
  Dupont Circle/Adams Morgan, 158–159, 162–170, 171–173
  Georgetown/Embassy Row, 140–141, 144–146
  National Mall area, 55–57, 58–60, 62–63, 64–80
  Northeast/Southeast, 256, 261, 262–265
  Northern Virginia, 276–278, 289–290, 296, 299
  Olde Virginia, 303, 306–313, 315–318, 320–330
  Tidal Basin, 127–131
  Uptown/Suburban Maryland, 227–228, 231–234, 236, 240–243, 244
  White House/Foggy Bottom area, 84, 95–100, 101

N

National Air and Space Museum, 66–68

National Aquarium, 84–85

National Archives, 181, 191–194

National Bonsai and Penjing Museum Collection, 256

National Building Museum, 207–208

National Capital Barbecue Battle, 339–340

National Capital Trolley Museum, 242–243

National Cathedral Flower Mart, 336

National Cherry Blossom Festival, 335

National Christmas Tree, 344

National Cryptologic Museum, 243–244

National Gallery of Art, 71–75

National Gallery of Art Sculpture Garden and Ice Skating Rink, 75

National Geographic Society, 172–173

National Grove of State Trees, 256

National Guard Memorial Museum, 49–50

National Harbor, 265–266

National Herb Garden, 256

National Japanese American Memorial, 46–48

National Law Enforcement Officers Memorial, 181, 206–207

National Mall, 55–82
  map, 57
  quick guide, 60–61

National Museum of African Art, 62–63

National Museum of American Art, 181

National Museum of American History, 78–80

National Museum of American Jewish Military History, 168–170

National Museum of Crime and Punishment, 196–198

National Museum of Health and Medicine, 232–233

National Museum of Natural History, 76–78

National Museum of the American Indian, 69–70

National Museum of the Marine Corps, 329–330

National Museum of Women in the Arts, 181, 186–187

National Portrait Gallery, 181, 201–203

National Postal Museum, 50–51

National Theatre, 364

National Weather Service, 298–299

National World War II Memorial, 110, 120–121

National Zoo, 215, 218–219

Nationals Stadium, 356

Native Cultures of the Americas (National Museum of Natural History), 76

Nature Centers, 352

Naval Heritage Center, 195

Navy Museum, 261

Netherlands Carillon, 291–294

New Big Wong Restaurant ✕, 203

New Hampshire Period Room/Children's Attic (DAR Museum), 99

Newseum, 181, 194
Newseum food court ✕, 194
Nine West (shop), 52
Nissan Pavilion, 364
Nordstrom (shop), 297
Northeast, 248–269
  map, 248
  quick guide, 250–251
Northern Virginia, 271–300
  map, 271
  quick guide, 274–275
Nurses Memorial, 284

O

O. Orkin Insect Zoo, 76–77
Octagon, The, 84, 96–97
Old Glory ✕, 146–147
Old Presbyterian Meeting House, 316–317
Old Stone House, 141–142
Old Town Alexandria, 303, 306–319
Olde Virginia, 302–332
  map, 302
  quick guide, 304–505
Onassis, Jacqueline Kennedy, gravesite of, 280–281
Opera House (Kennedy Center for the Performing Arts), 104
Organization of American States Building, 84, 101–102
Oriole Park at Camden Yards, 355
Orioles Baseball Store, 355

P

Packing, 14–15
Pageant of Peace/Lighting of National Christmas Tree, 344
Panda Café ✕, 216
Parish Hall (Christ Church), 314

Parks and gardens. ➪*Also* specific parks and gardens
  Capitol Hill area, 39–40
  Georgetown/Embassy Row, 137, 140–141, 143, 144, 149
  National Mall, 59, 62
  Northeast/Southeast, 249, 256–260, 263, 266–268
  Northern Virginia, 272, 294–295
  Olde Virginia, 313, 321, 325–326, 327–328
  Tidal Basin, 116–117
  Uptown/Suburban Maryland, 224, 228–231, 234–236, 238–239
  White House/Foggy Bottom, 93–94
Paula's Imports (shop), 176
Pavilion at the Old Post Office, 190–191
Pavilion Café ✕, 76
Peary, Robert Edwin, gravesite of, 285
Peirce Barn, 232
Peirce Mill, 231–232
Pentagon, The, 272, 296–297
Pentagon Memorial, 297–298
Pershing, John Joseph, gravesite of, 285–286
Phillips Collection, 162–163
Pho 75 ✕, 294
Pilgrim Observation Gallery (Washington National Cathedral), 224
Political Americana (shop), 52
Pope-Leighey House, 328–329
Pop's Old Fashioned Ice Cream ✕, 318

President Lincoln's Cottage, 255
Presidents' Day, 346
Pretzelmaker (shop), 147
Project ideas, 381–383
Puppet Company Playhouse, 365

Q

Quality Inn & Suites 🏨, 245

R

Radisson Reagan National Airport
    🏨, 300
Raku ✗, 164
Ramsay House Visitors Center,
    306–307
Rayburn Building Cafeteria ✗,
    37
Rayburn House Office Building,
    35
Recorded tours, 374
Red Onion Records and Books
    (shop), 170
Red Roof Inn 🏨, 213
Reflecting Pool, 116–115
Renaissance Festival, 342
Renwick Gallery, 84, 95–96
Residence Inn Marriott 🏨, 269
Restaurants. ⇨See Dining
Rifle Range Simulator (National
    Museum of the Marine
    Corps), 330
Ringling Brothers and Barnum &
    Bailey Circus, 334
River Inn, The 🏨, 106
Robert F. Kennedy Stadium, 356
Rock Creek Nature Center,
    228–231
Rock Creek Park Day, 342
Rocklands ✗, 153–154
Ronald Reagan Building and In-
    ternational Trade Center, 189

Ronald Reagan Washington Na-
    tional Airport, 17
Roof Terrace Restaurant & Bar ✗,
    104
Rough Riders Monument, 286
Round House Theatre, 365
Russell Senate Office Building, 35

S

Sabin, Albert, gravesite of, 287
Safety, 22–24
St. John's Church, 94
St. Matthew's Cathedral, 170–171
St. Patrick's Day Parade, 334
Sant Ocean Hall, (National Mu-
    seum of Natural History), 76
Savoy Suites Georgetown 🏨, 154
Scavenger hunt, 24–25, 379,
    384–386
Scoop Grill and Homemade Ice
    Cream ✗, 318
Scottish Rite Freemasonry Temple,
    173
Seasonal events, 43, 333–346
Second Story Books and Antiques
    (shop), 169
Self-guided tours, 374–375
Semper Fidelis Memorial Park
    (National Museum of the
    Marine Corps), 330
Senate, 27, 37–39
Senate Office Building, 27, 37
Senators' Dining Room ✗, 36
Sewall-Belmont House, 38
Shakespeare Free for All, 339
Shakespeare Theatre, 365–366
Shakespeare's Birthday at the Fol-
    ger, 336
Shaw neighborhood, 210
Sheraton Suites Old Town Alexan-
    dria 🏨, 331